BURDEN OR BENEFIT?

PHILANTHROPIC AND NONPROFIT STUDIES

Dwight F. Burlingame and David C. Hammack, editors

BURDEN OR BENEFIT?
IMPERIAL BENEVOLENCE AND ITS LEGACIES

Edited by Helen Gilbert and Chris Tiffin

INDIANA UNIVERSITY PRESS
Bloomington and Indianapolis

This book is a publication of

Indiana University Press
601 North Morton Street
Bloomington, Indiana 47404-3797 USA

http://iupress.indiana.edu

Telephone orders   800-842-6796
Fax orders   812-855-7931
Orders by e-mail   iuporder@indiana.edu

The paper used in this publication meets the minimum requirements
of American National Standard for Information Sciences—Perma-
nence of Paper for Printed Library Materials, ANSI Z39.48-1984.

Manufactured in the United States of America

Library of Congress Cataloging-in-Publication Data

Burden or benefit? : imperial benevolence and its legacies / edited by
Helen Gilbert and Chris Tiffin.
    p. cm. — (Philanthropic and nonprofit studies)
  Includes bibliographical references and index.
  ISBN-13: 978-0-253-35077-0 (cloth : alk. paper)
  ISBN-13: 978-0-253-21960-2 (pbk. : alk. paper) 1. Benevo-
lence—Great Britain—Colonies—History. 2. Social ethics—Great
Britain—Colonies—History. I. Gilbert, Helen, date II. Tiffin, Chris.
 BJ1474.B87 2008
 177'.7—dc22
                              2007035719
1 2 3 4 5 13 12 11 09 08

CONTENTS

ACKNOWLEDGMENTS

We would like to acknowledge the University of Queensland for seed funding of the project under its Small Grants scheme, and the members of the Queensland Postcolonial Group for wide-ranging and productive discussion in the development of several of the papers. Amanda Lynch provided research assistance to the project with customary energy, accuracy and imagination and Carol A. Kennedy scrutinised the manuscript with sympathetic yet forensic thoroughness. The editors would also like to thank the contributors for their generous responses to requests for clarification or supplementation of their arguments and for their patience as the book advanced to publication.

BURDEN OR BENEFIT?

1 Introduction: What's Wrong with Benevolence?

Chris Tiffin and Helen Gilbert

A cartoon in the *New Yorker* shows an executive on his way to work trying to avoid a panhandler who asks, "Spare a little eye contact?"[1] This cartoon wittily presents some of the ambivalence and awkwardness associated with that relationship variously called "benevolence," "philanthropy," "charity," or "humanitarianism." It bespeaks goodwill, but it also speaks inequality; it involves the willingness and power to give, but it also involves demands and obligations that are sometimes complicated and unwelcome. "Benevolence," like "peace" or "freedom," is a quality that seems axiomatically positive and unexceptionable. To wish for the well-being of others, to desire their happiness, is manifestly preferable to its antithesis. Yet in 1978 William Gaylin noted that it was "fashionable these days to view . . . benevolence as obscene."[2] Why should something so palpably positive for human life engender not only suspicion but even outright rejection? What's wrong with benevolence? This book proposes no glib answer, but rather raises a set of philosophical and historical questions that are as fascinating as they are complex.

Optimistic philosophers see benevolence as innate to humans. They propose that we are naturally attracted to other human beings and are disposed to wish for their happiness and betterment. Moralists such as the third Earl of Shaftesbury (and after him Francis Hutcheson) even made benevolence the definitional test for virtue, while Percy Shelley believed that two human beings had only to come together for the "social sympathies" to be aroused between them, and that love was "the great secret of morals."[3] For others, however, humans were either not naturally benevolent (Thomas Hobbes) or benevolent only within a specific range of contexts (David Hume).[4] Such limitations, of course, raise the question of the relationship between benevolence and self-interest. Shaftesbury was able to argue that self-interest was compatible with benevolence so long as the interest of the species or the whole order of creation was not compromised,[5] but a suspicion about self-interest has lingered, and genuine benevolence has been thought to exclude donor gain, to overlap with, if not be identical to, altruism.

Benevolence thus has some inherent ambivalence as a concept, but the real problems emerge only when we look at its practical implementation. The *practice* of benevolence is all-important, for we know benevolence not directly but by its consequences. Benevolence is essentially a disposition or attitude, but it manifests itself in practical relationships and actions, and it is only through those actions that the "good" of the benevolent attitude can be assessed.[6] Often when we speak of "benevolence" we are actually discussing "beneficence"—not willing well, but doing well. The major complexity comes with the consideration of the recipient of the benevolent action. It is useful, as David H. Smith has done, to consider benevolence within the economy of the gift.[7] Smith notes three levels of exchange, one a clear market transaction in which a good or service is offered in exchange for another (or a pecuniary sum), a second in which a gift is offered in expectation of a reciprocal offering within the social structure at some time in the future, and a third in which a gift is offered with no expectation that any reciprocal offering of any sort will be made. Smith's example of the last category is someone being suddenly given concert tickets by a complete stranger, and he notes that an element of "surprise" is often associated with this form of giving.[8]

The first category needs little explication because it is an overt exchange that makes no claim that any spirit of "willing well" is involved. Two parties simply "give" each other some good that furthers their individual self-interest without any motive apart from the satisfaction of that self-interest. We should note, however, that there is a long tradition of associating commercial trade with the mutual goodwill (and by extension, ethical positiveness) of the participants. Back in the eighteenth century, Joseph Addison ebulliently praised the Royal Exchange as a site that evoked general benevolence: "As I am a great lover of Mankind, my heart naturally overflows with Pleasure at the sight of a prosperous and happy Multitude. . . . I am wonderfully delighted to see such a Body of Men thriving in their own private Fortunes, and at the same time promoting the Public Stock."[9]

Smith's second category is clearly exemplified to different extents in a range of societies. In Western societies one is invited to a wedding banquet and expected to offer a gift to the newly wed couple. Not to do so would be to violate an unstated but clearly understood protocol. In Melanesian or Pacific American Native societies, however, the exchange conventions of *kula* or potlatch respectively can be far more complicated, with much more stringent rules about the circulation of wealth. These latter exchange networks remind us that while there is an element of reciprocity in all such gift exchanges, the exchanged gifts might not be equal. In fact, creating a deliberate imbalance by extravagant giving is a way of claiming or demonstrating one's higher status. Moreover, in a gift-exchange culture, exchanges may be, and often are, nonsimultaneous. One may offer a gift now in expectation of a reciprocal benefit sometime in the future. Religiously motivated giving can be seen as an extension of the exchange system. Formal religious gifting such as Christians tithing or Muslims paying zakat can be understood as involving an exchange in which a proportion of material wealth is sacrificed regularly for the promise of postmortem rewards.

In Western societies, public appeals and benefactions constitute a variation of this exchange system. The fact that only a very small percentage of donations are made anonymously suggests that public acknowledgment of donations (and hence enhanced social prestige) is a good that the benefactor receives in return for the donation. (Another interpretation of the desire to gift publicly, however, is that the public acknowledgment itself constitutes a further "donation" because it encourages others to contribute also.)[10] Just as public giving enhances prestige in some groups, so failure to give can incur censure and loss of prestige (being branded as miserly). Thus another type of return in a gift exchange is simply that of avoiding a negative result—that is, not being stigmatized as an ungenerous member of the group.

Smith's third category is the most interesting because it makes the greatest claims to complexity of attitude in the donor. In his example of the concert tickets, the apparent altruism is accentuated by narrating the story from the point of view of the recipient, thus preserving the opacity of the donor's motives. However, even purely "altruistic" donations demonstrate forms of reciprocity in that the donor requires (or at least expects) certain behaviors of the recipient. The aunt whose ongoing generosity is dependent upon appropriate expressions of gratitude is an obvious reminder that donors construct a gift situation as one in which they have certain prerogatives, and if these are not respected, they feel their position undermined. William M. Sullivan gives the example of U.S. donors to the 9/11 Appeal in 2001 feeling cheated on learning that their donations had been applied to purposes other than immediate relief to the New York and Washington victims, and being quite hostile toward the Red Cross as a result.[11] Donors were not satisfied to provide assistance that could be applied where it was most needed. Rather, they expected to control precisely how the money would be allocated, and felt betrayed to learn than it had been spent on other purposes. Although the instance is complicated by the Red Cross acting as agent in the process, it is still possible to deduce that such donors do not see their gift as conferring an unencumbered benefit on the recipient, but rather as establishing a relationship in which the recipient has on-going obligations to the donor.

Givers can have expectations of others in a gift dynamic, but they can also have expectations of themselves, and receive in exchange for their gift the plea-sure of matching that positive self-image. Even if the donation is anonymous, the gift is performed to the audience of self. Thus, virtually all forms of personal benevolence, even the most apparently altruistic, involve a structural relation-ship that situates the donor as a dominant, self-approving figure. Benevolence, then, is never simple, and its complications multiply exponentially when the case is not that of the individual within a contained culture, but rather that of an organization or nation acting across cultures.

Personal benevolence continues to enjoy its religious warrant even up to the present, but from the 1830s the idea of public benevolence, particularly within Britain, came under attack from the new science of political economy. Rather than accept the municipal responsibility of alleviating distress, the Malthusian view was that charity only increased dependence, and that people should be left to extricate themselves from their problems. Such thinking was implemented in the stringent workhouse system deliberately designed to make the experience of receiving public relief as physically and psychologically undesirable as possible. As Patrick Brantlinger shows, such thinking also underlined government (in)-action during the Irish Famine of the late 1840s. In fact, he goes on to argue, the success of benevolent projects in the middle of the nineteenth century largely depended on the degree to which they overlapped with new ideas of po-litical economy. Where a humanitarian project coincided with an economic ten-dency, as happened with the push to abolish slavery, it was able to succeed, but where an attempted project was either counter or irrelevant to the economic di-rection of the time, it sputtered for a time and then failed.

An act of benevolence can be the provision of mutually valued goods or ser-vices, as in giving money to a beggar, but it can also involve the communication of beliefs and practices that are valued by one party but not by the other. Such was the history of European colonialism, in which various colonizing powers found a justification for their expropriation of land and other resources in the as-sumption that their values and practices in language, beliefs, hygiene, medicine, and social organization were superior to those of the peoples they encountered, and that to instill those values in the natives was not only justifiable but truly benevolent. With this justification, imperialism could draw into its economic system "lazy" native societies whose constituents would be improved by their transformation into industrious, productive, and consuming units in the colonial economy. For this to happen, the colonizer had to reduce sectarian and tribal strife and ensure social stability, which could be done either by direct rule, using

Western principles of equalitarian law, or by harnessing and manipulating the hierarchical, customary power structures already existing in the society at hand.[12] At best, this sense of civilizing mission smoothed the hard edge off colonial greed; at worst it provided a justification for unconscionable and expedient practices. The Liberal view of colonialism positioned it as a process that, despite its temporarily destructive local effects, was ultimately grounded in good principles of liberty and progress, which would advance colonized societies. Confident of the superior utility of individualism, and equally sure of individualism's central role in human destiny, Liberal thought disparaged any theory or practice of benevolence that conflicted with utilitarian ideologies. As J. C. Furnivall succinctly puts it, "Humanitarian ideals may point the goal for political reforms, but human nature travels faster with self-interest for its guide."[13]

This book explores some of the paradigmatic ways in which benevolence—which might be seen as a particular crystallization of humanitarian thought—has been imagined, planned, implemented, modified, and even challenged in colonial and postcolonial contexts. We focus primarily, though not exclusively, on the British Empire as a major instance of imperialism that demonstrates the complexities and contradictions inherent in benevolent ideas and practices. For all its aggressive program of expansion and domination, there is ample evidence that Britain often saw its imperial and colonial projects as essentially benevolent, as suggested by the semi-official credo that colonial actions were (or should be) altruistic, and self-abnegating. Thus Sir Charles Dilke, writing in 1892, called for a colonial regime that validated itself by self-sacrifice:

> We are accustomed to regard as the type of moral perfection the character which prefers death to the abandonment of an ideal of duty. . . . If we are right in approving in the case of the individual man or woman the maxim "death before dishonour," it can hardly be right in the conduct of national affairs to adopt a mere calculation of commercial or material interests. The condition of moral strength that "Whoever will save his life shall lose it," applies not to the individual alone, but to the nation.[14]

This high-minded call for a colonial policy based on self-sacrifice is consistent with Dilke's estimation of British activities in India as both disinterested and anti-utilitarian: "The two principles upon which our administration of this country might be based have long since been weighed against each other by the English people, who, rejecting the principle of a holding of India for the acquisition of prestige and trade, have decided that we are to govern India in the interests of the people of Hindostan."[15] How, after the hysteria surrounding the reporting of the Indian Mutiny, the British public came to this conclusion remains unclear, but Dilke's investment in the ideals of benevolent rule is striking.

His denial of British self-interest can be compared with Anthony Trollope's more tempered comment: "It should be our greatest boast respecting India that we hold that populous country to the advantage of the millions by whom it is inhabited; but we do not hold it for the direct welfare of our own race, although greatly to the benefit of our own country."[16] Trollope agrees that imperial relations should not be based simply on commercial interests, and is keen to claim a basic benevolent intention in Britain's dealings with India, although admitting that there is a significant material benefit to Britain. In theory at least, the benevolent intention comes first.

There is a degree of moral triumphalism about this self-assessment that did not die with the nineteenth century. After India finally achieved independence in 1947, Ernest Baker described the British Empire as fundamentally differing from Roman or German ones by promoting the Liberal goal of freedom without coercion and without the attendant mercenary self-interest: "[T]he century which has elapsed since the publication of Lord Durham's report of 1839 . . . has turned an empire which was a mixture of a *Völkerwanderung* and a business proposition into a subtle and intricate structure for the development of human freedom. It is, in effect, an empire without *imperium:* an empire which has preferred the opposite principle of *libertas.* It is a contradiction in terms, and a living paradox."[17]

This is a formulation of benevolent empire: a conception of control that acts not for itself but for the controlled, and a notion of dominance that is not oppressive but libertarian. Liberal economics would find the resolution of this paradox of benevolent domination in the assurance that humanity is common although at different stages of development in different races, and that colonial domination confers a benefit to the native in bringing him or her into its developmental economic system, even if only at a lowly level. Baker sees the paradox implying a political ethic that accepts disparity in races and cultures and deliberately abstains from exercising its full power to coerce and absorb other groups.

Critical studies of imperialism in its past and present forms have demonstrated both the (limited) extent to which ostensibly benevolent empires have succeeded in ameliorating the lot of their subjects and the associated costs of cultural and economic intervention. Less attention has been paid to the ways in which benevolence, as a structural dynamic of Empire, has affected and informed specific domains of practice, for instance medicine, politics, economics, religion, and education. At the same time, such domains of practice have been significant not only in shaping the ways in which benevolence is conceived but also in positioning donors and recipients in relation to "gift" exchange. The essays gathered here examine imperial benevolence and its legacies in a wide variety of contexts, ranging from political tracts, antislavery campaigns, famine relief efforts, missionary evangelism, and independence struggles to contemporary indigenous sovereignty demands, migrant integration in the "new Europe," and recent environmental management programs. These case studies of personal and institutional benevolence are arranged in loosely chronological order of subject to sketch a trajectory from colonial to postcolonial practices and to give a sense of how the workings of benevolence and imperialism have articulated with each other across different eras and geographical locations. Collectively, the essays suggest that benevolence has been a rather expansive and even ambiguous concept over the centuries, as benevolent practices and principles have been adapted to respond to particular cultural, political, social, religious, and economic imperatives. This conceptual elasticity is what makes benevolence so fascinating in the context of Western imperialism, where it quickly came to encompass not only philanthropy (which seems to have a more narrow definition) but also forms of public, municipal, and humanitarian responsibility.

While this volume attempts to elicit connections between different, and sometimes disparate, instances of benevolence, it also maintains their contextual specificities. Nicholas Thomas argues, in this respect, that "[c]olonialism is not a unitary project but a fractured one, riddled with contradictions and exhausted as much by its own internal debates as by the resistance of the colonized."[18] The following essays illustrate Thomas's thesis in a range of historical contexts. Patrick Brantlinger's synopsis of selected humanitarian projects across two centuries of imperialism and Lisa O'Connell's analysis of one ideologue's vision of colonization both trace tensions in the modern formulation of benevolence to eighteenth-century thinkers, respectively tying these tensions to the related concepts of political economy and utilitarian philosophy. Subsequently, as Brantlinger and several other contributors show in detail, benevolence became a site of contestation between various strands of the colonial outreach. The planter or grazier who wanted natives to be docile, industrious workers at his total beck and call often came into conflict with missionaries who wanted them to be orderly, clean, church-attending crofters with the leisure to tend their gardens and read the Bible. Both sides could cite the master narratives of "civilization" and "progress" in defense of their vision. The most acute point of difference was, of course, the humanity and attendant rights of colonized peoples, an issue canvassed by Chris Tiffin in his study of polemical debates about slavery as conducted in the nineteenth-century British periodicals.

The confronting motto of the Society for Effecting the Abolition of the Slave Trade—"Am I not a Man and a Brother?"—had little resonance on the pastoral frontier in colonies where successful European settlement was seen to depend on the dispossession of native peoples and/or their coerced labor. Alan

Lester explores this conflict by charting antislavery reform discourses as they were transported to the Cape Colony and New South Wales via the humanitarian networks of the London Missionary Society, while Leigh Dale scrutinizes accounts of the actions and intentions of colonial governor Frederick Weld in response to settler aggression toward indigenes in Western Australia. As Dale's essay shows, colonial injustice cannot be whitewashed as regrettable but understandable in its historical moment; nor can it be conveniently separated by the protective filter of a century's distance from the structures of white privilege that remain unproblematized today. The insidiousness of colonial racism is further explored in Kirsten Holst Petersen's case study of Danish author Karen Blixen, whose writings have often been praised for their critique of colonialism. Blixen professed great affection for the Africans who worked on her plantation in Kenya, attempted to improve their health and education, and protested against (at least some of) the economic constraints imposed upon them by the Colonial Office, but her benevolence was, as Petersen reveals, that of someone living out a fantasy as an aristocratic landholder whose avowed commitment to African peoples alternated with revelations that she thought of them as clever children rather than as equals with rights to independence. This case example, along with Sarah Richardson's discussion of the signal role played by a number of British women in determining the contours of imperial philanthropy in response to poverty in Ireland and other colonies, confirms that benevolence was not the exclusive prerogative of Empire's men.

The latter part of the book chronicles more recent benevolent projects, beginning with Chris Prentice's essay on the modern legacies of the Treaty of Waitangi. Her historicized analysis of biculturalism in Aotearoa–New Zealand shows how even the most assiduous attempts at respecting minority rights struggle to avoid reinscribing the imbalances and misprisions of colonial encounters. Other instances of modern-day benevolence may be less directly connected with formal imperialism while still manifesting its ideologies. If the motifs of "benevolent" nineteenth-century European colonialism were Christianity and progress, to be pursued through cleanliness, order, piety, and industry, the twenty-first century seems to have taken as its watchwords freedom and democracy. Just as Victorian England thought that other peoples would be better and happier if they converted to the Christian faith and worked industriously on the farms and plantations of European settlers, so the current American-European alliance appears to believe that communities in the Middle East will be better and happier if they embrace Western-style political structures and market economies, and it is prepared to use force to make those people better, happier, and freer. Nevertheless, the contradiction of compulsory freedom is palpable.[19] The question of how readily Western countries should intervene in the social practices of other societies is raised by Wairimū Njambi's critique of the American feminist campaign against the circumcision of African women. She argues that effective campaigning must be grounded in an understanding of the specific cultural situations in which such practices take place and that Western conceptions of sexual identity cannot be assumed as normative and universal. Njambi shows that the righteous impatience such feminists display not only is ineffective as a rhetoric, but also is as belittling to the women the campaigners wish to emancipate as the colonial constructions of native peoples as childlike and incapable of improvement. She does not condone female circumcision but advocates a more "responsible and accountable intervention." If this essay is controversial in its treatment of highly emotive issues that might seem at first glance to have little political, historical, or moral ambiguity, it nonetheless provokes us to consider what cultural freight we bring to our efforts at benevolent intervention, even in its apparently necessary forms.

The financial world shows little of the caution about imposing its own values that Njambi calls for. What has happened over the last twenty years is that intergovernmental benevolence—foreign aid—has become more and more tied to the expectations of the donor country or institution.[20] The attempt to control the terms of this exchange has extended from the specific donation to the wider actions of the recipient country, sometimes subtly inverting fundamental beliefs and practices. Beneficiaries may thus find themselves "free to pursue their own self-interest but not free to reject the cultural conditioning that defined what that self-interest should be."[21] Foreign aid is usually made subject to a range of conditions: the donor country must approve the specific purpose to which the aid is to be put; it must supply the materials and project management for the enterprise (thereby clawing back some fiscal benefit to its own economy); the expenditure of resources must be documented and audited in particular ways; the receiving country must give the donor preferential access to the products of the project (for example, in the case of a mine) and so forth. At least some of these conditions can be defended on the grounds that the ongoing effectiveness of the project depends upon them. But donor countries have been willing to use foreign aid as a manipulator of smaller nations in much broader ways. While they "use their power to withhold or increase aid as a means of influencing the general economic policies of developing countries in specific directions,"[22] they also use it to harness political support on quite unrelated issues. Hence, we have the spectacle of small landlocked countries acquiring strong opinions on the liberalization of whaling after receiving aid from Japan.

Even in nonmonetary aid, the balance between what the recipient country or community needs and what the donor wishes to supply can be hard to strike. William O'Brien's essay, about the U.S. Army Corps of Engineers' environmental management work in the Florida Everglades and the Mesopotamian marshlands, suggests the difficulties in negotiating among different vested interests. O'Brien shows that the key concepts of environmental justice, participation, and benevolence inform each other, in theory and in practice, in the particular ecological restoration projects he analyses. Although the Corps is formally committed to a policy of local stakeholder involvement, this consultative process conflicts with the essential professionalism and specialization of its work. Moreover, there is a considerable difference in the extent to which different stakeholders can affect the project's design, with donor capital disproportionately shaping the possible outcomes.

One of the most important forms of nonmonetary aid in the world today is the acceptance and integration of refugees. Wars, ethnic persecution, and the growing imbalance of capital among nations means that wealthy countries are receiving enormous numbers of applications for residency from people seeking to escape less attractive living conditions. Most countries acknowledge a humanitarian responsibility, but fearing an erosion of their own social stability and prosperity if immigration is allowed promiscuously, wealthy countries have tried to balance those responsibilities with rather more pragmatic tests of the needs of the national workforce. Prem Rajaram argues that Europe, a generous immigrant host by world standards, undercuts the benevolence of its immigration policies by basing them on a model that considers its own culture as normative and static, a standard to which the refugee/migrant must assimilate. Rajaram argues that true benevolence would require a society to be more flexible in its assumptions about itself, and more able to adapt creatively to its evolving ethnic mix.

Unequal power structures not only the situation of potential benevolence, but also the actions that have brought that situation into being:

> Pity would be no more,
> If we did not make somebody poor;
> And mercy no more could be,
> If all were as happy as we.[23]

Here William Blake suggests that benevolence is less the positive reaching out of soul to suffering soul than the construction of a perverted moral claim from a structural injustice in the situations that benevolence seeks to address. Therefore, its "goodness" is inevitably compromised by bad situation if not by bad faith. In her essay, Rajeswari Sunder Rajan discusses two attempts by prominent Indian leaders to frame a political ethic that escapes this impasse as it had developed in colonialism. She argues that Mahatma Gandhi found his ethic in the adoption of voluntary poverty and of service to the lower castes.

Both of these practices involved renunciation, but Gandhi's renunciation of possessions was "not a giving *to* but a giving *up*"[24] and thus removed the trailing complications of expectation and reciprocation. It was a benevolence that repositioned the self, not one's goods. With such a renunciation, Gandhi stepped outside the major constraints occasioned by Western ideas of progress and property and into an uncompromised ethic.

What, then, is wrong with benevolence, and more specifically, what was wrong with colonial benevolence? Is benevolence always already corrupted by the asymmetries of power that produce its possibility? Is it a "good" impulse whose motives and effects can never truly be disentangled from self-interest? Is it at best an excuse for society's failure to provide justice to its members? Was it a product of eighteenth-century sentiment-based ethics that was simply superseded by the new science of political economy? Were the ideals of British colonialism simply rank hypocrisy of a nation that saw itself as the Darwinian inheritor of the earth?[25] Whatever critiques can be brought to bear on it, benevolence seems to be a reality at the individual, the social, and the international level. Whether innately or not, people *are* capable of wishing and acting well toward their fellows. However, the test of altruism does not clarify the issue, for we can hardly comprehend our own motives accurately, much less those of others. Perhaps the validation of benevolence comes from the retrospective assessment of its effects and outcomes, and perhaps also we need to accept, with Shaftesbury, that self-interest and public virtue are not incompatible in the quest for a better world.

NOTES

1. *New Yorker,* September 17, 2001, p. 84.

2. William Gaylin, "In the Beginning: Helpless and Dependent," in *Doing Good: The Limits of Benevolence,* ed. William Gaylin, et al. (New York: Pantheon Books, 1978), p. 32.

3. Percy Shelley, "A Defence of Poetry," in *Shelley's Prose, or the Trumpet of a Prophecy,* ed. David Lee Clark (Albuquerque: University of New Mexico Press, 1954), p. 278.

4. Ideas on the extent or limitation of benevolence in this period are capably explored by Evan Radcliffe, "Revolutionary Writing, Moral Philosophy, and Universal Benevolence," *Journal of the History of Ideas* 54, no. 2 (1993): 221–40.

5. Anthony Ashley Cooper, Third Earl of Shaftesbury, *Characteristics of Men, Manners and Opinions,* ed. Lawrence E. Klein (Cambridge: Cambridge University Press, 1999), p. 170.

6. "Benevolence" as a practice has been a conflicted label for many hundreds of years, at least since 1473, when, according to the *Oxford English Dictionary,* English King Edward IV used the term to gild a new impost he exacted from his nobles to show their "spontaneous goodwill" toward him.

7. David H. Smith, "Introduction: Doing Good," in *Good Intentions: Moral Obstacles and Opportunities,* ed. David H. Smith (Bloomington: Indiana University Press, 2005), pp. 1–13.

8. Ibid., p. 3.

9. Joseph Addison, *Spectator,* ed. Donald F. Bond, vol. 1 (May 19, 1711; Oxford: Clarendon Press, 1965), p. 292.

10. David M. Craig, "The Give and Take of Philanthropy," in Smith, *Good Intentions,* pp. 57–83.

11. William M. Sullivan, "Philanthropy in Question," in Smith, *Good Intentions,* p. 204.

12. J. S. Furnivall, *Colonial Policy and Practice: A Comparative Study of Burma and Netherlands India* (New York: New York University Press, 1956), p. 8.

13. Furnivall, p. 514.

14. Sir Charles Wentworth Dilke and Spenser Wilkinson, *Imperial Defence* (London: Macmillan, 1892), pp. 13–14.

15. Sir Charles Wentworth Dilke, *Greater Britain: A Record of Travel in English-Speaking Countries* (1885; London: Macmillan, 1907), p. 552.

16. Anthony Trollope, *Australia,* ed. Peter David Edwards and Roger Bilbrough Joyce (St. Lucia: University of Queensland Press, 1967), p. 48.

17. Ernest Baker, *The Ideas and Ideals of the British Empire,* 2nd ed. (Cambridge: Cambridge University Press, 1951), p. 8.

18. Nicholas Thomas, *Colonialism's Culture: Anthropology, Travel and Government* (Melbourne: Melbourne University Press, 1994), p. 51.

19. This paradox is gloriously satirized in Trey Parker and Matt Stone's movie *Team America: World Police* (Paramount Pictures, 2004). The heroes save Paris by eliminating a terrorist cell, but they manage to lay waste much of the city in the process.

20. The distinction between "peace-building aid"—aid that is used to defuse a situation of conflict that offers an immediate or medium-term threat to the donor country—and "rights-based aid"—aid that is given simply on recognition of another country's need—clarifies this change. Nadia Abu-Zahra argues that rights-based aid is being discontinued in favor of more strategic funding. "No Advocacy, No Protection, No 'Politics': Why Aid-for-Peace Does Not Bring Peace," *Borderlands* 4, no. 1 (2005), http://www.borderlandsejournal.adelaide.edu.au/vo14no1_2005/abu-zahra_aid.htm (accessed January 1, 2005).

21. Thomas Holt, quoted by Alan Lester, "Thomas Fowell Buxton and the Networks of British Humanitarianism," in this volume.

22. Teresa Hayter, *Aid as Imperialism* (Harmondsworth: Penguin, 1977), p. 17.

23. William Blake, "The Human Abstract," *The Poems of William Blake,* ed. W. H. Stevenson, text by David V. Erdman (London: Longman, 1965), p. 216.

24. Rajeswari Sunder Rajan, "Refusing Benevolence: Gandhi, Nehru, and the Ethics of Postcolonial Relations," in this volume.

25. See for example, Sir Charles Dilke, "The Two Flies," in *Greater Britain: A Record of Travel in English-Speaking Countries,* pp. 274–78.

2 A Short History of (Imperial) Benevolence
Patrick Brantlinger

Because most of this essay concerns just a few episodes from British imperial history in the 1830s and 1840s, perhaps I should have called it "A *Very* Short History of Benevolence." The episodes include the abolition of slavery in 1833, attempts to protect and convert Aboriginals in Australia, and relief efforts during the Irish Famine of 1845–1850. They all involve humanitarian benevolence in action, but only in the case of abolition was it effective. Why did it fall short in the other instances? A cynic might argue that benevolence, even in the case of the antislavery crusade, always falls short, or even that benevolence, like Santa Claus, does not exist. But it does exist at least as an ideal, though how often that ideal has been put into practice is a vexed question—as is the issue of whether ideals can be said to have histories apart from practices. The cynic would at least have to admit that benevolence is an important ideal in all the major religions, and also that many of the institutions established by those religions—missions, orphanages, almshouses, hospitals, and so forth—are humanitarian in aim.

Besides, that most cynical genealogist of morals, Friedrich Nietzsche, did not claim that benevolence is nonexistent or that it has no history. On the contrary, it has been a leitmotif in Judeo-Christian history for the past two millennia, one outcome of the triumph of "slave morality" over its "noble" antithesis. The slaves and their descendants—that is, we ordinary mortals—advocate pity, benevolence, and charity as weapons of the weak, ways of undermining aristocratic or "noble" values (see, for instance, Nietzsche's *On the Genealogy of Morals*).[1] Though he inverts the values of Liberal or Whig history by viewing as weakness and decadence what it treats as progress, Nietzsche agrees with its account of modern civilization as a gradual expansion of benevolence—that is, of the valuing of human rights and welfare. Most older histories of the British Empire are Whiggish in outlook; in other words, they tell a teleological story of increasing benevolence. The Empire wrought its "civilizing mission," according to these accounts, by an expansion of imperial trusteeship and "commonwealth,"[2] through which the Empire grew from less to more humane. From the time of the Warren Hastings trial (1788–1795) and the abolition of the slave trade in 1807, there were certainly many humane officials, missionaries, and others who worked to make the Empire benevolent. In the case of abolition, they did so very successfully; but abolition was far from typical of British imperial practice.

Benevolence was a major factor in ending slavery in part because it found an ally in the new science of economics. But there was no such fit between benevolence and economics concerning either how Aboriginals were treated or how the Irish Famine was dealt with. On the contrary, in those situations, the principles of political economy overruled humanitarian intentions. At least from the early 1800s on, for humanitarianism to be effective on any large, sociopolitical rather than merely individual scale, it has had to march to the tune of economic orthodoxy. As an aspect of the "dialectic of Enlightenment,"[3] the rift between sentiment and science—or more specifically, between benevolence and economics—has made putting political and social humanitarianism into practice difficult or impossible.

During the 1700s, benevolence was much discussed as part of the larger debate about human nature and the course of history. From Shaftesbury through Kant, one line of thinkers argued that humans are fundamentally benevolent. In his 1755 *System of Moral Philosophy*, for instance, Francis Hutcheson writes that "it is of the nature" of the "generous affections" to aim at "universal benevolence" without expecting any return. "The kind heart acts from its generous impulse, not thinking of its own interest."[4] Kant's "categorical imperative" works in the same disinterested manner. Further, radicals such as Tom Paine and William Godwin believed that revolution would usher in the age of universal benevolence through either democracy or anarchy.[5]

Against such benevolently minded speculation, an opposed tradition—anticipating Nietzsche—argued that, as Helvétius put it in his *A Treatise on Man* (1772), "What we call in man his goodness or moral sense, is his benevolence to others; [but] that benevolence is always proportionate to the utility [others] are . . . to him. . . . Benevolence to others is therefore the effect of love for ourselves."[6] In other words, benevolence is never disinterested. This second, cynical tradition that smells bad faith in all high ideals perhaps reflects the Christian doctrine of original sin, but in modern, secular form it can be traced from Machiavelli through Thomas Hobbes, Bernard Mandeville, and many others down to Nietzsche and beyond—to, for example, Jacques Derrida, who in

Given Time argues that all "gifts" are always compromised, double-crossed, or crossed out by some expectation of reciprocity.[7] But again, this second, cynical tradition usually does not contend that there is no such thing as benevolence—only that there is no pure, disinterested benevolence.

The concept of benevolence changed significantly between the Enlightenment and the 1830s. The difference between Adam Smith's two major works, *The Theory of Moral Sentiments* in 1759 and *An Inquiry into the Nature and Causes of the Wealth of Nations* in 1776, is symptomatic. In the earlier work, Smith echoes his mentor Hutcheson by claiming that "sympathy," a close relative of benevolence, is the most basic of the "moral sentiments."[8] "Benevolence may [even] be," Smith writes, "the sole principle of action in the Deity. . . . It is not easy to conceive what other motive an independent and all-perfect Being . . . can act from."[9] But in *Wealth of Nations,* sympathy and benevolence drop below the horizon, replaced by supposedly rational self-interest and the profit motive. The few times the word "benevolence" appears, it is in opposition to self-interest, the motor of commerce, as when Smith declares: "It is not from the benevolence of the butcher, the brewer, or the baker, that we expect our dinner, but from their regard to their own interest."[10] Needless to say, as the founding text of the new social science of economics, it was *Wealth of Nations* rather than *Theory of Moral Sentiments* that most influenced nineteenth-century thinking. It is not the case that Smith turned from a positive assessment of the goodness of human nature to a negative or cynical one. But in the move from moral philosophy to economics, "moral sentiments" such as benevolence came to seem almost irrelevant.[11]

In the world according to David Ricardo and James Mill, there definitely is no free lunch; everything has its price.[12] As numerous nineteenth-century books with titles such as *The Principles of Political Economy* proclaim, economics is "the science" of value or wealth; and "principles" refers not to morality, but to something akin to or identical with the "laws" of nature. Nevertheless, such texts ordinarily also assert or imply that this science encompasses all values. Thus, from the start, economics—at least, orthodox, capitalist economics—has reduced all values to money or material wealth. And benevolence, according to the modern and modernizing science of economics, is often unwittingly costly —that is, uneconomical. One does not have to venture far into the nineteenth century before encountering—in debates over the New Poor Law of 1834, for example—the economists' argument that benevolence, at least in the form of organized charity, runs counter to economic principles. According to the Reverend Thomas Malthus's *On Population* (1798),[13] the sole way to alleviate poverty was for the poor to curtail their birthrate. Charity only encouraged them to overpopulate. Even Christian economists—and Malthus, of course, was one—

could argue vehemently against state-supported poor relief, as did also the Reverend Thomas Chalmers, an influential Scottish Malthusian.[14] For both Chalmers and Malthus, individual charity to the poor was a religious duty; but the only cure for poverty was through self-help on the part of the individual pauper.

Malthusianism gave "sentimental radicals" like Charles Dickens much fuel for satiric wrath on topics encompassing the trauma of the Irish Famine and beyond.[15] But in terms of law and social policy, sentiment was no match for science. In Dickens's novels, those jolly, Christmassy, unbelievable characters who save the day for the victims of social injustice are just that: unbelievable. Figments of Dickens's petit-bourgeois wishful thinking, the benevolent Cheeryble Brothers save the day for Nicholas Nickleby and Smike, but they also save the day for capitalism, bourgeois individualism, and class inequality. Benevolence in Dickens, and in capitalist culture more generally, has been ideologically useful, because it provides just enough social amelioration to allow the wheels of social injustice to go on turning. Or so Karl Marx and Friedrich Engels suggest, for example in their scathing remarks about "reactionary socialisms" in the second section of *The Communist Manifesto* (1848).[16]

Given its tentative hold on the Western philosophical imagination, how did benevolence achieve such a triumph with the abolition of slavery in all British territory in 1833? According to Eric Williams in *Capitalism and Slavery* (1944),[17] abolition occurred only when it squared with the imperatives of early industrial capitalism, or in other words, only when slavery came to be uneconomical from the standpoint of the emerging mode of production. Williams contended that even the benevolence of an evangelical "saint" such as William Wilberforce was far from being economically disinterested. Certainly slavery came into increasing contradiction with laissez-faire capitalism; but it does not follow that this contradiction gave rise to the benevolence evident in the words and deeds of the leading abolitionists. Rather, in the complex historical conjuncture of the late 1700 and early 1800s, benevolence, especially of an evangelical stripe, achieved a fusion with economic doctrine that gave the antislavery cause much of its ideological power. In *Wealth of Nations,* Smith had contended that "the work done by slaves, though it appears to cost only their maintenance, is in the end the dearest of any" form of labor.[18] For Smith and all later orthodox economists, slavery was antithetical to free trade; for an evangelical such as Wilberforce, it was also a national "sin" that had to be atoned for through its eradication. That slavery was both meant its days were numbered.

In his recent account of imperial trusteeship and humanitarianism, Andrew Porter contends that emancipation "took hold" once "the superior efficiency of free labour . . . emerged as conventional wisdom, adding a 'capitalist' argument to the humanitarian armoury."[19] Similarly, in *The Age of Atonement*, Boyd Hilton has traced the union of economics with evangelicalism in such figures as Wilberforce, Malthus, and Chalmers. David Brion Davis adds that the abolitionists believed "slave emancipation" both "unleashes the [economic] forces for universal progress" and "purifies and strengthens Christian civilization."[20] Would slavery have been abolished without a benevolence that was simultaneously religious and economic in inspiration? Together with Porter, Hilton, and Davis, I suspect the answer is no—or at least that slavery might have lasted a lot longer everywhere in the world without an economically correct version of religious benevolence working to undo it.

Abolition followed closely upon the passage of the Reform Bill of 1832; in the new climate of reform of the 1830s, humanitarianism came to the fore in governing the expanding British Empire. Presiding over the Colonial Office in London were two evangelical abolitionists, James Stephen and Charles Grant, Lord Glenelg.[21] In that favorable climate, Thomas Fowell Buxton, parliamentary leader of the antislavery crusade after Wilberforce, gained approval for a select committee to investigate the plight of Aboriginals in South Africa and other parts of the Empire. The committee's 1837 Report is a major document in the history of attempts to render the British Empire genuinely humane— that is, to realize the ideal of trusteeship that had emerged during the Warren Hastings trial.[22] "What have we Christians done" for the savages? asked the evangelical Buxton: "We have usurped their lands, kidnapped, enslaved, and murdered [them]. The greatest of their crimes is that they sometimes trespass into the lands of their forefathers; and the very greatest of their misfortunes is that they have become acquainted with Christians. Shame on such Christianity!"[23] From the outset, the committee recognized that, throughout the Empire as well as in the United States and Latin America, indigenous peoples were rapidly being exterminated. Many of its witnesses believed that Aboriginals everywhere were "doomed" to complete extinction. Even so, all agreed that their demise should be rendered as painless as possible. The committee made various recommendations for their protection, including increasing support for missionaries.

The work of the Aborigines Committee led to the founding of the Aborigines Protection Society (APS) in 1837, with Buxton as its first president and Quaker humanitarian Dr. Thomas Hodgkin as its leader and mainstay until his death in 1866. The APS remained active into the early 1900s; in 1909, it merged with the Anti-Slavery Society, which is still active as an indigenous people's rights organization. While a full history of the APS needs to be written, it would probably show that it was most effective in its first five years, from

1837 into the early 1840s, when evangelical humanitarians were in charge of colonial affairs.[24] In *Victorian Anthropology*, George Stocking notes that "by 1842, there was clearly a feeling [within the APS] that the opportunity provided by the [Aborigines] Committee had been lost."[25] Stocking relates the "increasing pessimism" of the APS to a "more general ebbing of the humanitarian tide," and also to another instance of the division between sentiment and science with the emergence of the new science of anthropology as what James Clifford has called a "salvage" enterprise[26]—no longer saving Aboriginals, but rather documenting their cultures before they vanished forever.[27] The APS, Stocking observes, "may be regarded as the oldest lineal ancestor of modern British anthropological institutions."[28] In 1842, it revised its statement of objectives: "rather than 'protecting the defenceless,' it would 'record the[ir] history,' and a resolution was passed to the effect that the best way to help Aboriginals was to study them."[29]

In the Australian colonies during the 1830s and early 1840s, offshoots of the APS were established, but these were no more effective than the London-based APS.[30] Also, several early missions closed after failing to protect and convert the Aboriginals in their regions. The so-called Friendly Mission of George Augustus Robinson in Tasmania had the blessing of the Aborigines Committee, the APS, and the Colonial Office.[31] After the farce of the so-called Black Line in 1830, when white settlers, soldiers, and convicts tried to round up the surviving Aboriginals, Governor George Arthur sent Robinson to do so. Out of a preinvasion population of perhaps 7,000, Robinson corralled only 203 survivors, whom he resettled on a reservation on Flinders Island, which historian Lloyd Robson has called the world's "first concentration camp."[32] Nevertheless, Robinson's reports from Flinders Island were upbeat about his benevolent efforts to convert his 203 charges to Christianity and a version of penny capitalism.[33] He believed his most important innovation was the establishment of a "circulating medium"—that is, money—among them, as a stimulus toward recognizing the values of private property and of work. But he had to acknowledge that they continued to die at an alarming rate.[34] When Robinson left Flinders Island to become head of the Port Phillip Protectorate in 1838, he took a small group of indigenous Tasmanians with him. In this new, strange land, two of them got into a struggle with a couple of whites, whom they killed. The two Tasmanians were tried and executed, constituting an early Australian sensation, in part because these were the first public executions in Melbourne. Meantime, with the blessing of the Colonial Office and the APS, Robinson and four assistant protectors assumed their new duties of protecting Aboriginals in the Port Phillip area.[35] But both this and later attempts to protect Aboriginals throughout Australia were dismal failures. In 1849, the New South Wales Legislative

Council concluded that the Port Phillip Protectorate "had totally failed in its object,"[36] and recommended its closure. Among other issues, its critics pointed to its "great expense of £61,000 in thirteen years." The Council was "unable to recommend any other measures as a substitute."[37] Not that the Protectorate, given its meager budget and staff, could ever have done much good.

Granted that Robinson and the other protectors of the Aboriginals were motivated partly by benevolence, why were the efforts to save the last Tasmanians and then the Aboriginals around Port Phillip failures? It was not because of anything Robinson did or did not do. Ironically, by trying to turn the Tasmanians into penny capitalists, he had the right idea. Not only in Australia but throughout the Empire, indigenous peoples stood little chance of "protection" and "preservation" if they did not behave in economically rational ways—that is, in capitalist ways. Where the rift between benevolence and economics first appears in Australia is not with Robinson, who after all tried to combine humanitarianism and economics, but with the First Fleet—or more precisely, with the doctrine of *terra nullius*, which meant that the Aboriginals were written out of the script of modern history. They had no conception of property; they owned nothing—certainly not the land; they did not know the meaning or value of labor, much less of money; and they were therefore not economically rational. *Terra nullius* was only the negative version of the standard liberal doctrine of what constituted economic rationality and citizenship.[38] Whether they retreated into the bush or stood their ground and fought to retain it, Aboriginals seemed to prove that their dispossession made economic good sense, because what had for ages been mere "waste lands" could now be converted to productive use. For most settlers, livestock made economic good sense, but the Aboriginals did not.[39] In 1877, Edward Curr told a Royal Commission that only if they "were as valuable commercially as short-horned cattle, or merino sheep" could the Aboriginals be saved from total extinction.[40]

Just as Robinson's Friendly Mission and the Port Phillip Protectorate were failing, so was the Reverend Lancelot Threlkeld's mission near Sydney (1826–1841). Threlkeld is interesting partly because he was the first colonist to study and attempt to codify Aboriginal languages. He believed that the Aboriginals' incapacity for civilization was a "convenient assumption,"[41] especially for "the murderers of the blacks [who] boldly maintained that [they] were only a specie[s] of the baboon, that might be shot down with impunity, like an Ourang Outang."[42] Threlkeld started with high hopes, praising his Aboriginal charges for their willingness to labor and learn. By 1841, however, he had to acknowledge failure, his mission going the way of Robinson's in Tasmania. In his final report, he declared: "This Mission to the Aborigines has ceased to exist, not for want of support from the British Government, nor from the inclination of the agent, but purely from the Aborigines themselves becoming extinct in these parts."[43] Perhaps, however, Threlkeld's use of the term "extinct" was hyperbolic. While disease and violence certainly decimated the Aboriginals of New South Wales, it must have been difficult for Threlkeld to acknowledge that he could not make and retain converts. Many of the Aboriginals first drawn to his mission, perhaps by curiosity, probably just wandered away back into the outback, so to speak. But "extinct" was a double-edged word: Threlkeld wanted to blame the failure of his mission on the "false principles of economy" of the London Missionary Society, which withdrew its support because of its unhappiness with his expenditures and his poor results.[44] In criticizing that organization for following "economic" instead of religiously benevolent motives, Threlkeld was also accusing it, albeit indirectly, of genocide.[45]

Threlkeld might have blamed the Aboriginals for their intractability or irrationality, but he did not do so. Even if he could not protect them from "extinction," he was their defender in cultural terms. After the first year or two, however, he must have realized that the Aboriginals preferred not to stay in one place for long, and, no matter how deferential they seemed, they saw no reason to relinquish their beliefs and customs for ones that made little sense to them. In any event, besides Threlkeld's, several other Australian missions closed between the 1820s and the late 1840s. These include William Shelley's "native institution" at Parramatta and then Black Town, as well as the Yarra Mission established by George Langhorne in 1837 but closed just two years later for lack of clientele.[46]

Versions of benevolent failures such as Robinson's and Threlkeld's have been frequent during the last several centuries. Indigenous peoples everywhere have been decimated by imported diseases and genocide, and while many missionaries and humanitarians have striven to protect and convert them, those efforts have usually failed, in part because "savage" or "primitive" customs have been interpreted by Western colonizers as economically retrograde.[47] Today numerous indigenous societies are still threatened with extinction if they fail to become economically productive in hegemonic terms.

If the Aboriginals were seen as economically irrational, so were starving Irish peasants both before and during the Famine of 1845–1850. Unfavorable comparisons of the Irish both to "savages" and to slaves were commonplace. From the outset of the potato blight, both governmental and nongovernmental attempts were made to prevent starvation. Yet one million died and another million and a half emigrated by the mid-1850s. Why didn't the combination of official and unofficial benevolence work in this case? As with the protection of Aboriginals, famine relief was too little, too late. The British government was prepared to spend £20 million to compensate West Indian planters when slavery was abolished, but it spent only £9.5 million on famine relief, and half of that amount was supposedly a loan. That the "potatophagous" peasants were seen as a drag upon the economic modernization of Ireland *and* that unrestrained charity or benevolence toward them was viewed as uneconomical compounded the disaster.

Starvation by political economy has been a key accusation against the British government. Young Irelanders asserted that the peasantry was being exterminated according to economic dogma. In 1847, the Catholic priests of Derry blamed "the Murders of the Irish Peasantry . . . [in] the name of economy [on] the administration of [Lord John Russell's] professedly Liberal . . . government."[48] Conservatives in Parliament, including Benjamin Disraeli, also blamed the Whig regime for adhering too strictly to economic dogma, thereby failing to save lives. Sadly witnessing the Famine at the end of her life, novelist Maria Edgeworth accused the government of being "reined, curbed and ridden by political economists," causing "its unnatural, unwise, impolitic and disastrous resolves."[49] And Irish socialist leader James Connolly later declared: "England made the Famine by a rigid application of the economic principles that lie at the base of capitalist society."[50] The official response was miserly because Treasury secretary Charles Trevelyan and other members of Russell's Whig regime were thoroughgoing Malthusians and believers in laissez-faire, free trade economics. They saw Ireland as a sort of accidental experiment that proved Malthus right. For both officials and economists, poverty meant too many mouths to feed, while government had a scientific responsibility *not* to give food to the overpopulating hungry. The Famine was God's way of rectifying the conditions that had caused the Famine in the first place: overpopulated Ireland would be depopulated, to its future benefit.

Trevelyan was an evangelical of the Clapham Sect variety, which had provided many abolitionist leaders, and he was as fundamentalist in economics as in religion. He believed that "perfect Free Trade is the right course" in dealing with all economic matters,[51] and he strove mightily to cut costs and to minimize the government's role.[52] Nothing should be given as a handout, he argued, because it would only lead to dependency: "if the Irish once find out there are any circumstances in which they can get" any form of assistance for free, "we shall have a system of mendicancy such as the world never saw."[53] That Ireland had already become a "nation of beggars" seemed self-evident,[54] and Trevelyan believed that the only cure was to make the beggars work for their livings.

In *The Irish Crisis,* which he published in 1848 to defend the relief efforts that he directed, and to declare—prematurely—that those efforts had helped to end the Famine, Trevelyan asserted that government action was insignificant compared to the long-range benefits of the Famine itself, the very handiwork of Providence: "[P]osterity will trace . . . to [the] famine . . . a salutary revolution in the habits of a nation long . . . unfortunate, and will acknowledge that . . . Supreme Wisdom has educed permanent good out of transient evil."[55] As Peter Quinn notes, in the discourse of Trevelyan and other supporters of the government's relief policies, "Providence and economics [were] mashed together in the mortar of politics."[56] But in this emergency, Providence did not favor benevolence. As an orthodox economist, Providence was, it seems, a true believer in its own invisible hand.

For Trevelyan, and from the hegemonic perspective of English public opinion, it was the bad national "habits" of the Irish—poverty, idleness, ignorance, superstition, sex, potatoes, whiskey—that had produced the Famine. "The great evil with which we have to contend," Trevelyan claimed, is "not the physical evil of famine, but the moral evil of the selfish, perverse and turbulent character of the [Irish] people."[57] Indeed, to Trevelyan and many other non-Irish observers, the bad national habits of the Irish made even Aboriginals seem superior. Trevelyan declared that the "domestic habits" of the Irish were "of the . . . most degrading kind."[58] Their standard of living was "on the lowest scale of human existence," and yet they were "perfectly content" with this poverty and ignorance.[59] Moreover, he likened the Irish to "South Sea" savages—lowest of the low, he implied, on the human totem pole. If anything, the Irish were even more abject than savages, because as white Europeans they ought to know better: they should be, but were not, civilized.

Together with widespread anti-Irish and anti-Catholic stereotyping, Malthusian coupled with laissez-faire economic doctrine was the main ideological factor that turned the potato blight into mass starvation. In her latest book on the Famine, Christine Kinealy cites Amartya Sen, who contends that famines are caused not by food shortages, but by adverse patterns of entitlement and distribution. Even in the poorest countries, according to Sen, "famine mortality could be averted if good will existed."[60] In the Irish crisis, Kinealy notes, "Good will did exist but its proponents were overwhelmed by a lethal cocktail of commercial greed, parsimony, providentialism and political economy."[61] She is expressing the consensus among historians today when she writes that official intervention could have dealt with the "ecological disaster" of the potato blight, but that the disaster was met only by the "failure" of "Irish merchants, landlords, and the policy makers within the British government." It was their stingy response that "transformed . . . blight" into the Famine.[62]

During the Famine, besides the stingy—that is to say, economically orthodox—government response, there was much private benevolent activity, but it was not enough to do more than stave off some indeterminate greater amount of starvation.[63] Trevelyan spoke for many non-Irish observers when he declared that God had "sent the calamity to teach the Irish a lesson, [and] that calamity must not be too much mitigated."[64] Similar providential "lessons" were being taught to Aboriginals on colonial frontiers throughout the Empire, and there too Providence was first and foremost an economist with little sympathy for unrestrained benevolence, including even missionary activity on behalf of Providence.

If we translate the economic Providentialism of Malthus, Chalmers, and Trevelyan into the modern, secular language of economic development, the results are strikingly similar. From the standpoint of transnational corporate capitalism—that is to say, from the standpoint of the IMF, the World Bank, and the WTO, institutions whose declared aim has been to help the world's poor by promoting development—benevolence toward the so-called underdeveloped world is supportable only if it adheres to orthodox economics. Instead of helping Africa and the rest of the Third World out of poverty and dependency, these international financial institutions have dramatically worsened their plight. Third-World indebtedness to the West has greatly increased over the past forty years. According to the 2001 International Forum on Globalization, "The income gap between the fifth of the world's people living in the richest countries and the fifth in the poorest doubled [between] 1960 [and] 1990, from 30 to 1 to 60 to 1. By 1998, it had jumped again, with the gap widening to an astonishing 78 to 1."[65] The Word Bank acknowledges that in 2000, "Excluding China, there [were] 100 million more poor people living in developing countries than a decade [earlier]."[66] That supposedly benevolent institution also now admits that "Globalization appears to increase poverty and inequality. . . . The costs of adjusting to greater [economic] openness [that is, to so-called free trade] are borne exclusively by the poor."[67] When NAFTA was ratified in 1994, the leader of the Zapatista movement in Chiapas, Mexico, Subcomandante Marcos, rightly declared: "NAFTA is a death sentence for indigenous peoples."[68] On average, Mexicans are poorer by 20 percent than they were twelve years ago, prior to NAFTA. Once again, benevolence restricted by the principles of economic orthodoxy has been too little, too late—although really, in the case of postcolonial economic dependency, benevolence is almost beside the point. What is occurring under the sign of globalization is economic imperialism via the interests of transnational corporate capital.

What is to be done? As many critics of the IMF, the World Bank, and the WTO contend, true benevolence—that is to say, genuinely effective aid toward eliminating instead of increasing world poverty—would entail "globalization from below," including:

(1) Strengthening instead of undermining local and regional patterns of production and exchange.

(2) "Enhancing [instead of subverting] people's abilities to exercise democratic control over all decisions that affect them."

(3) Abandoning "the paradigm of unlimited economic growth" in favor of "environmental sustainability" and prosperity through community stability.

(4) Recognizing "the rights and sovereignty of indigenous peoples" everywhere.

(5) Encouraging "biodiversity, cultural diversity, and diversity of social, economic, and political forms."

(6) Strengthening the United Nations and international laws, policies, and agreements, such as the Kyoto Protocol, that would work toward all of these goals.[69]

Obviously the advocates of economic orthodoxy, including the minions of the IMF, World Bank, WTO, and the Bush and Blair regimes, are not interested in "globalization from below." The upshot is that their version of benevolence, like that of Trevelyan and the other officials who tried to relieve the Irish Famine along economically orthodox lines, is no benevolence at all. Today the rich are getting richer and the poor poorer at such a dizzying rate and at such enormous cost to the global environment that it is difficult to see how there can be any way out of the mess. But, starting with Seattle in 1999, the mass protests around the world against "economic globalization" via transnational capitalism offer a glimmer of hope for a better outcome. One way of thinking about that better outcome is to consider what humanity's future might be if benevolence governed economics rather than the other way around.

NOTES

1. Friedrich Wilhelm Nietzsche, *On the Genealogy of Morals/Ecce Homo*, ed. Walter Kaufmann, trans. Walter Kaufmann and R. J. Hollingdale (New York: Vintage Books, 1967).

2. George R. Mellor, *British Imperial Trusteeship, 1783–1850* (London: Faber and Faber, 1951).

3. For "the dialectic of Enlightenment," see Max Horkheimer and Theodor Adorno, *Dialectic of Enlightenment*, trans. John Cumming (New York: Continuum, 1987).

4. Francis Hutcheson, "Concerning the Moral Sense," extract from *System of Moral Philosophy* (1755), in *The Portable Enlightenment Reader*, ed. Issac Kramnick (New York: Penguin, 1995), p. 278.

5. "Benevolence," Kant argues, has "an intrinsic worth," because it aims only at the "privilege . . . of participating in the giving of universal laws . . . [for] a possible kingdom of ends"—a kingdom, that is to say, autonomous from the influence of worldly means and selfish "interests." Immanuel Kant, extract from *Fundamental Principles of the Metaphysics of Morals* (1785), in Kramnick, *Portable Enlightenment Reader*, p. 304.

6. Claude-Adrien Helvétius, "A Treatise on Man," extract from *A Treatise on Man: His Intellectual Faculties and His Education* (1772), in Kramnick, *Portable Enlightenment Reader,* p. 294.

7. Jacques Derrida, *Given Time: 1. Counterfeit Money,* trans. Peggy Kamuf (Chicago: University of Chicago Press, 1992).

8. Adam Smith, *The Theory of Moral Sentiments* (London: A. Millar, 1759), p. 442.

9. Smith, *Theory of Moral Sentiments,* pp. 446–47.

10. Smith, *An Inquiry into the Nature and Causes of the Wealth of Nations,* ed. Edwin Cannan, vol. 1 (1776; Chicago: University of Chicago Press, 1976), p. 18. In *Theory of Moral Sentiments,* Smith notes that "Beneficence . . . is less essential to the existence of society than justice," p. 125, and that merchants can do their business "from a sense of . . . utility, without any mutual love or affection," p. 124. See also Christopher J. Berry, *Social Theory of the Scottish Enlightenment* (Edinburgh: Edinburgh University Press, 1997), pp. 133–34.

11. This difference or even contradiction between *Theory of Moral Sentiments* and *Wealth of Nations* used to be called "the Adam Smith problem." Recent commentators have minimized it or even declared that there is no "problem." It's likely that Smith didn't see any contradiction. The man of "prudence" in *Theory of Moral Sentiments* is no doubt the forerunner of the man governed by rational "self-interest" in *Wealth of Nations,* as Samuel Hollander in *The Economics of Adam Smith* (London: Heinemann Educational Books, 1973), pp. 313–14, and Donald Winch in *Adam Smith's Politics: An Essay in Historiographic Revision* (Cambridge: Cambridge University Press, 1978), pp. 105–106, 415, both claim. Nevertheless, sympathy and benevolence are foregrounded in the earlier text, but are not necessary in the later one for explaining the workings of commerce.

12. David Ricardo, *The Principles of Political Economy,* ed. Edward C. K. Gonner (London: G. Bell and Sons, 1891); John Stuart Mill, *Principles of Political Economy with Some of Their Applications to Social Philosophy,* ed. William J. Ashley (1848; London: Longmans, Green, and Co., 1909).

13. Thomas Robert Malthus, *On Population* (1798; New York: Random House, 1960).

14. Boyd Hilton, *The Age of Atonement: The Influence of Evangelicalism on Social and Economic Thought, 1795–1865* (Oxford: Clarendon Press, 1988), p. 101.

15. Walter Bagehot first called Dickens a "sentimental radical" in 1858. See Bagehot, *Literary Studies,* vol. 2 (1911; London: Everyman's Library, 1950), p. 191.

16. Karl Marx and Friedrich Engels, *The Communist Manifesto* (1848; London: Verso, 1998).

17. Eric Williams, *Capitalism and Slavery* (Chapel Hill: University of North Carolina Press, 1944).

18. Smith, *Wealth of Nations,* p. 411.

19. Andrew Porter, "Trusteeship, Anti-Slavery, and Humanitarianism," in *The Oxford History of the British Empire,* ed. Andrew Porter, vol. 3 (Oxford: Oxford University Press, 1999), pp. 203–204. Roger Anstey notes in *The Atlantic Slave Trade and British Abolition, 1760–1810* (Atlantic Highlands, N.J.: Humanities Press, 1975) the centrality of the idea of benevolence for those eighteenth-century thinkers, both religious and secular, who opposed slavery. These include Hutcheson, Smith, and most of the other intellectuals of the Scottish Enlightenment, as well as many of the French philosophes.

20. David Brion Davis, *Slavery and Human Progress* (New York: Oxford University Press, 1984), p. 122.

21. See Paul Knaplund, *James Stephen and the British Colonial System, 1813–1847* (Madison: University of Wisconsin Press, 1953); and Mellor, *British Imperial Trusteeship*, p. 249.

22. See Mellor, *British Imperial Trusteeship*.

23. Charles Buxton, ed., *Memoirs of Sir Thomas Fowell Buxton, Baronet, with Selections from His Correspondence* (London: Murray, 1848), pp. 368–69.

24. Patrick Brantlinger, *Dark Vanishings: Discourse on the Extinction of Primitive Races* (Ithaca: Cornell University Press, 2003), pp. 74–93.

25. George W. Stocking Jr., *Victorian Anthropology* (New York: Free Press, 1987), p. 244.

26. James Clifford, "On Ethnographic Allegory," in *Writing Culture: The Poetics and Politics of Ethnography*, ed. James Clifford and George Marcus (Berkeley: University of California Press, 1986), p. 112.

27. Stocking, *Victorian Anthropology*, p. 244.

28. Ibid., p. 240.

29. Aboriginal Protection Society (APS), quoted in Stocking, *Victorian Anthropology*, p. 244.

30. See Henry Reynolds, *This Whispering in Our Hearts* (Sydney: Allen and Unwin, 1998).

31. See Brantlinger, *Dark Vanishings*, pp. 124–30; Henry Reynolds, *Fate of a Free People* (Camberwell, Victoria: Penguin, 2004).

32. Lloyd Robson, *A History of Tasmania*, vol. 1 (Melbourne: Oxford University Press, 1983), p. 220.

33. See George Augustus Robinson, "Report on the Aboriginal Establishments at Flinders' Island," Enclosure no.2 in "Copy of a Despatch from Lord Glenelg to Governor Sir George Gipps, Dated Downing-street, 31 January, 1838," *Copies of Extracts of Despatches Relative to Massacre of Various Aborigines of Australia, in the Year 1838, and Respecting the Trial of Their Murderers. British Parliamentary Papers* 1839 vol. 34, pp. 6–19; also "Report from the Select Committee on Aborigines (British Settlements) with the Minutes of Evidence, Appendix and Index," *British Parliamentary Papers* 1836 vol. 7.

34. By 1843 the number of Tasmanian Aborigines on Flinders Island had dwindled to fifty-four. In 1846, this shrinking remnant was shipped back to Tasmania and placed in a reserve at Oyster Cove, not far from Hobart. There, these depressed, docile bodies "guzzled rum," writes Robert Hughes, "which was thoughtfully provided by their keepers; they posed impassively for photographers in front of their filthy slab huts; and they waited to die." *The Fatal Shore: A History of the Transportation of Convicts to Australia, 1787–1868* (London: Collins Harvill, 1987), p. 423. By 1855 there were just sixteen survivors, including Truganini, regarded as the last full-blooded Tasmanian when she died in 1876, and William Lanney, the last man of his race.

35. Manning Clark, *A History of Australia*, vol. 3 (Melbourne: Melbourne University Press, 1973), pp. 104–12.

36. Ibid., p. 431.

37. Ibid.

38. See Henry Reynolds, *The Law of the Land* (Ringwood, Victoria: Penguin Australia, 1992).

39. Jan Kociumbas, *The Oxford History of Australia*, vol. 2 (Oxford: Oxford University Press, 1986), p. 144.

40. Edward Curr, quoted in Geoffrey Blainey, *A Shorter History of Australia* (Sydney: Vintage, 2000), p. 46.

41. Lancelot Edward Threlkeld, *Australian Reminiscences and Papers of L. E. Threlkeld, Missionary to the Aborigines, 1824–1859*, ed. Niel Gunson, vol. 1, Australian Aboriginal Studies 40, Ethnohistory Series 2 (Canberra: Australian Institute of Aboriginal Studies, 1974), p. 46.

42. Ibid., p. 69.

43. Ibid., p. 170.

44. Ibid., p. 147.

45. Brantlinger, *Dark Vanishings*, p. 132.

46. Clark, *History of Australia*, p. 111.

47. See Christopher Bracken, *The Potlatch Papers: A Colonial Case History* (Chicago: University of Chicago Press, 1997).

48. Christine Kinealy, *This Great Calamity: The Irish Famine 1845–52* (Boulder, Colo.: Roberts Rinehart, 1995), p. 102.

49. Maria Edgeworth, quoted in Christine Kinealy, *The Great Irish Famine: Impact, Ideology, and Rebellion* (New York: Palgrave, 2002), p. 48.

50. James Connolly, quoted in Cormac Ó Gráda, *The Great Irish Famine* (New York: Macmillan, 1989), p. 57.

51. Charles Trevelyan, quoted in Cecil Woodham-Smith, *The Great Hunger: Ireland 1845–1849* (New York: Penguin, 1991), p. 123.

52. As James S. Donnelly Jr says, "This . . . was to make a religion of the market, and to herald its cruel dictates as blessings in disguise." "'Irish Property Must Pay for Irish Poverty': British Public Opinion and the Great Irish Famine," in *Fearful Realities: New Perspectives on the Famine*, ed. Chris Morsah and Richard Hayes (Blackrock: Irish Academic Press, 1996), p. 299.

53. Trevelyan, quoted in Woodham-Smith, *Great Hunger*, p. 171.

54. Ned Lebow, "British Images of Poverty in Pre-Famine Ireland," in *Views of the Irish Peasantry, 1800–1916*, ed. Daniel Casey and Robert Rhodes (Hamden, Conn.: Archon Books, 1977), p. 67.

55. Charles Trevelyan, *The Irish Crisis* (London: Longman, Brown, Green, and Longmans, 1848), p. 1.

56. Peter Quinn, Introduction, *Éire-Ireland* 32, no. 1 (1997): 14.

57. Trevelyan, quoted in Woodham-Smith, *Great Hunger*, p. 156.

58. Trevelyan, *Irish Crisis*, p. 7.

59. Ibid., pp. 4–5.

60. Amartya Sen, quoted in Kinealy, *Great Irish Famine*, p. 29.

61. Kinealy, *Great Irish Famine*, p. 29.

62. Kinealy, *Great Calamity*, p. 345. Cormac Ó Gráda also concludes that "the pre-Famine economy, for all its problems and injustices, did not contain the seeds of its own inevitable destruction by famine." *Ireland before and after the Famine: Explorations in Economic History, 1800–1925* (Manchester: Manchester University Press, 1991), p. 40. But the scale of the emergency and the ideological myopia of Trevelyan, Russell, and other officials turned crop failure into demographic catastrophe. Concerning the plight of agricultural laborers in the aftermath of the Famine, Marx writes: "according to the

unanimous testimony of the [Poor Law] inspectors, a sombre discontent runs through the ranks of this class . . . they long for the return of the past, loathe the present, despair of the future, give themselves up 'to the evil influence of agitators', and have only one fixed idea, to emigrate to America. This is the land of Cockaigne, into which the great Malthusian panacea, depopulation, has transformed green Erin." *Capital: A Critical Analysis of Capitalist Production,* trans. Samuel Moore and Edward Aveling, ed. Friedrich Engels, vol. 1 (Moscow: Progress Publishers, 1974), p. 663.

63. Private charity was substantial through 1847, but dwindled after that, apparently partly because of "famine fatigue," but also because Trevelyan and other officials were announcing that the worst was over. On philanthropy and private donations, see Kinealy, *Great Irish Famine,* pp. 61–89.

64. Trevelyan, quoted in Hilton, *The Age of Atonement,* p. 113.

65. International Forum on Globalization (IFG), *Does Globalization Help the Poor?* (San Francisco: August, 2001), p. 2.

66. The World Bank, quoted in International Forum on Globalization, p. 2.

67. The World Bank, International Forum on Globalization, p. 1.

68. Subcomandante Marcos, quoted in Sarah Anderson and John Cavanagh with Thea Lee, *Field Guide to the Global Economy* (New York: New Press, 2000), p. 92.

69. This list of goals is based on the "Social Movement's Manifesto" and the "Charter of Principles" of the World Social Forum. See William F. Fisher and Thomas Ponniah, eds., *Another World Is Possible: Popular Alternatives to Globalization at the World Social Forum* (Black Point, Nova Scotia: Fernwood, 2003), pp. 346–57.

Part 1
Colonial Burdens?

3 Thomas Fowell Buxton and the Networks of British Humanitarianism

Alan Lester

This essay emerges from two key, closely interrelated understandings of British colonialism in the nineteenth century. Scholars from a number of disciplines have derived these understandings by refining a postcolonial analysis of the discursive regimes that underpinned, legitimated, and, some would argue, gave rise to European colonialism in general. The first understanding concerns what Fred Cooper and Ann Laura Stoler have called the "tensions of empire."[1] Partly forged in sympathetic critique of the homogenizing tendency of Edward Said's *Orientalism*,[2] it recognizes that there was never a single European colonial project or a single colonial discourse associated with it. Rather, the agendas of colonial interests and their representations of colonized places and peoples were not only differentiated, but often constructed in opposition to one another.[3] The second understanding is almost inextricable from the first. It is that colonial projects were forged in and between multiple and connected sites, rather than within any one metropolitan or colonial site in isolation. The discursive regimes accompanying colonialism never simply emanated from Europe to be cast around the globe. Rather, they were the result of contests and communications that stretched across imperial spaces, connecting people in the colonies with those in the metropole and with those in other colonies in enormously varied, intricate, and complex ways. The political campaigns that ensued from the "tensions of empire" were thus always both local and trans-imperial (indeed, often extra-imperial), their success dependent on the mobilization of certain empowering geographies of connection.[4]

Within this combination of understandings, this essay seeks to examine in more detail the ways in which one particular imperial discourse, and the network through which it was energized, came to be constituted and implemented. This was a network first created in the late eighteenth century largely by evangelical antislavery reformers, and maintained and considerably expanded during the early nineteenth century in different ways by Thomas Fowell Buxton and the women of his family circle in particular. It was a politicized discourse and network from the first, clarifying its basic tenets in opposition first to slaveowning planters in the West Indies, and subsequently, to the activities and representations of emigrant Britons in new colonies of settlement, largely in the southern hemisphere. Its organizing secular principle was benevolence toward the victims of empire, but this principle was founded upon an evangelical Christian project that rendered it irredeemably ethnocentric.

BUXTON AND THE EVANGELICAL ALLIANCE

At the hub of the trans-Atlantic antislavery campaign during the late eighteenth and early nineteenth centuries were the evangelicals associated with William Wilberforce and comprising the Clapham Sect. They mobilized the texts, images, and artifacts sent to them by the Nonconformist missionaries who acted as their main informants in the West Indies, and who sponsored the tours of Britain by witnesses able to testify against slavery from their own experience. Aside from Wilberforce himself, politically prominent men such as Granville Sharpe and Thomas Clarkson and their families formed the core of the group during the 1780s. As it expanded thereafter, the sect developed an even more extensive web of evangelical connections. By the 1820s, intermarriage between the Clapham Sect's founding families, as well as the inclusion of new, likeminded reformers, had given rise to a "second generation" led by Thomas Fowell Buxton.

Although an Anglican, Buxton was the son and husband of Quaker women, and he became a key supporter of the Bible and missionary societies as well as a director of the Nonconformist London Missionary Society (LMS). He was brother-in-law to the Quaker reformer Elizabeth Fry and shared her concern with prison reform. In 1823, with the slave trade having been outlawed for some sixteen years, it was Buxton whom the ailing Wilberforce asked to take over the campaign to emancipate those already enslaved in the British colonies. As member of Parliament for Weymouth, Buxton devoted much of his considerable energy to the pursuit of this objective. But he also maintained his own prior reformist interests. Giving a characteristic snapshot of the intersection between his pious domestic and overseas concerns, in 1823 he wrote: "How can I promote the welfare of others? In private, by . . . sparing on my own pleasure and expending on God's service. In public, by attending to the Slave Trade, Slavery,

Indian widows burning themselves, the completion of those objects which have made some advance, viz. Criminal Law, Prisons, and Police."[5] Evidently, such was the fame, or rather, notoriety that Buxton attained as the most persuasive parliamentary figure challenging colonial practices, that even the rumor of a missionary being in correspondence with him could be enough to arouse colonists' ire. In 1825 Buxton felt obliged to declare in the House of Commons, "I never received from or wrote to [the Wesleyan missionary based in Barbados, William Shrewsbury] a single letter; nor did I know that such a man existed, till I happened to take up a newspaper, and there read, with some astonishment, that he was going to be hanged for corresponding with me!"[6] Ironically, as we will see, having been transferred to southern Africa, Shrewsbury would become one of the colonial settlers' most valuable allies against Buxton's humanitarian "interference."

As the antislavery campaign was entering its final stages during the early 1830s, an increasing proportion of Buxton's correspondents were based in the new colonies of settlement in the southern hemisphere. With his sister Sarah Maria, his daughter Priscilla, and, most importantly, his wife's cousin Anna Gurney undertaking the compilation of his enormous correspondence and (although unacknowledged except in Buxton's private communications) doing much of the writing, Buxton maintained regular contact, for instance, with the senior Anglican minister Samuel Marsden in New South Wales (and later New Zealand), Governor George Arthur in Van Diemen's Land, the British Resident James Busby in New Zealand, the Quaker missionary James Backhouse, who moved between various parts of Australia and the Pacific, and a number of LMS missionaries in the Cape Colony led by Dr. John Philip.[7]

These correspondents' narratives established links between the condition of enslavement against which Buxton had long struggled in the West Indies and the situation of indigenous peoples confronting expanding British settlement. Buxton was explicit about the connection:

> Great Britain has, in former times, countenanced evils of great magnitude, —slavery and the slave trade; but for these she has made some atonement; for the latter by abandoning the traffic; for the former, by the sacrifice of 20 millions of money. . . . An evil remains very similar in character, and not altogether unfit to be compared with them in the amount of misery it produces. The oppression of the natives of barbarous countries is a practice which pleads no claim to indulgence.[8]

Particular correspondents scattered across the imperial frontiers, most of them missionaries, would prove vital to Buxton's task of countering this "oppression" in the British metropole.

DR. JOHN PHILIP AND THE CAPE COLONY

Buxton's most prolific colonial correspondent during the 1830s was his fellow LMS director and superintendent of its missionaries in the Cape Colony, John Philip. As Porter notes, Philip "corresponded widely with the organisers of other missionary societies and their employees in the field," both within the Empire and outside it, particularly in the U.S.A. He felt that too few people appreciated "how much of our active benevolence we owe to our sympathy with the great affairs of the world, and these great things cannot affect us if they are not known to us."[9] Philip was vehemently opposed to the "antiquated" and "degrading" measures, including pass controls and compulsory apprenticeship, which bolstered colonial masters' control over their indigenous Khoesan labor force in the Cape. He was convinced that the Khoesan's plight was no better than that of the enslaved peoples of the West Indies. Indeed, it was probably worse since the Khoesan did not constitute the legal property of their master and were thus more likely to be mistreated. His prescriptions for their salvation, both material and spiritual, were also very much in line with those proposed by evangelicals in the West Indies. Philip made it clear to the Khoesan that he could alleviate their plight only if they conformed to the expectations of their missionary benefactors. He urged on the converts of the LMS's Bethelsdorp mission station, for instance, "the advantage which an improvement in their houses, and in their industry and mode of living, would afford to their friends, in pleading their cause."[10]

Philip's campaign on behalf of the Khoesan began when he returned for a visit to Britain in 1822. There, he arranged a meeting with Buxton and Wilberforce. It was partly as a result of this meeting, and Buxton's close contacts with the Colonial Office, that the commissioners of inquiry, J. T. Bigge (chief justice of Trinidad) and W. M. G. Colebrooke (Indian army officer and later governor of a series of West Indian islands), were sent to investigate colonial policy in the Cape, Mauritius (another of Buxton's longstanding interests), and Ceylon. In 1824, Buxton examined the reports from these commissioners specifically for useful information on the Khoesan, and in 1826 Philip was back in England, maintaining the metropolitan momentum. The campaign culminated in 1828, the same year that Philip published his *Researches in South Africa*.[11] Buxton noted that the book "excited much attention."[12] In fact, it caused a furor in both the Cape and Britain. Philip's narrative of the violent dispossession of the Khoesan led to his being successfully sued for libel by a number of Cape colonists.[13] In Britain, Buxton had to rally his friends to pay Philip's costs by subscription. It was during the controversy caused by the book that Buxton raised the issue of the Khoesan formally in Parliament. In the event, he agreed not to speak to the subject as long as the government consented to grant them "freedom." Philip himself was in the House of Commons to witness the motion passed, and shortly afterward he wrote to Buxton that its passage was momentous: "[It] is intimately connected with all the great questions now before the public, which have for their object the amelioration of the coloured population in every region of the globe; it is one of the principal stones in the foundation of that temple which Mr. Wilberforce has been so long labouring to rear, for the protection of the oppressed."[14]

Also under pressure from Philip, the Anglo-Irish Whig and acting governor of the Cape, Sir Richard Bourke, passed Ordinance 50 just two days later.[15] This more concrete piece of legislation abolished the pass laws and released the Khoesan from apprenticeship requirements. It also explicitly recognized their right to own land.[16] The colonial secretary heard of the ordinance in January 1829 and ratified it, prohibiting any future alteration by any colonial authority. The ordinance, however, by no means met with universal approval in the Cape itself. For the British settlers established on the eastern frontier in 1820, it was a disaster. Thomas Stubbs spoke for many settlers when he described the ordinance as "that abominable false philanthropy which made [the Khoesan] free and ruined them. . . . They were a people that required to be under control, both for their own benefit and the public; the same as the slaves in this country."[17] J. C. Chase, one of the most voluble of a select group of self-appointed settler spokesmen, felt that the colony's Khoesan had been favored by "the pious but gulled John Bull," duped by the representations of Philip and his allies.[18]

Ordinance 50 was just the beginning of Buxton's interest in the Cape and his connection with Philip. The process of Christianization and "civilization" in the Kat River Valley, where some of the freed Khoesan had been granted land, aroused deep emotions in Buxton during the remainder of the 1820s and early 1830s and kept alive a prolific correspondence with Philip and other Cape missionaries. Of these the LMS's James Read was one of the most significant, despite his scandalous past (see below). Read helped set up missionary schools in the new settlement, one of them financed personally by Buxton in the village named after him, and assisted in securing supplies for a flourishing agriculture. In 1835, Read exulted: "The improvement of the Hottentots was such that their friends supposed them now to be taking their final exit from that state to which slavery naturally reduces a people. Their enemies stood aghast."[19] After receiving the latest news of the settlement in one of Philip's letters, Priscilla Buxton reported: "My Father walked up and down the room, almost shedding tears of joy to hear of the prosperity and well-being of these dear people."[20]

Buxton later used the improving tale of the settlement in parliamentary debates to agitate for the early ending of freed slaves' apprenticeship in the West Indies.

Again, the British settlers in the vicinity did not look upon the success of the Khoesan in the Kat River Valley kindly. T. J. Biddulph, the settler who was later, and disastrously for its inhabitants, appointed as the settlement's superintendent, described its foundation as "the most transparent piece of humbug ever practised upon the public to serve the purposes of unscrupulous, intriguing people,"[21] and the Cape's new governor from 1847, Sir Henry Pottinger, characterized the settlement as "a concourse of rebellious, idle paupers."[22] With such invective, and associated punitive intervention directed against them from locally powerful interests, it is not surprising, first, that many of the settlement's inhabitants rebelled during the 1850–1852 frontier war and, second, that the settlement was then effectively broken up by the local government.

In 1833, however, with Ordinance 50 in a protected position on the statute books and the Kat River settlement apparently flourishing, Philip felt confident that the Cape's "Hottentot question was settled." But, he wrote to an American colleague, "there is another evil of great magnitude which I have to contend against . . . the colonists will think of nothing but an extension of territory and more land. . . . The indulgence of those feelings by the extension of the colonial frontier is attended with . . . the destruction of the natives who have been killed in defending their territories, or have perished by the evils which have followed their expulsion."[23] Unbeknown to the British settlers, they had been allocated land from which the Ndlambe Xhosa chiefdom had recently been expelled and across which a war had just been fought. The settlers were intended by local officials to act as a "buffer" shoring up the frontier against retaliatory Xhosa raids. Having been subjected to a number of such raids by the early 1830s, prominent settlers, and notably Robert Godlonton, who edited the settlers' *Graham's Town Journal*, were beginning to orchestrate a representation of the "typical" Xhosa as a rapacious cattle thief. Such a representation helped to legitimate calls for the Xhosa's further punitive dispossession in order to allow for the expansion of newly profitable settler sheep farms.[24]

Philip visited the frontier in 1830, and spoke with Xhosa chiefs. He also made fruitful contacts with the LMS and Glasgow Missionary Society (GMS) missionaries living among the Xhosa, as well as consolidating his connection with James Read in the Kat River settlement. Most of these missionaries would become vital channels of the Xhosa grievances that Philip would modify and relay to Buxton. By the early 1830s, the *South African Commercial Advertiser*, edited by Philip's son-in-law, John Fairbairn, was increasingly coming into conflict with Godlonton's *Graham's Town Journal* as a result of their different visions of "progress" along the frontier. The *Advertiser* saw in Godlonton's program of

land appropriation and Xhosa punishment the potential for the ultimate betrayal of Britain's civilizing and Christianizing mission. Fairbairn derided those
colonists who attempted to "search for new principles of action in the minds of
men who differ from us only in the colour of their skin."[25] In a series of letters to
Buxton, as well as in the colonial press, Philip foresaw the Xhosa sharing the
historical fate of the colony's Khoesan if the British settlers were to have their
way: land deprivation and servitude.

The contest between humanitarian and settler agendas in the Cape was
brought to a head from 1834 to 1836, when all-out war raged along on the eastern frontier. As Philip was keen to point out, the attack that initiated the war had
been provoked by a series of colonial aggressions that the Xhosa associated with
the British settler presence. Twenty-four settlers were killed in the first onslaught. This "Sixth" Frontier War soon had its counterpart in a discursive war
between the settlers and their evangelical critics as prominent settlers declared
that "many of the missionaries have been labouring under the greatest delusion
and although living for years amongst the Kafirs, they have not been able to form
anything like a correct estimate of the character of the people around them."[26]

Not all missionaries in the Cape opposed settler projects or were participants in Buxton's humanitarian network. Settlers found moral authority for
their views in the speeches and letters of frustrated Wesleyan missionaries, some
of whom had themselves emigrated as settlers and turned to missionary work
only after their arrival. Encountering widespread resistance to his evangelical efforts across the frontier, the Reverend Shrewsbury—the same man who had
been ejected from Barbados by planters objecting to his presumed correspondence with Buxton ten years before—had declared even before the war, "[W]ere
it not that I desire to promote the salvation of their souls, I would not dwell
amongst such a wretched people another hour."[27] After the war, and much to the
embarrassment of the WMS Directors in London, whose meetings were chaired
by Buxton, Shrewsbury suggested the execution of any Xhosa who had taken
colonial lives and the tagging of others so that they could be monitored while
they were put to "merciful" hard labor building colonial roads.[28] The Cape's new
governor, General Sir Benjamin D'Urban, shared Shrewsbury's sentiment, and,
declaring that the Xhosa were "irreclaimable savages," he determined that after
their surrender, their land should be seized by the colony, distributed among
British settler sheep farmers, and renamed Queen Adelaide Province.

THE ABORIGINES COMMITTEE AND THE POLITICS OF COLONIAL BENEVOLENCE

In disputing the future of the Xhosa within Queen Adelaide Province, settlers, missionaries, and their respective metropolitan supporters were prompted,

in large part by Philip, Gurney, and Buxton, to discuss the processes, purposes, and morality of British colonization as a whole. Their frame of reference expanded to incorporate all those diverse territories where Britons were "encountering" non-European peoples. This was when the early-nineteenth-century network of colonial benevolence orchestrated by Buxton would be implemented to greatest political effect.

The colonial secretary at the time was Lord Glenelg, son of Clapham Sect luminary Charles Grant. Glenelg's colleague as under-secretary at the Colonial Office, James Stephen, grew up within the same tradition, his father-in-law being Clapham's rector, John Venn. Given the small size of the Colonial Office's staff, it could always prove susceptible to the particular interests of its personnel, and it is not surprising that during the mid-1830s Buxton considered both Glenelg and Stephen to be important allies. So did exponents of humanitarian discourse in the colonies themselves. When Glenelg was first appointed colonial secretary, Fairbairn declared to his readers in the Cape: "The People of England will now bear with all its clearness, with all its nobleness, with all its wisdom, on every branch of our Colonial Policy."[29]

On hearing of the Cape frontier war, Buxton wrote to Philip, "It will be of great importance to get the ear of the Ministers before they shall have time to form an opinion on the Governor's Despatches on this subject, and one word from you in the present state of England will be enough to prevent them taking the wrong course."[30] Anna Gurney compiled a digest of Philip's letters to be presented before the colonial secretary. Buxton also made a series of personal visits to Glenelg, introducing him to the LMS secretary, William Ellis, who was receiving his own independent stream of letters from Philip, Read, and the other LMS missionaries in the Cape. Ellis reinforced Buxton's assertions that warmongering officials and acquisitive settlers had provoked the war. After one of his meetings with Glenelg, Buxton reported that he had been able to give the colonial secretary "a disquisition to [his] heart's content on the treatment of savages, . . . the atrocities of white men, and above all, on the responsibilities of a Secretary of State." "I believe," he added, "that Lord Glenelg feels both soundly and warmly on the subject."[31]

While Buxton's personal and informal campaign was influential, it was the formal evidence given before the select committee he established in London in 1835 that proved decisive and that would have the most effective impact beyond the Cape as well as within it. Prompted initially by Gurney, Buxton had first agitated for a committee to inquire into the humanitarian allegations about Cape frontier policy in 1834, before the outbreak of the war.[32] He had written to Philip asking to be furnished with the facts,[33] and news of the Xhosa attack provided an opportunity to bring the attention of metropolitan groups to bear directly on the provocations that had caused it. Referring to Philip's letters on "the wickedness of our proceedings as a nation, toward the ignorant and barbarous natives of countries on which we seize," Buxton wrote: "My object is to enquire into past proceedings, for the purpose of instituting certain rules and laws, on principles of justice, for the future treatment of the aborigines of those countries."[34]

In May, again prompted by Gurney, Buxton moved successfully in Parliament for the inquiry. The Aborigines Committee, with Buxton as its chair, was given powers to investigate colonial policy not just across southern Africa, but also in the Canadas, Newfoundland, New South Wales, and Van Diemen's Land. It also received and published information on New Zealand and the South Sea Islands, where many Britons resided.[35] After hearing testimony from colonists, officials, and above all missionaries from each of these sites, in January 1837 Buxton invited Philip to travel once again from the Cape and help him write the committee's report at Northrepps, his Norfolk home. There, Buxton, Philip, Gurney, and Priscilla Buxton all contributed, with Gurney undertaking the drafting and checking.[36]

The committee's report supplied the definitive humanitarian, missionary-informed analysis of the evils of settler-led colonialism. Whether in "the south and west of Africa, Australia, the islands in the Pacific Ocean, a very extensive district of South America," or in the "immense tract which constitutes the most northerly part of the American continent," the report commented that "the intercourse of Europeans in general, without any exception in favour of the subjects of Great Britain, has been, unless when attended by missionary exertions, a source of many calamities to uncivilized nations. Too often their territory has been usurped; their property seized; their numbers diminished; their character debased; the spread of civilization impeded."[37] In order to get the committee's report accepted by the end of the 1837 parliamentary session, Gurney and Buxton were forced to compromise on the most scathing criticisms that they had intended to make of the Cape's colonial authorities and the British settlers. Even so, the hearings of the select committee influenced Glenelg directly during 1835. After some procrastination, the secretary of state decided to renounce Queen Adelaide Province and hand it back to independent Xhosa chiefly rule.[38]

This act of retrocession was to be the most significant policy initiative arising out of missionary and humanitarian influence during the first half of the nineteenth century. It enraged the British settlers in the Cape, who accused the humanitarians and the Colonial Office of endangering their lives and the security of the Empire through their betrayal. Buxton's own reaction was recorded in a letter to Gurney: "[T]he hand of the proud oppressor in Africa has been, under Providence, arrested, and a whole nation, doomed to ruin and exile, and death, has been delivered and restored to its rights. . . . Only think how delighted must our savage friends be. . . . This is, indeed, a noble victory of right over might."[39] In the wake of the committee's hearings, Dr. Thomas Hodgkin was galvanized to establish a permanent organization in order to pursue the matters that the committee had raised.[40] His British and Foreign Aborigines' Protection Society was instituted in 1837, with Buxton as its first president. The society aimed "to assist in protecting the defenceless and promoting the advancement of Uncivilized Tribes" by guiding colonial policy through the publication of materials and the mobilization of "popular opinion."[41] The committee also prompted offshoots in the colonies.

As the establishment of an Aborigines Protection Society during 1838 demonstrates, it was not only the Cape Colony that was directly affected by the deliberations of the Aborigines Committee and its missionary informants. As a direct result of the Aborigines Committee, New South Wales's Governor Gipps issued a public notice declaring "that each succeeding dispatch from the Secretary of State, marks in an increasing degree the importance which Her Majesty's Government, and no less Parliament and the people of Great Britain, attach to the just and humane treatment of the aborigines."[42] Protectors of Aborigines were then appointed to each of the Australian colonies. The unprecedented prosecution and execution of some of the culprits of the Myall Creek massacre of Aboriginal people in 1838 also stemmed from the pressure brought to bear by Buxton's committee.[43] In New Zealand, similarly, a Protectorate of Aborigines was established,[44] while the Treaty of Waitangi arose out of the concerns the Committee expressed about the effects on the Maori of increased British settlement.[45]

The restoration of land, establishment of protectorates, and foundation of treaties were notable successes for Buxton's network during the late 1830s, and they helped persuade British settlers across the southern hemisphere that the benevolent vision of Christian humanitarians presented them with real threats. However, this network was by no means as seamless, as omnipresent, nor always as powerful as it seemed. As with all social networks, Buxton's excluded and marginalized some even as it connected others. Lancelot Edward Threlkeld's experiences help to demonstrate the effects of such exclusion.

LANCELOT EDWARD THRELKELD AND EXCLUSION FROM THE NETWORK

Two main testimonials were presented to Buxton's Aborigines Committee concerning New South Wales. They both came from prominent figures based in Sydney, Archdeacon Broughton and the Presbyterian minister J. D. Lang. Unlike in the Cape, where Philip effectively marshaled evidence from the LMS missionaries on frontier stations, there was an important discrepancy between these men's testimony and the evidence supplied by humanitarian missionaries on the Australian colonial frontiers. Broughton and Lang told the committee that many Aborigines had been killed by convict stockmen in the outer reaches of the British settlements, but they and, accordingly, the committee were loath to imagine that anything like systematic murder at the hands of "respectable" Britons was being carried out.[46] Broughton's evidence on the "diminution" of Aborigines was what was quoted in the final report: "[W]herever Europeans meet with them they appear to wear out, and gradually to decay: they diminish in numbers; they appear actually to vanish from the face of the earth."[47] For missionaries embroiled in the local politics of the frontier, however, although the "indirect" processes of disease and infanticide (associated with the abuse of Aboriginal women by white men) were acknowledged, the "disappearance" of Aborigines could also be much less mysterious. Many of them emphasized the deliberate attempts of relatively well-off and "respectable" squatters to "exterminate" the Aborigines persisting on "their" land, rather than blaming the spontaneous actions of colonial "riff raff." Lancelot Threlkeld was perhaps the most vocal, if also the most politically isolated, of these "men on the ground."[48]

Threlkeld, a Methodist, had been sent to Polynesia as a missionary by the LMS in 1816 and arrived in Australia in 1824. His station was on Lake Macquarie near Newcastle, and he was soon in conflict with local settlers over his attempt to prevent the systematic abuse of Aboriginal women and killing of Aboriginal men. He acted as a local compiler of information on the atrocities, naming prominent culprits and passing on reports to other missionaries, government officials, and members of the judiciary. He also gave an impassioned speech at the founding meeting of the Reverend John Saunders's Aborigines Protection Society in Sydney. His 1837 report to the LMS directors in London, which detailed some of the local abuses, was read sympathetically by Governor Gipps, but the following year's report went too far for the governor in implicating Major James Nunn, the colony's senior military officer, in the mass killing of innocent Aborigines during his campaign along the Gwydir River and its tributaries.[49]

Threlkeld was more vocal than many other humanitarian missionaries, but he was also less successful at inserting himself into the powerful humanitarian networks to which Buxton was key. Although his work in translation of parts of the Bible was mentioned in Broughton's evidence to the Aborigines Committee, and Buxton asked about his background, his direct testimony was absent from the rather more moderate evidence presented there.[50] In a long letter left with Buxton before he returned to New South Wales, Lang had actually inveighed against Threlkeld's "reckless" expenditure of LMS funds and his acceptance of financial help from the established church.[51] Threlkeld managed to alienate both influential churchmen in the colony, such as Lang and Samuel Marsden, and the LMS directors in Britain. They had cut him off from further funding by 1826. As Anna Johnston notes, "while Threlkeld could produce large amounts of information about the Awabakal people, in particular, and what he assumed was their 'need' for salvation, he could not promote their cause in an appealing enough manner to ensure important moral support from Britain."[52] This was in part due to the particular financial circumstances in which Threlkeld found himself, but it is also revealing of the contingent ways that "truth" and "knowledge" traveled from colony to metropole through the imperial networks of the day.

James Read in the Cape was at least as controversial a figure as Threlkeld. He married a Khoesan woman, had a "mixed race" son, was found guilty by the LMS of adultery, and campaigned for the prosecution of colonists who beat their Khoesan servants. And yet his testimony was taken seriously by Buxton, helping to shape the understandings of powerful humanitarian interests at the center of the Empire. This was largely because of the unusually close and productive cross-continental relationship that Philip had forged with Buxton. Activist missionaries in Australia, such as Threlkeld, but also figures such as Dr. Louis Giustiniani of the Western Australia Missionary Society, lacked the kind of mediation between their local concerns and the agenda of metropolitan agencies that Philip could provide for the LMS missionaries in the Cape. The Aborigines Committee was thus left reliant upon the more muted and restrained testimony of figures such as Broughton and Lang who either knew little of the activities of remote "frontier" missionaries or, as in Threlkeld's case, were actually in dispute with them. The committee's findings on Australia were premised accordingly on the notion that, with the backing of the "respectable" class of settlers, protectors would be sufficient to curtail the abuse of Aborigines.

THE FRAGMENTATION OF THE HUMANITARIAN NETWORK

By the mid-1840s, there was growing metropolitan opposition to the humanitarian model of colonization that the Aborigines Committee had defined and that Buxton's network had coordinated, if unevenly, across vastly different colonial terrains. Settlers who had long resented that model of colonialism found their voices heard more readily, and their representations accepted more willingly "at home," both among the public and in government circles. While a dispute between local missionaries and settlers over the causes of the Wairau "Affray" was still ongoing in New Zealand during 1843, the *Nelson Examiner* was aware that its humanitarian enemies were no longer so powerful in Britain. It complained only that "having ceased or worn out at home," the humanitarianism associated above all with Buxton "still [had] life and activity" in the person of government officials in New Zealand: "[T]he waves continue to roll when the storm that raised them is laid."[53]

The diminished political potency of the humanitarian network during this period was the result of a variety of interconnected developments at and between sites located across the British imperium, which this essay does not have the space to explore in any depth. They certainly included immediate, short-term, but quite decisive events, such as the loss of Buxton's parliamentary seat at Weymouth in 1838 and of Glenelg's post at the Colonial Office in 1839, as the now entrenched bourgeois British electorate became more wary of Whiggish reformism. But they also included the sense of disillusionment among many humanitarians at the outcome of the emancipation "experiment" in the West Indies (a sense derived from the refusal of the freed slaves to conform to missionary prescriptions)[54] and a similar sense of disappointment at the results of Buxton's grand attempt to regenerate West Africa through the ill-fated Niger Expedition.[55] At a time when an increasing proportion of the British population had family and friends emigrating to the colonies, those humanitarians who persisted in their activism also encountered increasing sympathy for settlers in places where violent indigenous resistance was peaking, such as the eastern Cape in 1847–1848 and 1850–1852, New Zealand in the mid-1840s and 1860s, and India in 1857.[56]

As these developments, combined with the mockery of humanitarian "sentimentalists" by prominent figures such as Thomas Carlyle, Matthew Arnold, and Charles Dickens,[57] undermined colonial humanitarianism's purchase among metropolitan observers, the cruelest blow to humanitarian aspirations in the colonies themselves was the movement toward settler self-government. This was a movement propelled initially by the Durham Report of 1838, which advocated self-government in a federated Canada in order to secure settler loyalty and prevent a recurrence of the American Revolution. It was reinforced from the late 1840s, as the need to reduce metropolitan military expenditure led to the encouragement of free trading colonies that would be economically and militarily self-sufficient. The Aborigines Committee's insistence that "native policy" be reserved for a more distanced and more philanthropically inclined metropolitan government was effectively abandoned as settler legislatures took on the "responsibility" for "managing" indigenous societies.[58]

In both the Cape and New Zealand, the utilitarian Governor George Grey (former explorer and governor of South Australia) proved instrumental in working with settler-dominated assemblies to overturn humanitarian precepts "on the ground," whilst upholding them rhetorically.[59] During his first period as governor in New Zealand, Grey closed down the protectorate, and during both spells, he concentrated on combating Maori sovereignty through military force.[60] In the intervening period, he oversaw the crushing of Xhosa resistance on the Eastern Cape frontier and consolidated British rule once more over Queen Adelaide Province, now known as British Kaffraria, by settling swathes of it with colonial farmers. He did not encounter any real opposition from the old stalwarts of the missionary-humanitarian complex in the Cape, Philip having retired from political involvement and Fairbairn having become disillusioned, like many other Cape humanitarians, with the Xhosa's capacity for "civilization" in the face of their continuing resistance to the missionaries' evangelical endeavors.[61]

In the Australian colonies, by the end of the 1840s, most mission stations were in a state of collapse, having lost access to government funds because of their failure to attract settled converts. The Protectorate of Aborigines itself was abolished in 1849. Broughton had anticipated the disillusionment of Australia's missionaries and protectors when he had told the Aborigines Committee some ten years before that the Aborigines' "want of fixed attention is the great obstacle we have to contend with [in their Christianization]; the impossibility of inducing them to settle in one place, or to attend to one subject."[62] As in the Cape and in the West Indies before it, then, the refusal of those "saved" by Christian humanitarians to conform to apparently universal, but deeply ethnocentric, notions of "civilized" conduct was interpreted as both a lack of gratitude to their benefactors and evidence of their incapacity to "progress." Even where a significant proportion of indigenous people were adopting Christianity, as they were in the Cape and New Zealand during the mid-nineteenth century, the syncretic way in which they appropriated and adapted Christian practices and beliefs alienated many of the original supporters of the missionary enterprise. While Buxton himself remained committed to the cause that he had done so much to further in the late 1830s, he was rendered less politically potent by his electoral defeat, and something of a figure of fun by the disaster of the Niger Expedition.[63]

CONCLUSION

In areas of new colonial settlement, not just in the Cape, but in New South Wales, and New Zealand too, during the 1830s and 1840s, there were real and meaningful conflicts between settler communities on the one hand and colonial and metropolitan humanitarians on the other, about the proper treatment of indigenous peoples and land allocation. Although there were often disjunctures between the view of missionaries "on the spot," such as Threlkeld in New South Wales, and the representations marshaled in by Buxton, colonial missionaries and metropolitan reformers were nevertheless sufficiently well articulated to present a powerful, trans-imperial challenge to prevailing settler colonizing practices. This challenge was based in part on the notion of benevolence toward the victims of empire.

Ultimately, however, the cause of humanitarians' disillusionment during the mid-nineteenth century lay in the nature of their own evangelical prescriptions. As Nicholas Thomas puts it, their "benevolence and their will to control were indissoluble."[64] In general, missionaries and humanitarians were far more comfortable speaking *for* rather than *with* the indigenous peoples whose souls they sought to save and whose lands they sought to preserve. Thomas Holt's description of the Christian humanitarian prospectus for Jamaican slaves applied just as well to the Khoesan and Xhosa in the Cape, Aborigines in Australia, and Maori in New Zealand: "They would be free to pursue their own self-interest but not free to reject the cultural conditioning that defined what that self-interest should be."[65] Buxton's biographer felt that, throughout his political struggles, Buxton was motivated primarily by "sheer horror at the idea that thousands of . . . fellow-creatures were unable to read the gospels [or] possess the clothes and habits that were the outward example of the pure and cleanly life."[66] When indigenous peoples in the colonies of settlement rejected this version of a "pure and cleanly life" and continued striving to live life on their own terms, the Christian humanitarian benevolence that Buxton, Gurney, and their contacts had helped to marshal was fundamentally weakened.

NOTES

1. Frederick Cooper and Ann Laura Stoler, eds., *Tensions of Empire: Colonial Cultures in a Bourgeois World* (Berkeley: University of California Press, 1997).

2. Edward Said, *Orientalism: Western Conceptions of the Orient* (London: Penguin, 1978).

3. See Martin Daunton and Rick Halpern, eds., *Empire and Others: British Encounters with Indigenous Peoples, 1600–1850* (London: UCL Press, 1999); Catherine Hall, *Civilizing Subjects: Metropole and Colony in the English Imagination, 1830–1867* (Cambridge: Polity, 2002); Thomas C. Holt, *The Problem of Freedom: Race, Labor, and Politics in Jamaica and Britain, 1832–1938* (Baltimore: Johns Hopkins University Press, 1992); and Alan Lester, *Imperial Networks: Creating Identities in Nineteenth-Century South Africa and Britain* (London: Routledge, 2001).

4. See Alison Blunt and Cheryl McEwan, eds., *Postcolonial Geographies* (London: Continuum, 2002); Hall, *Civilizing Subjects;* Lester, *Imperial Networks;* and David Lambert, *White Creole Culture, Politics and Identity during the Age of Abolition* (Cambridge: Cambridge University Press, 2005).

5. Charles Buxton, ed., *Memoirs of Sir Thomas Fowell Buxton, Baronet, with Selections from His Correspondence* (London: Murray, 1848), p. 125.

6. Ibid., p. 155.

7. Zoë Laidlaw, "Aunt Anna's Report: The Buxton Women and the Aborigines Select Committee," *Journal of Imperial and Commonwealth History* 32, no. 2 (2004): 1–28.

8. "Report from the Select Committee on Aborigines (British Settlements) with Minutes of Evidence, Appendix and Index," *British Parliamentary Papers*, 1836–37 vol. 7, p. 75.

9. Andrew Porter, "North American Experience and British Missionary Encounters in Africa and the Pacific, c. 1800–50," in Daunton and Halpern, *Empire and Others*, p. 352; see also Porter, *Religion versus Empire? British Protestant Missionaries and Overseas Expansion, 1700–1914* (Manchester: Manchester University Press, 2004), pp. 80–83, 109–17.

10. Andrew Ross, *John Philip (1775–1851): Missions, Race and Politics in South Africa* (Aberdeen: Aberdeen University Press, 1986), pp. 212–13.

11. John Philip, *Researches in South Africa: Illustrating the Civil, Moral, and Religious Condition of the Native Tribes: Including Journals of the Author's Travels in the Interior*, 2 vols. (London: James Duncan, 1828).

12. Buxton, *Memoirs*, p. 210.

13. Andrew Bank, "The Great Debate and the Origins of South African Historiography," *Journal of African History* 38, no. 2 (1997): 258–75.

14. Buxton, *Memoirs*, pp. 211–12.

15. Zoë Laidlaw, "Richard Bourke: Irish Liberalism Tempered by Empire," in *Colonial Lives across the British Empire: Imperial Careering in the Long Nineteenth Century*, ed. David Lambert and Alan Lester (Cambridge: Cambridge University Press, 2006), pp. 113–44.

16. William M. Macmillan, *The Cape Colour Question: A Historical Survey* (London: Faber and Gwyer, 1927); Elizabeth Elbourne, "'The Fact So Often Disputed by the Black Man': Khoekhoe Citizenship at the Cape in the Early to Mid Nineteenth Century," *Citizenship Studies* 7, no. 4 (2003): 379–400.

17. Thomas Stubbs, quoted in W. A. Maxwell and R. T. McGeogh, eds., *The Reminiscences of Thomas Stubbs* (Capetown: A. A. Balkema, 1978), p. 71.

18. J. C. Chase, quoted in M. J. McGinn, "J. C. Chase—1820 Settler and Servant to the Colony" (master's thesis, Rhodes University, 1975), p. 8.

19. James Read, quoted in Elizabeth Elbourne, *Blood Ground: Colonialism, Missions, and the Contest for Christianity in the Cape Colony and Britain, 1799–1853* (Montreal: McGill-Queen's University Press, 2002), p. 271.

20. Priscilla Buxton, quoted in Elbourne, *Blood Ground*, p. 272.

21. T. J. Biddulph, quoted in Tony Kirk, "Self-Government and Self-Defence in South Africa: The Inter-relations between British and Cape Politics, 1846–1854" (Ph.D. thesis, Oxford University, 1972), p. 180.

22. Ibid.

23. John Philip, quoted in Porter, "North American Experience," p. 353.

24. See Lester, *Imperial Networks*.

25. John Fairbairn, editorial, *South African Commercial Advertiser*, June 27, 1829, n.p.

26. Robert Godlonton, editorial, *Graham's Town Journal*, January 23, 1835, n.p.

27. Hildegarde H. Fast, ed., *The Journal and Selected Letters of Rev. William J. Shrewsbury, 1826–35* (Johannesburg: Witwatersrand University Press, 1994), p. 75.

28. Alan Lester and David Lambert, "Missionary Politics and the Captive Audience: William Shrewsbury in the Caribbean and the Cape Colony," in Lambert and Lester, *Colonial Lives*, 2006.

29. Fairbairn, *South African Commercial Advertiser*, September 5, 1835, n.p.

30. Thomas Fowell Buxton, quoted in Jan Gabriel Pretorius, *The British Humanitarians and the Cape Eastern Frontier, 1834–1836* (Pretoria: Government Printer, 1988), p. 128.

31. Ibid., p. 129.

32. See Laidlaw, "Aunt Anna's Report."

33. Pretorius, *British Humanitarians*, p. 12.

34. Buxton, *Memoirs*, p. 360.

35. "Report from the Select Committee on Aborigines," p. iii. For the networks of correspondence that Buxton maintained with humanitarians in New Zealand and Australia, see Alan Lester, "Missionaries and White Settlers in the Nineteenth Century," in *Missions and Empire*, ed. Norman Etherington (Oxford: Oxford University Press, 2005), pp. 64–85; Henry Reynolds, *This Whispering in Our Hearts* (Sydney: Allen and Unwin, 1998); and Anna Johnston, *Missionary Writing and Empire, 1800–1860* (Cambridge: Cambridge University Press, 2003).

36. Buxton, *Memoirs*, p. 415; Laidlaw, "Aunt Anna's Report."

37. "Report from the Select Committee on Aborigines," p. 5.

38. See R. Vigne, "'Die man wat die Groot Trek veroorsaak het': Glenelg's Personal Contribution to the Cancellation of D'Urban's Dispossession of the Rarabe in 1835," *Kleio* 30 (1998): 30–48.

39. Buxton, *Memoirs*, p. 369.

40. "Report from the Select Committee on Aborigines," p. 455.

41. Quoted in Ronald Rainger, "Philanthropy and Science in the 1830s: The British and Foreign Aborigines' Protection Society," *Man* 15 (1980): 707–708; see also Roderick E. Mitcham, "Geographies of Global Humanitarianism: The Anti-Slavery Society and the Aborigines Protection Society, 1884–1933" (Ph.D. thesis, Royal Holloway, University of London, 2002).

42. Governor Gipps, quoted in George R. Mellor, *British Imperial Trusteeship, 1783–1850* (London: Allen and Unwin, 1951) pp. 292–93.

43. Alan Lester, "British Settler Discourse and the Circuits of Empire," *History Workshop Journal* 54, no. 1 (2002): 24–48; Roger Milliss, *Waterloo Creek: The Australia Day Massacre of 1838, George Gipps and the British Conquest of New South Wales* (Sydney: University of New South Wales Press, 1992).

44. See C. H. Wake, "George Clarke and the Government of the Maoris: 1840–45," *Historical Studies: New Zealand and Australia* 10, no. 39 (1962): 339–56.

45. Claudia Orange, *The Treaty of Waitangi* (Melbourne: Bridget Williams Books, 1987); Reynolds, *Whispering*.

46. As are some historians today: see Gregory D. B. Smithers, "Reassuring 'White Australia': A Review of *The Fabrication of Aboriginal History: Volume One, Van Diemen's Land 1803–1847*," by Keith Windschuttle, *Journal of Social History* 37, no. 2 (2004): 493–505, for instance, on the debate between Henry Reynolds and Keith Windschuttle.

47. "Report from the Select Committee on Aborigines," pp. 10–11.

48. See Reynolds, *Whispering;* Johnston, *Missionary Writing.*

49. See Milliss, *Waterloo Creek.*

50. "Report from the Select Committee on Aborigines," p. 20.

51. See Milliss, *Waterloo Creek,* pp. 123–27.

52. Anna Johnston, "Mission Statements: Textuality and Morality in the Colonial Archive," in *Australian Literary Studies in the 21st Century: Proceedings of the 2000 ASAL Conference, Hobart, 6–9 July 2000,* ed. Philip Mead (Hobart: Association for the Study of Australian Literature, 2001), p. 157.

53. Supplement to the *Nelson Examiner and New Zealand Herald,* December 23, 1843, n.p.

54. See Holt, *Problem of Freedom;* Hall, *Civilizing Subjects.*

55. See Buxton, *Memoirs.*

56. Elizabeth Elbourne, "The Eastern Cape and International Networks in the Early Nineteenth Century," Working Paper no. 43, University of Fort Hare, South Africa: Fort Hare Institute of Social and Economic Research, August 2003, p. 29.

57. See Hall, *Civilizing Subjects;* Lester, *Imperial Networks.*

58. See Julie Evans, et al., *Equal Subjects, Unequal Rights: Indigenous Peoples in British Settler Colonies, 1830s–1910* (Manchester: Manchester University Press, 2003).

59. For a particular version of Grey's ideological leanings, see Jeffrey B. Peires, *The Dead Will Arise: Nongqawuse and the Great Xhosa Cattle-Killing Movement of 1856–7* (Johannesburg: Ravan Press, 1989); for an analysis of some of the self-created mythologies surrounding him, see Leigh Dale, "George Grey in Ireland: Narrative and Network," in Lambert and Lester, *Colonial Lives,* 2006.

60. See James Belich, *The New Zealand Wars and the Victorian Interpretation of Racial Conflict* (Montreal: McGill-Queen's University Press, 1986).

61. See Lester, *Imperial Networks.*

62. "Report from the Select Committee on Aborigines," p. 16.

63. See Buxton, *Memoirs;* Ralph Hale Mottram, *Buxton the Liberator* (London: Hutchinson, 1946).

64. Nicholas Thomas, *Colonialism's Culture: Anthropology, Travel and Government* (Cambridge: Verso, 1994), p. 61.

65. Holt, *Problem of Freedom,* p. 53.

66. Mottram, *Buxton the Liberator,* pp. 36–37.

4 Settler Colonialism, Utility, Romance: E. G. Wakefield's *Letter from Sydney*

Lisa O'Connell

In the mid-1770s, two critical accounts of colonization were published that broke with established discursive frameworks for thinking about colonialism. The first, by Adam Smith, appeared in chapter 7 of Book 4 of his treatise on political economy, *The Wealth of Nations* (1776); the second, published two years earlier in Germany by Johann von Herder, was an essay-length attack on Voltaire, and more particularly on Voltaire's philosophy of history that is known in English as "This too a Philosophy of History for the Formation of Humanity" (1774). From very different positions, Smith and Herder challenged legitimations of colonialism that turned around concepts such as paganism and conversion, or savagery and civilization, or innocence and corruption, or philanthropy and ignorance.

Adam Smith approaches colonialism less as a topic for its own sake than as an opportunity to bolster his attack on state-based mercantilisms in the name of laissez-faire economics. For him, colonialism is best understood not in terms of religion, or of civilization as a particular set of practices or values, but as a project with its own specific political-economic rationality. Settler colonies, which he defines as territories where a "civilised nation" "takes possession either of a waste country, or of one so thinly inhabited, that the natives easily give place to the new settlers," have the potential to "advanc[e] more rapidly to wealth and greatness than any other human society."[1] But they also distort the economies of the home countries, first by rewarding the export of capital and labor, then by encouraging policies that control trade through the creation of monopolies that restrict the free development of global commerce and the unimpeded expansion of the home economy, and last by becoming expensive to protect and administer on their own account. Furthermore their history has in fact been marked by "folly and injustice,"[2] a charge that Smith believes can be laid even more strongly against territories that are controlled and exploited by, but have not been settled by, Europe—such as those of the Asian subcontinent, where new forms of oppression and economic distortion have appeared. In sum, Smith casts a skeptical eye on colonialism, not simply on moral or spiritual or humanitarian grounds, but on economic and political ones.

Herder was a still harsher critic of colonialism, but for his own particular moral and political reasons. For him, modernity, as celebrated and promulgated by apologists for Enlightenment such as Voltaire, meant the triumph of the mechanical and of universals, or, otherwise put, the defeat of difference and the destruction of a world collectivity once constituted by autonomous peoples and cultures, each with their own norms and beliefs. Europe's universalizing and mechanical global victory was, however, unstable. Apostrophizing colonized peoples, Herder wrote: "The more we Europeans invent means and tools to enslave, cheat, and plunder you other continents, the more it may be left to you to triumph in the end! We forge the chains by which you will pull us [one day], and the inverted pyramids of our constitutions will be righted on your soil—you with us."[3]

How to prevent this? Herder wished to encourage an organic and holistic world system, which, ironically, shared something with that of Adam Smith. He hoped for the "natural" (i.e., nongovernmental) development of links and connections between different and separate peoples through travel and commerce (there being, for him, no hard division between the savage and the civilized). Such informal links would enable the use of a new hermeneutical tool by which different cultures could come to understand and communicate with one another. This tool Herder named, untranslatably, *Einfühlung* (literally "feeling one's way in"). As Michael Forster, Herder's translator, has argued, *Einfühlung* does not denote a form of understanding of another culture though "empathy" or sympathy—Herder was suspicious of such notions because they implied too complete an identification with the Other.[4] It denotes, rather, a learned, critical knowledge of and familiarity with other languages and lifeways to such a degree that interpreters can respond to the world as if they were indeed members of the other culture with whom they were in contact. At any rate, Herder breaks with the sentimentalism and emphasis on compassionate feeling that, for instance, was already a motif of anticolonialist thought (as, for instance, in the popular fiction *Yarico and Inkle*) and would soon help motivate the abolitionist movement. He did so largely because he saw difference as a cultural value in and of itself under the universalizing conditions of modernity.

Herder and Smith were writing at the same time as James Cook, quite independently, was opening up the Pacific for European expansion. Recent scholarship has shown that this expansion occurred outside of any coherent and controlling governmental or rationalized plan and, indeed, without agreement as to its function and benefits. As Jonathan Lamb has argued, the establishment of the Pacific dimensions of Britain's second empire was characterized less by deliberate policy than by accident and confusion in the face of the unknown.[5] In this sense, and with a couple of exceptions, the "enlightened" engagement with the Pacific looks back to the older discourses of expansion and even to tropes of wonder and curiosity that organized early modern speculations about the austral unknown, as much as it looks forward to the increasingly systematized conceptions of empire that came to organize nineteenth-century settler colonial projects, under the more or less direct sway of Adam Smith, and with Herder's concept of cultural difference unable wholly to be discounted, or kept out of play. Thus it was that celebrations of Cook (all the more intense in Britain, of course, because of the recent loss of the American empire) typically called upon values of sympathy and benevolent improvement, often centered on the thematics of fertility and population regeneration that had helped guide the mercantilism that Smith had critiqued as well as the enlightened progressivism against which Herder set himself.

It was in these terms that writers such as Erasmus Darwin and Johann Reinhold Forster articulated the ties of feeling and decency that in theory bound Europeans to the inhabitants of the newly chartered regions. For instance, in his allegorical poem *The Temple of Nature; or, The Origin of Society* (1803),[6] Darwin figured the historical advancement of civilization as the globe-encompassing march of a dazzling triumvirate of Reason, Sympathy, and Hymen. Forster, on the other hand, presents his encounter with the Tahitian natives during Cook's second voyage as a form of fellowship that evokes the *sensus communis* of all mankind. The Tahitians, he says,

> are nearer to happiness than any other nations we met with. . . . Their hearts are capable of the warmest attachment, of the most generous friendship, and of the most tender connexions. . . . [W]hat a great and venerable blessing benevolence is . . . when . . . it connect[s] all mankind as it were into one family . . . [and] the inhabitant of the polar region, finds a warm and generous friend in the torrid zone or in the opposite hemisphere. . . . I could not help repeatedly wishing, that our civilized Europeans might add to their many advantages, that innocence of heart and genuine simplicity of manners, that spirit of benevolence, and real goodness, which these my new acquired friends so eminently possessed.[7]

Forster's understanding of contact as extending what might be called "the family of man," along with his Rousseauvian sense of the islanders as innocent and natural versions of himself—available to sympathetic recognition—epitomizes the sentimental strain of colonialism whose long slow death knell was already being tolled by Herder.

Yet the older settler colonialism of mercantilism, Christianity, and sensibility was to be most effectively transformed into a post-Smithian, post-Herderian settler colonialism by Edward Gibbon Wakefield, arguably colonization's first systematic theorist, who was closely aligned, in his early days, with Jeremy Bentham. At a time when Bentham and other philosophic radicals viewed colonies, as did Smith, as little more than throwbacks to the mercantilist past (that is, as diminutions of political and economic freedom and utility), Wakefield argued passionately for their potential benefits. Remarkably, he extended the principles of the "classical" economics founded by Smith into a theory of imperialism that envisaged self-governing settler colonies as loyal and happy participants in a British free-trade empire. He believed that colonies could provide labor markets for Britain's "redundant population," as well as new opportunities for capital investment, and commodity markets for English manufactures, without distorting the home economy. Benevolent improvement, he argued, was contingent upon wealth creation alone. Thus for instance, slavery "exists, not to gratify the hearts of cruel men, but to fill the pockets of those who, without slavery, would be poor and insignificant. It will never be abolished by appeals to the hearts of slave-owners."[8] To prove his point, Wakefield's colonial writings routinely staged fictionalized renunciations of sympathy on the part of colonial capitalists and landowners, whereby English gentlemen colonists, men of feeling at the outset of their settler ventures, become hard-headed men of utility upon their exposure to the frontier. Indeed, they become figures not unlike Wakefield himself: passionate advocates for an economistic, means-end orientated colonial policy that displaces moral sense, and moral argument, within post-Smithian calculations of a common good or general utility.

Wakefield's systematic theory was first articulated in relation to New South Wales. He proposed an ingenious and technically sophisticated scheme for the restricted sale of colonial "waste lands" (his term, partly borrowed from Smith) that would fund the passage of immigrant workers from Britain so as to deploy the oversupply of labor at home to relieve a labor shortage in the penal settlement. The fixing of a so-called sufficient price for colonial lands would achieve two related ends. First, it would regulate the numbers of laborers who could become landowners, thereby producing the requisite balance between land under cultivation and labor supply to keep wages low and markets profitable for colonial capital. Second, it would concentrate the settler population (the proportion of people to territory, as Wakefield was to put it) in such a way as to produce the conditions (that is, the cheap labor) upon which the accumulation of wealth and its attendant cultural benefits (leisure, knowledge, and "civilization") were understood to depend.

Wakefield's theory was essentially an adaptation of David Ricardo's analysis of the relations between land, labor, and capital—one that understood the setting of a fixed price for land as a means of tweaking the three-factor economy in the colonial context, where large expanses of territory otherwise threatened supply-side advantage by inflating the value of labor and diminishing capital returns. But more than other political economists of his day, Wakefield saw and theorized the connection between a managed economy and social relations (or what he called in the context of settlement, "civilized" values), and he was able to do so precisely because he understood himself to be projecting sound economic principles into the apparently blank space of the colonies. His working definition of colonization was "the creation and increase of *everything but land,* where there is *nothing except land*"[9]—an invocation of terra nullius that paradoxically helped bring the social and cultural relations of colonial capital more clearly into view. For Wakefield, European traditions, tastes, and manners were the agents of civilized values, the means by which the chaos of the colonial wilderness could be brought to order. Settler societies were otherwise at risk of lapsing into barbarism or "newness"—the forms of cultural degeneration caused by the isolation and deprivation of the colonial frontier—of which America was Wakefield's primary exemplification.

It was this "insight" about the social relations of capital that later led Marx to acknowledge Wakefield as the leading political economist of his period and that, conversely, licensed Wakefield to merge policy-oriented analysis with extravagant fantasy and rhetorical excess. Take for example the following conceit from his first major text on colonization, *Letter from Sydney* (1829). It imagines happy colonial and metropolitan communities as by-products of a futuristic imperial economy in which labor and land (and their economic/cultural indices, everything and nothing) have struck a perfect balance: "[T]he mother country and the colony would become partners in a new trade—the creation of happy human beings; one country furnishing the raw material—that is, the land, and the dust of which man is made; the other furnishing the machinery—that is, men and women, to convert the unpeopled soil into living images of God."[10] Here the global sympathy to which eighteenth-century benevolent sentimentalists appealed is figured as something like the industrial production of human beings. But it is not just that older tropes of colonial familialism have been reconstructed within a utilitarian calculus of the free-trade economy for which raw materials + machinery + trade partners = happy human beings. We need to notice that Wakefield attributes a godly creative power to his colonial model of that economy, and particularly to "sufficient price" as the single mechanism by which land, labor, and capital could be coordinated in the new colonies so as to generate civilizations from nothingness.[11]

As it happens, Wakefield was wrong about "sufficient price," as he was about most aspects of his theory. By the 1840s, systematic colonization had spawned a number of ventures in Australia and New Zealand (and later also in Brazil), but none came close to realizing Wakefield's forecasts, and all demanded that he modify or abandon his principles in the face of local conditions. It took just a few years for South Australia, the very first Wakefieldian settlement, established in 1836, to discredit Wakefield's claims for "sufficient price." In theory, a fixed price would regulate the expansion of settlement and generate proportional immigrant labor supply. In fact, it had merely enriched British investors, who failed to employ local labor and readily resold their land for huge profits that were lost to the colony. And experiments with Wakefieldian land reform in New South Wales pointed to the impracticality of so-called concentrated settlement in the colonial context. Wakefield had theorized culture as an effect of population mass, and calculated that restricted land sales would enable class and property relations to be finessed in such a way as to optimize civilized social outcomes.[12] What he hadn't understood was that an artificially "concentrated" economy could only hobble development in New South Wales, where ventures such as sheep farming required vast amounts of acreage to be profitable.

Of course the vulnerability of any systematic theory is precisely its systematicity; one false premise can bring down the entire house of cards. Wakefield seems to have known this, and in the face of the failure of his policy experiments, he showed an extraordinary readiness to revise elements of his theory. As early as 1836, he had jettisoned one of his key principles, that land sales ought to be pegged to immigration flow, and in the 1840s he conceded that concentrated settlement was ill-conceived.[13] Nonetheless, he never recanted from systematic colonization per se, and he retained an indefatigable appetite for new colonial projects through which his system might be realized. Historians continue to debate his merits: throughout the nineteenth century he remained—and to some degree remains—a controversial figure. Yet there is little disagreement about his influence: if his system was misguided, his broader vision was prescient.[14] Colonialism as a great philanthropic enterprise of economic and cultural improvement, emigration as a means of alleviating the condition of Britain's poor and creating new horizons for its emerging "uneasy" classes, and empire as a glorious, happy, self-governing system—these are the contours of the Wakefieldian dream as it bound home and colony together like no vision of colonialism before it and gave expression to high-minded white settler visions of Australian and New Zealand development.

There can be little doubt that the legacy of Wakefield's settler vision is ideologically retrograde. Indeed for today's scholars and historians systematic colonization is little more than an intellectual ruin that attests to the folly and hubris of Victorian and proto-Victorian imperialisms. It does so on two counts. First, it sought to replicate English economic and social structures in the colonial environment. In the words of Philip Temple, Wakefield's latest biographer, Wakefield set out "to manufacture kitset Little Englands" in the Antipodes.[15] As early as 1848, the socialist Labour League criticized systematic colonization as simply a "facsimile of English society with its classifications,"[16] identifying Wakefield's scheme with the "ameliorative" politics of the middle-class reform movement. From this point of view, systematic colonization merely extends the yoke of capitalism into a new, liberal imperium by using assisted emigration schemes to siphon off revolutionary energies at home and fixed-price land sales to subordinate labor in the colonies. More recent criticism has foregrounded the cultural politics of Wakefield's system. For him, successful colonization would take the form of "little Englands" because England was the index of economic prosperity and civilized values. But there was some circularity in his thinking, so that later in his career Wakefield came to view Englishness as a requirement rather than merely an effect of colonial prosperity. In *A View of the Art of Colonization,* for instance, he concluded that "colonial prosperity . . . only attains the maximum in colonies peopled by the energetic Anglo-Saxon race."[17]

This brings us to the second key objection to Wakefield's work—that his understanding of colonial settlement as a form of mimesis involved, by default, the systematic erasure of indigenous cultures. After all, his theory was premised upon the concept of *terra nullius,* and so it took no account of the native peoples' prior possession of the "waste lands" it proposed to package and cultivate. Nor did it concern itself with the questions of law and sovereignty that underpinned its assumption that secure private property would form the basis of colonial settlement. This is all the more obvious since Smith himself had lamented the "misfortunes" of colonized native peoples,[18] and the first generation of philosophic radicals were such forceful critics of colonialism, and in Bentham's case, of the legal grounding of the New South Wales settlement in particular.[19]

As we might expect, Wakefield's failure to conceive of indigenous rights and sovereignty has made him a bête noir for postcolonial studies, and most particularly for scholars of colonial and postcolonial New Zealand, where his theory extended furthest and shaped the course of Maori/Pakeha conflicts over land to this day. Indeed it is entirely appropriate that Wakefield's dubious modern reputation has been forged within the farcical circumstances surrounding the British claim to sovereignty in New Zealand and the signing of the Treaty of Waitangi in 1840. Wakefield's New Zealand Company agents arrived without a charter, forcing the hand of the British government by buying as much Maori land as possible in anticipation of annexation. When the settlers arrived, most of the 20 million acres that had been precipitously exchanged in bogus deals with North Island tribes were the subject of disputes that escalated into the wars of the 1860s.

It is perhaps unsurprising, then, that having once been celebrated as a heroic figure—a great "founding father" and an "architect of the British Commonwealth"—Wakefield is now routinely viewed as the ideologue of a British settler culture that was Anglophilic, racist, and class-bound. Yet this stereotype does not do justice to the radical, utilitarian roots of systematic colonization, nor indeed to the distinctive style and utopian eccentricity of a text such as *Letter from Sydney*. Indeed Wakefield's early writing has tended to be swallowed up (and is now tainted) within characterizations of his project as a whole, and this is partly because he himself treated *Letter from Sydney* as a rudimentary draft of the theory that he went on to revise and develop in later writings. Yet there is a case to be made for that text's particularity, and it lies not least in the extraordinary circumstances of its production.

Wakefield wrote *Letter from Sydney* from Newgate prison, where he was serving a three-year sentence on charges of conspiracy relating to his abduction of Ellen Turner, a fifteen-year-old schoolgirl and heiress to a Manchester banking fortune, in March 1826. With the help of his brother William, Wakefield had kidnapped Turner from her boarding school and spirited her away to Gretna Green, where she had married him, believing the union would save her father from financial ruin. This was the second time Wakefield had eloped with an heiress, and his father, uncles, and brothers had all been involved in similar matrimonial adventures. After having been moderately enriched by his first wife, Eliza Pattle, and left alone with two young children by her premature death, he turned again to stratagem to secure his future, hoping to receive, along with Ellen Turner's hand, her father's fortune and political backing. The plan failed when Ellen Turner renounced him after being rescued by her family. Wakefield was prosecuted, and after a very public trial involving his vociferous self-defense, the marriage was dissolved by a special act of Parliament. Wakefield himself was imprisoned. He escaped the death penalty, but he had forfeited his reputation and with it any chance of a political future or a public career.

The point of recalling *Letter from Sydney*'s sensational "back story" is to remind ourselves of the extremity of the disjunction between the text's authorial and fictional worlds. Narrated in the persona of a disgruntled colonial landowner, yet composed in a prison cell in London, *Letter from Sydney* was published in nine anonymous installments in the *Morning Chronicle*, and then issued as a book edited under the name of Wakefield's friend and fellow radical reformer, Robert Gouger, in December 1829.[20] Wakefield had never been to Australia, or to any of the colonies, so he had asked his uncle Daniel to bring every available published account of the Botany Bay penal colony to his cell. The text he wrote wove the details appropriated from these colonial texts into the analytical categories of classical economics by presenting itself deceptively, or at least fictively, as the letters of a reform-minded colonist.

So *Letter from Sydney* was motivated by a combination of reckless adventurism, reformist enthusiasm, and self-redemptive ambition. Its grandiose rhetorical style bespeaks Wakefield's belief in the transformative power of the new political economy and in the principles of philosophic radicalism systematized and applied to New World contexts. Indeed Wakefield believed he had done nothing less than mastermind the penal colony's development into a civil society with a free-trade economy, all from the vantage point of his prison cell.[21] The text does indeed transform the grim consequences of his elopement into the fabric of a new vision of (a privately funded, public-spirited) benevolent colonialism. It does so by means of a number of ingenious substitutions and connections between old world and new: surplus metropolitan labor is offset by surplus colonial land, and Wakefield's own disgrace and imprisonment in Newgate, which he called his "terra incognita," is refigured as a glorious, prosperous future for all British subjects, premised, as we've seen, upon the allure and promise of terra nullius.

Wakefield was by no means the first British writer to view the colonies as a theater of self-redemption—Richard Savage, another maverick cultural figure and confidence man, had done so almost a century earlier.[22] But the story that underpins Wakefield's colonial dreaming reminds us that *Letter from Sydney* was just that—an imaginary narrative, a colonial fantasy—one that belongs to the long tradition of precolonial utopias focused upon the austral regions as places of fabulous inversion (I am thinking here of the work of Henry Neville and Therese Huber, for instance, with which it shares a sexual frisson).[23] Viewed in this light, the failures of systematic colonization begin to take on a different complexion. Wakefield's inability to account for local conditions, or to imagine prior possession of the lands he fetishized, or indeed, significantly to depart from a mimetic vision of colonial worlds—are clumsy, giveaway clues to the text's compensatory impulse and the intensely fictional, indeed fantastical status of the Australasia it portrays. Here, in its very first iteration, Wakefield's systematic vision is yet to congeal into an orthodox settler ethic, or, as we will see, any kind of ethic at all.

This is not to suggest that we read *Letter from Sydney*'s nascent colonial plan in narrowly biographical terms. The text is not adequately understood, as some recent critics have suggested, as an extension of the character traits that led Wakefield to abduct Ellen Turner (though there is clearly an important link between the adventurism of his life and his work).[24] Nor is it a simple fantasy, though I would argue that its interest for readers today is partly as an unrevised theoretical document, a piece of pure speculation, untried and unimpeded by any experience of the colonial world it purports to represent. Rather the text's significance lies in its particular blend of utopian dreaming and utilitarian policy formulation. *Letter from Sydney* anchors its colonial utopia—a new world that enjoys the virtues and refinements of the Mother Country but is free from all of its evils—in a detailed economic plan for fixed-price land sales in New South Wales, mixing the nuts and bolts of land tenure, labor relations, investment forecasts, and colonial reportage with an all-encompassing, systematic vision. Alloyed in this manner, it looks toward the public-spirited settler projects of the Victorian period while retaining links to early Pacific colonialisms of sensibility and whimsical self-projection.

I want to conclude by touching upon *Letter from Sydney*'s unorthodox treatment of three key issues for the early Australian colonies: labor, population, and national identity as it turned upon race. I am focusing on these issues because they have been relatively neglected in Wakefield scholarship and because they provide a framework for recognizing the text as a radical document. Wakefield's argument proceeds by stealth. The colonist-narrator promotes his "sufficient price" system by false advocacy, detailing the policy *alternatives* by which a profitable balance of land, labor, and capital might be secured. These alternatives include the introduction of "negro slavery" to address the demand for labor;[25] the mass importation of English prostitutes to correct the disproportion of the sexes in the colonies;[26] and finally and most audaciously, a plan to channel Chinese immigrant labor to Australia, at the rate of "millions" per year, to create sufficient population density in the new colony.[27] Offered merely as "pseudo solutions" to the problem of colonial labor supply, each proposal is patently less desirable than the sufficient price system, though equally effective in terms of pure utility. What we need to notice here is that for all the guile with which Wakefield details the abject cruelty, sexual delinquency, and overwhelming foreignness that might yet thrive in the fledgling colony, it is still the case that he was able to imagine multiple experimental political and cultural futures for Australia (even while he prescribed those futures within narrow, economistic measures). We are reminded, for instance, that radical utility would have New South Wales be a prosperous extension of China as readily as of Britain. The key to the text's extraordinary latitude in this regard is its trenchant critique of benevolent sympathy in favor of benevolent improvement for the common good. This licenses Wakefield to flirt with what we might think of as a systematic amoralism with regard to the colonies. And in this latitude it enables us—even today—to catch sight both of the contingencies of history and of alternative possibilities for Australia: colonial Australia based on slave labor; an Australia populated not by European settlers, but by the Chinese; and Australia as an experiment in reformed social existence for sexual renegades. Imagining these Australias along with Wakefield has, I would suggest, the salutary effect of making us less complacent about, and less secure in, the Australia that history bequeathed us.

NOTES

1. Adam Smith, *An Inquiry into the Nature and Causes of the Wealth of Nations,* ed. Edwin Cannan (1792; New York: Modern Library, 1937), pp. 531–32.

2. Ibid., p. 555.

3. Johann Gottfried Herder, *Philosophical Writings,* ed. and trans. Michael N. Forster (Cambridge: Cambridge University Press, 2002), p. 352.

4. Michael Forster, Introduction, in Johann Gottfried Herder, *Philosophical Writings,* trans. Michael Forster (Cambridge: Cambridge University Press, 2002), p. xvii.

5. Jonathan Lamb, *Preserving the Self in the South Seas, 1680–1840* (Chicago: University of Chicago Press, 2001), p. 4.

6. Eramus Darwin, *The Temple of Nature; or, The Origin of Society* (1803), in *Literature Online,* http://lion.chadwyck.com (accessed March 12, 2005).

7. Johann Reinhold Forster, *Observations Made during a Voyage Round the World,* ed. Nicholas Thomas, Harriet Guest, and Michael Dettelbach (Honolulu: University of Hawai'i Press, 1996), pp. 222–23.

8. Edward Gibbon Wakefield, *Letter from Sydney,* in *The Collected Works of Edward Gibbon Wakefield,* ed. Muriel F. Lloyd Prichard (London: Collins, 1968), p. 113.

9. Ibid., p. 135.

10. Ibid., p. 168.

11. In posing the effects of "sufficient price" terms, which flirt with the divine power of generation, Wakefield offers an uncanny insight into the mystical dimension of Smithian political economy. For it, the laissez-faire market functions as a hidden hand whose effects amount to something akin to a manifestation of intelligent design in the economic sphere.

12. That is, the restriction of land sales would both protect the value of existing land holdings and prevent laboring classes from becoming property holders too readily.

13. Eric Richards, "Wakefield and Australia," in *Edward Gibbon Wakefield and the Colonial Dream: A Reconsideration,* ed. Friends of the Turnbull Library (Wellington: GP Publications, 1997), pp. 92–93.

14. Wakefield was a tireless propagandist and agitator in support of his theory, bringing his fellow philosophic radicals (with the exception of John Arthur Roebuck and John Bowring, the editor of the *Westminster Review*), the Colonial Office, and the public alike around to a new kind of colonial policy.

15. Philip Temple, *A Sort of Conscience: The Wakefields* (Auckland: Auckland University Press, 2002), p. 134.

16. Labour League, quoted in Temple, *A Sort of Conscience,* p. 132.

17. Wakefield, *A View of The Art of Colonization,* in Lloyd Prichard, *Collected Works,* p. 800.

18. Smith, *Wealth of Nations,* p. 590.

19. See "Panopticon versus New South Wales: or, The Panopticon Penitentiary System, and the Penal Colonization System, compared," in *The Works of Jeremy Bentham,* vol. 4 (Bristol: Thoemmes Press, 1995), pp. 173–249.

20. Temple, *The Wakefields,* p. 134.

21. In the attempt, he had restored himself to the good opinion of his family, all committed philanthropists and reformers in the Nonconformist tradition. His father was an associate of Bentham and Mill, and his grandmother, Priscilla Wakefield, invented savings banks as a means of empowering the poor and wrote a series of morally instructive children's books and travel tales extolling the virtues of knowledge and industry.

22. Savage published a poem, "Of Public Spirit," in 1737, which contains an attack on colonial commerce and an encouragement to settler colonialism. It is implicitly an attack on Walpole and speculative schemes such as the South Sea Company. Lamb notes that it is an "allegory" in which "Discovery is sent out at the behest of Public Spirit to find space for Population." *Preserving the Self,* p. 212.

23. Henry Neville's *The Isle of Pines, or, A Late Discovery of a Fourth Island near Terra Australis* (London: Cadell, 1768) was set in a presettlement utopia in the South Seas where sexual desire was imagined to flow freely. Therese Huber's *Adventures on a Journey to New Holland,* trans. Rodney Livingstone (1793; Melbourne: Lansdowne Press, 1966) was the first novel set in the new Australian colony. Huber was an exponent of experimental marriage and used the novel to present a fictionalized account of her simultaneous relationships with her husband, Georg Forster, the son of Johann Reinhold Forster, who had accompanied his father on Cook's second voyage, and her lover, Ludwig Huber, for whom she later left Forster.

24. See, for example, Ged Martin, "Wakefield's Past and Futures," in *Edward Gibbon Wakefield and the Colonial Dream,* pp. 29–44; and Lydia Wevers, "My Mrs Harris," in *Edward Gibbon Wakefield and the Colonial Dream,* pp. 179–85.

25. Wakefield, *Letter from Sydney,* p. 112.

26. Ibid., p. 138.

27. Ibid., p. 171. The assumption was that a Chinese labor force would be as productive as a British one, perhaps more so.

5 Benevolence, Slavery, and the Periodicals
Chris Tiffin

The periodical reviews that appeared at the beginning of the nineteenth century in that turbulent time of the Napoleonic Wars exercised an authority over public thought in Britain that has probably been unmatched at any other period of British history. While the audience was politically polarized, it was still encompassable by the writers. As R. G. Cox commented, "It was still possible to write for the reading public as a whole just as it was still possible for the reviewers to examine the whole output of the publishers."[1] The *Edinburgh Review*, edited by Scottish lawyer Francis Jeffrey, appeared in 1802 and was so successful in advocating its Liberal position that the Tories felt obliged to counter it with their own journal, the *Quarterly Review*, in 1809.[2] Far more intellectual and polemical than such journals of record as the *Annual Register* and the *Gentleman's Magazine* that had flowed through from the eighteenth century, the new *Reviews* consisted of long anonymous essays ostensibly reviewing particular publications, but often simply using them as jumping-off points for freewheeling, magisterial essays on the topic at hand. Perhaps most familiar to literary scholars for their savaging of Keats and allegedly hastening his death, the *Reviews* played a significant role in the campaign for the abolition of slavery. This essay analyzes the stance the *Reviews* took on the slavery question and the ways in which benevolent positions were defined against issues of partisanship, Christianity, the law, and economic interest.

Slavery has a history as long as humanity, but it took its modern European form with the settlement of the Americas in the sixteenth century to provide labor for the New World plantations. From being one of the initial leaders of the African slave trade, Britain began to campaign for its abolition in the eighteenth century. In 1807 Britain and the United States abolished the slave trade to their colonies and agitated for the universal abolition of slavery. In 1834,

Britain abolished slavery in its colonies, although full emancipation did not come until 1838. An extensive, violent economic system is not transformed overnight, however, and the first few decades of the nineteenth century show contested progress toward the abolition of this system. The *Reviews* played a significant role in this progress, monitoring government reports, scouring colonial travelers' books, and debating with writers of pamphlets. Closely connected with the respective major political parties, they addressed as much the country's lawmakers as the private reader and continued debates that had been conducted in the House of Commons. The *Edinburgh* mounted a more concerted campaign since abolition was a major interest of one of its most prolific contributors, Henry Brougham, director of the African Institution. As early as 1803, his first book, *An Inquiry into the Colonial Policy of the European Powers*, had concluded with a denunciation of both the slave trade and slavery itself. The *Quarterly*'s essays on the slavery question were more disparate, being contributed by a number of writers rather than mostly by a single champion like Brougham. The articles ranged from high-minded endorsements of reformist principles to cautious and even reactionary pronouncements about the necessity of maintaining the existing economic structures. Painting itself as reasoned and balanced, the *Quarterly* exhorted Britain "to adopt and to sustain a steady line of policy, consistent with national honour, and not to be warped either by sordid views of interest, or by any vague notions of undiscriminating philanthropy."[3] There was greater agreement between the two journals when the topic was the Foreign Slave Trade, as benevolent principle and competitive patriotism then coalesced. When the topic was the emancipation of the West Indian slaves, the *Quarterly* was far more sympathetic to the position of the West Indian planters living in London. For John Barrow the issue was not one of the rights and wrongs of slavery, but rather between the competing claims of the slaves and their planter masters. In fact, Barrow argued that the planters (and the colonial legislatures) should be the agency through which emancipation, when it arrived, should proceed. It would be invidious for the Imperial Parliament to legislate against the planters for the benefit of the slaves: "Let us be careful then that the full tide of our philanthropy for the blacks sweep not away the lives and fortunes of the whites. Whatever is done with a view to emancipation, must flow, as a boon, from the proprietors of the slaves not be forced from them by any enactment of the British parliament."[4]

The typical Brougham article on the slave trade lists a number of publications, including parliamentary speeches and commissioners' reports, memoirs of colonial travel, pamphlets by the African Institution, and counter-pamphlets by the plantation lobby. The article argues a case about some aspect of the trade, drawing evidence from the works. It does not usually provide a close examination of the works themselves but absorbs them into its own polemic. Rhetorically, even when the argument is primarily about economics, the article opens with graphic descriptions of the privations and suffering that characterize the slave experience, so that the reader comes to statistics on sugar markets and colonial trade well primed with a sense of the misery endured by humans whom the trade designated as "chattels" for the sake of an argument about insurance.[5] Two motifs in particular recur as the icons of the inhumanity of slave practice: the suffocating overcrowding of the slave ships and the separation of families at slave sales once the slaves had landed.

It is usual for those prosecuting a disinterested cause to believe that cause just, and the connection between benevolence and right behavior is usually taken to be a close one. But this is not always true, so when Henry Brougham in the *Edinburgh* reviews the trial of some slave traders in Sierra Leone, he finds a sticking point that prevents him from taking the sort of satisfaction in the slavers' being convicted that we might have expected. As a lawyer and member of Parliament, Brougham shows a fine sense of the importance of due process, even when recounting the most heinous of crimes and cruelties. His stance is explicitly pedagogic: he reviews the report of the trial in some detail "for the sake of the colonial functionaries entrusted with the administration of the new law."[6]

The legal point at which Brougham jibs is one of jurisdiction. Britain's jurisdiction was limited to British subjects and foreigners acting on British soil. The slaver in this case, Samuel Samo, claimed he was a Dutchman, and as his slave-trading operation had been conducted outside a British area, he argued that he did not come under British law. The judge at Sierra Leone disagreed and continued the trial, but Brougham argues that this was poor proceeding, and that it was the responsibility of the prosecution to establish the identity and allegiance of the accused or the judge should have released him. The judge in sentencing showed much eloquence in excoriating the enormities of which Mr. Samo had been guilty, a response that the abolition movement could admire. However, the *Edinburgh* argues that the cause of abolition was not served by indulging in humanitarian zeal to the neglect of the law:

> [I]f force of language were the only, or even the principal requisite in the judicial character; or if zeal in behalf of a good cause, could authorize the dispensers of justice to gratify any private feelings on the Bench, we should not have a word to say upon any part of these proceedings. But a judge has one duty only to perform; and if any man should be free from all passion, nay, from all feeling, (were it possible), it is he who sits on the judgment seat.[7]

In Sierra Leone, where these trials took place, there was considerable support among the white population for the abolition movement, and in such a case the judge may have found himself in the peculiar position of quasi protector of someone whose deeds were manifestly abhorrent. Hence, Brougham argued, "It was therefore peculiarly the duty of the judge to stand between the accused and this popular feeling,—exactly as in the other colonies the first duty of the magistrate undoubtedly is, to stand between the negro and his oppressors,—that the deep-rooted prejudices of the whites may not carry away before them all law, humanity and justice."[8] Brougham makes a clear distinction here between the processes of law and the endorsement of an unquestionably good cause. Benevolence is a feeling that issues in the pursuit of practical campaigns for socially desirable ends, but those good ends cannot justify a distortion of the sequence of due process. The claims of the law are paramount even if they frustrate the progress of the abolitionists.

Writers point to a similar frustration in the context of intercepting slave ships at sea. During the Napoleonic wars Britain's naval superiority had had the side effect of repressing the slave trade, but the peace had restored it. Britain sought to establish antislaving treaties with the other European powers, including reciprocal authority to intercept and search suspect vessels, and in 1818 posted a navy squadron to the west coast of Africa to intercept slaving ships and to emancipate their cargoes. Their jurisdiction, however, extended only to ships of those countries that were signatories to specific anti-slave-trade conventions.[9] By flying the flag of a nonsignatory country, a ship could assure itself of immunity. The British would sometimes intercept such ships, discover slaves in appalling conditions, but be able to do nothing toward liberating them. The *Quarterly* cites an interception of a ship that was thought to be Brazilian at a time when Brazil was interdicted from slaving north of the equator, although it was still permitted to trade further south. The slaver had fled for thirty hours before it was overhauled by the British. It had been intercepted above the equator, and the slaves on board claimed to have been from areas north of the equator. All the circumstantial evidence pointed to its being in breach of the law. Nevertheless, "the captain . . . was provided with [i.e., possessed] papers, which exhibited an apparent conformity to the law, and which, false as they may have been, yet could in no way be absolutely disproved." Thus, as the *Quarterly* writer laments, no action could be taken: "The reader will be not a little disappointed to learn that, with all this, the case was deemed too doubtful, in point of legal proof, to bear out a detention; and the slaver, therefore, after nine hours of close investigation, was finally set at liberty, and suffered to proceed."[10]

Even where a treaty existed, slave trading persisted with the apparent connivance of the respective foreign governments. In 1821, the *Edinburgh* described a recent French slave voyage during which an ophthalmic disease broke out, blinding all of the slaves and most of the crew, including the captain and the surgeon.[11] The incident was fully written up in a French medical journal, which featured such matter-of-fact details as the blinded slaves' being thrown overboard as no longer salable.[12] However, when the French government was pressured into investigating this breach of the slave-trade treaty, it eventually reported that a "strict enquiry" elucidated the information that the captain of the vessel had no knowledge of any French slave-trading activity but that he had heard at St Thomas that it was the custom of Spanish and Portuguese slave ships that had encountered French ones to adopt their names,[13] although he did not know the motive for this. The *Edinburgh*'s forensic analysis of this Gallic Sir Humphrey Appleby evasion was calculated to pressure the Home government into pursuing the French on the matter. The *Review*s understood governmental inertia, and the need constantly to push and prod.

The question of law is raised also by T. B. Macaulay in the *Edinburgh* in dealing with the objection made by colonists that the abuses and cruelty on plantations that abolitionists cited were extreme examples, that random crimes could be found in all societies, and that it is improper to judge the whole society or system by them.[14] Macaulay follows James Stephen in laying out the legal constraints on the West Indian plantation slave to show that before the law he was literally a chattel, subject in every way to his master, with the sole constraint that the master did not have the right to kill him. The actual legal basis of the slaves' existence is shown to be intolerable. Macaulay dismisses the further colonist claim that, while the formal law may be restrictive, in practice the system is "lenient and liberal," with the tart observation that "public feeling, though an excellent auxiliary to laws, always has been, and always must be, a miserable and inefficient substitute for them" because it acts strongly on the sensitive but is ignored by the brazen.[15] As a moderator of practice in a slave-owning situation, public opinion must fail since the slave's opinion counts for nothing; therefore the idea that public opinion can be both balanced and self-correcting is illusory. "The opinion then, which is to guard the slaves from the oppressions of the privileged order, is the opinion of the privileged order itself."[16] Macaulay elaborates an argument that basically says legal license invites abuse, concluding, "There is only one way in which the West Indians will ever convince the people of England that their practice is merciful, and that is, by making their laws merciful."[17]

Benevolence is an attitude, an emotion that eschews worldliness, so it finds its strangest and most difficult arguments when it encounters economics. The emancipation movement had always to counter the argument that Britain and its colonies could not *afford* to abandon slavery. It was standard belief that whites *could* not perform the heavy labor of the sugarcane fields, and that blacks *would* not without coercion. To abolish slavery but still ensure that the former slaves carried out the work, some form of moral coercion had to be introduced to replace the physical coercion of the whip. According to R. J. W. Horton, this substitute might take the form of training the naturally indolent Negro in acquisitiveness—inculcating "a new series of feelings and opinions, creating an interest in property, and a fixed and unshaken desire to better the condition of himself and his family."[18] Such training could easily be accomplished under the sign of Christianity since the desired attributes, such as thrift and industry, were exactly in line with Protestant teaching. It would, however, be a slow and lengthy process.

The relationship between slavery and Christianity as figured in the *Quarterly Review* is strangely paradoxical. While slavery could be denounced as an absolute evil, and Bishop Warburton praised for his sermons rejecting the slavers' equation of humans with property,[19] Christianity could be summoned also to support arguments that seemed ingeniously tolerant of slaving practices. In fact the *Quarterly* writers showed some deftness in admitting the antislavery tendency of Christianity, but not thereby feeling that Christians had an obligation actively to oppose slavery. Robert Horton accords the MP George Canning the last word on the topic in quoting his speech in the House of Commons: "Assuredly no Christian will deny that the spirit of the Christian religion is hostile to slavery, as it is to every abuse and misuse of power: it is hostile to all deviations from rectitude, morality and justice; but if it is meant that in the Christian religion there is a special denunciation against slavery, that slavery and Christianity cannot exist together, I think the proposition is historically false."[20] This passage seems to contain a remarkable evasion. It admits both that Christianity has an essential hostility to injustice and abuse of power and, by implication, that slavery involves both, yet seems to think that there are historical reasons that remove the onus on modern Christians to alter their behavior according to its dictum. Canning goes on to argue, in fact, that Christianity has been very successful in adapting itself to many social and political situations, and that the faith has provided consolation to the oppressed, just as it has provided "lustre" to the great. Canning seems to see Christianity as having a role to play in human life that is supportive of the oppressed but not constraining on the oppressors. Using biblical precedents, John Gibson Lockhart also considered that Christianity took no clear position against slavery. Lockhart denounced slavery as evil, but in the case of the West Indies endorsed its continuance during a transition period that might last for "real *bona fide* human generations."[21] His paper found support for this view in Christian Scripture since the Old and New Testaments contain many references to slavery, yet nowhere do they explicitly denounce it. Therefore, he argued, it must be assumed that both the evil of slavery and the injudiciousness of attempting to eradicate it rapidly were ideas central to the earliest Christian practice and belief.

> That the existence of slavery is an evil—who is he that will deny? Upon that point there can be no dispute surely among Englishmen.—But the question is not whether slavery be or be not an evil; but whether, once existing, it be or be not an evil capable of reaching a hasty termination otherwise than in the creation of evils greater than itself. Now, if we assume—as who can hesitate about assuming?—that the evil of slavery was abundantly appreciated by the inspired founders of our religion, it is, we must say, absolutely impossible to explain the conduct they pursued in regard to the slavery of the Roman empire, otherwise than by holding them to have deliberately formed and uniformly acted upon the latter of these two opinions.[22]

The key words here are, perhaps, "once existing." The *Quarterly* seemed susceptible to the planters' view that whatever the rights or wrongs of slavery in the abstract, it existed, and a huge amount of English capital and endeavor had been devoted to it. Slavery underwrote an economic project that was vital to the progress and well-being of both the colonies and Britain. It was characterized by relations of dependency and comparative intimacy. These complex economic and personal relationships could not be suddenly ruptured by a fiat of Parliament; they must be allowed to atrophy and dissolve over a very long time.

The subversion of principle by pragmatism can be seen in the same essay in a quotation that the *Quarterly* finds "honest and manly." Henry Nelson Coleridge, the author of *Six Months in the West Indies*, engages with the central question of freedom:

> I would not sell my birthright for a mess of pottage; yet if my birthright were taken from me, I would fain have the pottage left. So I scorn with an English scorn the creole thought that the West Indian slaves are better off than the poor peasantry of Britain; they are not better off, nothing like it; an English labourer with one shirt is worth, body and soul, ten negro slaves, choose them where you will. *But it is nevertheless a certain truth that the slaves in general do labour much less, do eat and drink much more, have much more ready money, dress much more gaily, and are treated with more kindness and attention, when sick,* than nine-tenths of all the people in Great Britain under the condition of tradesmen, farmers and domestic servants. . . . It seems to me that where English freedom *is not and cannot be,* these things may amount to a very consolatory substitute for it.[23]

This shows a similar rhetorical pattern to that of the previous passage, with the principle (the desirability of freedom) acknowledged but marked as irrelevant because unobtainable, just as a slave-free world was not possible. The desirable thus acknowledged and dismissed, the writer can concentrate on the lesser processes and conditions of the real world. By framing the dilemma thus, the writer can claim allegiance to the ideal principle without actually having to try to promote it, since it has already been declared impossibly remote or redundant. "If my birthright were taken from me" corresponds with "freedom is not and cannot be" in that both phrases describe a situation that purports to be established and irreversible, thereby authorizing complicity with the system as offering some "consolations."

The *Quarterly*, which sometimes seemed as annoyed by the intemperate expression of an opposing argument as by its substance, even swayed so far toward the planters' view on occasion as to depict slavery not as a present evil that could be eradicated only gradually but rather as an inherently benevolent system encouraging mutually fulfilling emotional and social relations. With no apparent irony, it ventriloquized the planters' argument that both parties had much to lose from their present situation that was too intangible to be quantified in monetary terms.

> You talk, say they, of compensation. . . . Who will compensate to us and to our slaves, for the interruption of charities which, whatever strangers may say or fancy, have been, and are, dear and valuable both to us and to them? [W]ho will compensate for the pride of kind protection taken away—the gratitude of humble hearts congealed—the daily habits of confidential intercourse broken—the sense of mutual dependence and good will extinguished?[24]

This is an extreme version of the idealized planter-slave "family," but it is clearly an image that many planters recognized and adopted, however remote from reality it was. The arguments against emancipation often included the reminder that whereas slaves were provided for until death, as free persons they would be responsible for their own upkeep and aged care.

The *Quarterly* could be pragmatic, and once emancipation in the colonies was at last proclaimed, it sought to make the most of the situation and to renew the call to unite against the real enemy, the foreign powers that persisted in the practice of slave trading. Grandly pronouncing that "from this time forth, policy and sympathy coincide" and that "the aspirations of philanthropy are no longer in conflict with any claims of property,"[25] the journal asserted that metropolitan Britons, colonial planters, and the newly emancipated slaves now had a common enemy in the foreign slave trade. The abolition of slavery may have appeared a religious and ethical question, but it subtended a string of economic and political ones. These must be recognized and anticipated or Britain would lose all the good of her abolitionist campaign and compensation monies paid to the planters. The reality was that Britain's abolition of slavery in her colonies added a proportionate cost to the production of sugar there that immediately priced it out of the Continental market. Since that market had previously taken one-sixth of the total exports from the British West Indian colonies, it could be expected that one-sixth of the West Indian planters would be driven out of business, but by adjusting tariffs and maintaining protection on its domestic consumption, Britain could ensure that the balance of the plantations were kept viable and that the freed Negroes would have work.

The *Quarterly* considers the suggestion that Britain abandon her West Indies colonies and look instead to Hindustan to produce sugar at the same cheap rates as had previously been enjoyed. It rejects this plan, though, as it would mean abandoning the newly emancipated slaves as well as the planters, and destroying the viability of the British West Indian colonies would make them vulnerable to reoccupation by slaving societies, thereby undoing all the work of the emancipation. The *Review* envisages the Negro being drawn into a working-class consumer society that will ensure the future of the sugar industry:

> [With] negroes working for wages, our colonial industry must stand upon a basis more firm and lasting than slavery could ever have constructed. Our emancipated Creoles, gradually learning, from their new state of society, and from their more equal intercourse with the whites, to entertain artificial wants and appetites, and more and more generally accustoming themselves, as their growing population diminishes their facilities of comfortable subsistence, to engage in stipendiary labour as the only means by which such wants and appetites can be gratified, will form a community of labourers ready and able to extend the operations of the British planter in the continental markets, as the produce of the foreign colonies falls off; for the diminution of foreign production will have been raising prices in those markets toward their proper level—that is, toward the level at which free labour may be employed with a profit.[26]

Emancipation from the forced labor of slavery is thus only the first step toward true beatitude. The Negro is to develop "artificial appetites" in emulation of the British, which the easy subsistence living afforded by the fertile tropical climate cannot satisfy. Hence the Negro will become available for paid labor and may help the planters regain some of the markets lost through Britain's high-mindedness.

As James Walvin points out,[27] the emancipation of the slaves did not lead to their satisfactory emplacement as a contented, free, industrious peasantry. Without the artificial supports of slave labor and preferential tariffs, the British West Indian sugar industry largely collapsed, and the former slaves either settled into a subsistence poverty or emigrated to find work on ships or in more

successful colonies. In a peculiarly sad irony, the disappointment of the abolitionists at the reluctance of successful peasant societies to spring up was laid at
the door of the ex-slaves themselves, and they were seen as too indolent to cap-
italize on their freedom. Thus one of the arguments used to justify the use of
slave labor—that the Negro was naturally lazy and incapable of industrious ambition—was deemed to have proved correct. Later in the century, Anthony
Trollope succinctly summarized this disappointed assessment: "[The Negro]
seldom understands the purpose of industry, the objects of truth, or the results
of honesty. They are a servile race, fitted by nature for the hardest physical work,
and apparently at present fitted for nothing else."[28]

The *Reviews* took a prominent role in the serious discussion of public affairs in Britain at a time when wars and revolution abroad induced repression
and censorship at home. In such a climate, the *Reviews* sought (not always successfully) to articulate a benevolent position on the slave question that rose
above party politics, that grounded any amelioration of the slave condition in
legal foundation, and that dealt with the economic ramifications of what would
be a seismic shift in Britain's colonial and domestic economies. Fundamentally
in agreement about the abstract injustice of the slavery itself, their discussion of
right remedies shows a fascinating range of skillful polemic and ingenious compromise.

NOTES

1. R. G. Cox, "The Great Reviews," in *Selections from Scrutiny*, vol. 2 (Cambridge:
Cambridge University Press, 1968), p. 242.

2. Samuel Smiles, *A Publisher and His Friends*, vol. 1 (London: John Murray, 1891),
p. 93.

3. [Richard Colley Wellesley], "Spain and Her Colonies," *Quarterly Review* 17
(1817): 551. Articles in the *Reviews* were headed simply by the list of publications being
reviewed. I follow the convention of referring to the articles by the short title used as a
running head.

4. John Barrow, "The Slave Trade," *Quarterly Review* 28 (1822): 178.

5. Averil Mackenzie-Grieve, *The Last Years of the English Slave Trade: Liverpool
1750–1807* (London: Frank Cass, 1968), p. 140. In this notorious case of the *Zong*, a
captain on a delayed voyage with diminishing food and water supplies had thrown sick
slaves overboard and claimed their deaths were caused by the adverse weather conditions
that had run down the food supplies. Adverse weather meant there would be insurance
cover, whereas if the slaves had died from "natural causes" the loss would not be covered.
In the course of putting forward a case for the ship's owners, legal counsel argued that a
captain had the right to throw the slaves overboard, as they were simply chattels like a
cask of biscuit.

6. [Henry Brougham], "The Trials of the Slave-Traders," *Edinburgh Review* 21
(1813): 76.

7. Ibid., pp. 78–79.

8. Ibid., p. 79.

9. Britain signed anti-slave-trade conventions with Holland in 1822, Brazil in 1826, and France in 1833. See W. E. F. Ward, *The Royal Navy and the Slavers: The Suppression of the Atlantic Slave Trade* (London: George Allen and Unwin, 1969).

10. [J. G. Lockhart], "The Foreign Slave-Trade," *Quarterly Review* 55 (1835): 256–57.

11. [Henry Brougham], "Foreign Slave Trade," *Edinburgh Review* 36 (1821): 34–52.

12. In the first edition. Brougham records that a second edition of the issue was published suppressing some details in order not to offend the French colonial lobby.

13. A common claim; see [John Barrow], "The Slave-Trade," *Quarterly Review* 28 (1822): 169.

14. [T. B. Macaulay], "The West Indies," *Edinburgh Review* 41 (1825): 474–75.

15. Ibid., p. 475.

16. Ibid.

17. Ibid., p. 477.

18. [R. J. W. Horton], "West India Colonies," *Quarterly Review* 30 (1824): 568.

19. [Thomas Whitaker], "Hurd's Edition of Dr Warburton's Works," *Quarterly Review* 7 (1812): 403.

20. [Horton], "West India Colonies," pp. 584–85.

21. [John Gibson Lockhart], "Six Months in the West Indies," *Quarterly Review* 33 (1826): 514.

22. Ibid., p. 503.

23. Ibid., p. 507.

24. Ibid., p. 515.

25. [Lockhart], "Foreign Slave-Trade," p. 250.

26. Ibid., p. 254.

27. James Walvin, *Black Ivory: Slavery and the British Empire,* 2nd ed. (Oxford: Blackwell, 2001), pp. 279ff.

28. Anthony Trollope, quoted in Walvin, *Black Ivory,* pp. 281–82.

6 "This Nineteenth Century of Progress and Humanity": The Life and Times of Frederick Weld (1823–1891)

Leigh Dale

I can say that I am not aware of any act of my public life which was not based on the desire of doing what was for the public good.[1]

—FREDERICK WELD

When I led my men of the 1st Battalion, Royal Irish regiment across the border into Iraq we believed we were going to do some good.[2]

—TIM COLLINS

This essay focuses on the life and work of a British subject, New Zealand colonist, and imperial governor, Sir Frederick Weld. It attempts to consider the paradoxes of Weld's reputation for benevolence as an administrator, most particularly through his role in contesting violence on the colonial frontier of Western Australia. This contestation occurred when he intervened to ensure that a white colonist was charged with murder for killing an Aboriginal man. My aim is to consider the nature of benevolent intention and its role in the imperial process, particularly in the context of the often unspoken assumption that there is a gradual and inevitable improvement in the quality of justice. The inquiry is made from a position that is "postcolonial," by which I do not mean that Australian culture has "outgrown" or "moved on" from colonization, but the opposite: that colonization has so profoundly shaped Australian society that almost no cultural analysis can legitimately reject a consideration of its impact. The "post" in postcolonial, therefore, does not mean "after" colonization, but signals an ongoing engagement with its legacy.

It is a truism to note that the Empire of Britain drew much of its legitimacy—at least in the mind of its proponents—from its claims that the ultimate motives of its key agents and proponents were altruistic ones. Few have a greater reputation in that arena than James Stephen (1789–1859), who in addition to being closely associated with the antislavery movement, was the permanent under-secretary (the most senior bureaucrat) in the Colonial Office from 1836 to 1848. The Colonial Office was the administrative heart of the British Empire, overseeing the government of British colonies other than Ireland and India. Notwithstanding its title, the policies of the Colonial Office reflected British or "imperial" political interests; these often differed from—and indeed could be diametrically opposed to—those of colonists.[3] Near the end of his long and distinguished career Stephen asserted that the British values that inspired colonization were "the most precious treasures of a great nation," and Empire the greatest gift that Britain could bestow on humanity: "[W]hen were such national powers ever employed more wisely than, or magnanimously, or beneficially, than when we converted the American and Australian wildernesses into the abodes of populous commonwealths, the inheritors of our Christianity and civilisation, and impressed with the very image and superscription of our ancient constitutional monarchy?"[4] He went on to note that it is "the right belief, or at least the traditional belief . . . that to emigrate and to colonise is the prescriptive, the hereditary, and the exclusive privilege of the race which it is the fashion to call Anglo-Saxon."[5] His qualifications here—"at least the traditional belief," "the fashion"—are the markers of Stephen's awareness of his own hyperbole, while at the same time they sanctify the dispossession of land on the basis of race. They hint at a knowledge, even among Empire's most fervent evangelists, of the cost of colonization to those who did not enjoy the "exclusive privilege" of calling themselves "Anglo-Saxon."

If Stephen's life and work give ample evidence of a strongly felt and long sustained commitment to the cause of a benign empire (along with an awareness of the difficulties of actually creating such a thing), the remarkable elasticity of faith in benevolent purpose is indicated by its residual influence in the most unexpected of places. Jennifer Rutherford argues that in the late twentieth century, supporters of Australia's One Nation party are able to "identify with and defend [a] moral code of the good Australian,"[6] while at the same time acknowledging the violence of colonialism.[7] This view is summed by a One Nation supporter interviewed by Rutherford who claimed that, in the past, "the soldiers would come out, round them [the Aborigines] up, shoot a few and do all sorts of things. They're asking for an apology for this sort of thing but that's how they dealt with things in those days. That's how they dealt with their justice. They didn't have courts like we do now."[8] The essence of the interviewee's claim is that acknowledging colonial violence is somehow anachronistic. It is the desire to examine this assumption that underpins my analysis of the life and

work of Frederick Weld; the essay also aims to demonstrate the enduring capacity of individuals to deplore individual acts of violence, while at the same
time taking for granted the legitimacy of white privilege.

Although he first took up an imperial role two decades after Stephen had
retired from the Colonial Office, Frederick Aloysius Weld's sense of his "imperial self" owed much to his faith in the benign purposes of the British Empire.
Unusually, Weld had been given an appointment after having risen to prominence through pastoralism and a career in New Zealand politics. As a colonial,
and a Catholic, with no formal military experience, he was an anomalous recruit
in a profession in which the most prized appointments were generally reserved
for senior members of the nobility and the more fashionable regiments. Weld's
experience as a colonist nurtured the assumption that he would take the "colonial" rather than the "imperial" view, by which was understood sympathy toward
the colonists rather than the land's original owners. A few months after taking
up his position in Western Australia in September 1869, Weld wrote chirpily to
a friend in England: "I am getting on very well here & I am told have a firm
hold on the people already—the 'Melbourne Argus' (the leading Australian paper) has written me up on several occasions & so have other papers out of this
colony—and here I have no opposition that can lift its head."[9] These things
would change.

On June 18, 1872, after deliberation with the members of his Executive
Council, Weld moved to suspend magistrate Edward Landor from office.[10] This
was consequent upon Landor's decision, made in collaboration with three colleagues, to reduce the seriousness of the charge against Lockier Clere Burges.[11]
Burges, a colonist, had shot and killed an Aboriginal man, a fact that was not in
dispute. In Weld's view, Landor and his colleagues were at fault in determining
that Burges should be charged not with murder, but with what was described as
the "minor charge of shooting a native with intent to do bodily harm."[12] The
view of the Colonial Office was revealed when Landor was reinstated, and subsequently promoted.[13] Burges was tried and sentenced to five years in jail, but
the Colonial Office again intervened, this time reducing the sentence from five
years to one.[14] The ostensible basis of these decisions was that Weld and his colleagues had made procedural errors.[15] Weld's biographer Jeanine Graham is
adamant that Weld was wrong in terms of law and of process, asserting he had
intruded "into a sphere of law which it was not within [his] competence to discuss."[16]

Graham gives little weight to the determination of Landor and his colleagues to ignore or to call into question the evidence of an Aboriginal witness
to the shooting, whose name is given as "Chum Chum." She notes that they justified their view on the grounds that his view had been impeded by "bushes"

(notwithstanding his statement to the contrary), that he could not have seen what had happened because he was minding a second captive, and that it was not possible for a person who had been shot to have dropped to the ground in the manner the witness described.[17] Graham does, however, note Weld's own coda to the incident: reference to a letter from Burges to another colonist, not surfacing until 1873, which seemed to imply his guilt.[18] Graham asserts that Weld erred because he sought "to apply in Western Australia a native policy which he had evolved and deemed appropriate in New Zealand,"[19] but Weld himself appealed to an Australian precedent. Writing to the Colonial Office, he noted, "Years ago, when I was a young colonist, Sir George Gipps fought the same battle for justice to the Australian native against the whole force of a powerful squatter aristocracy" in New South Wales.[20] In fact, Weld was fifteen and at school in England when the incident he cites occurred: the 1838 Myall Creek massacre and the ensuing prosecution of white stockmen, seven of whom were hanged.[21]

Weld's letters to his friends and colleagues about the Burges/Landor incident offer a rueful acknowledgement of public opinion among colonists, while carefully withholding comment on the views and actions of the Colonial Office. His own interpretation of the widespread criticism of his actions seems to have owed as much to his sense of the persecution of Catholics in England as to the colonial context, judging from a letter to Bishop Salvado (whose New Norcia mission was home to a significant number of Aborigines): "It is painful to see how little people think of the murder of a native, petitions are being signed and much sympathy displayed for Mr Landor and I am talked of as the 'persecutor' of Mr L.C. Burges. Some of the very far sighted even see a Popish plot but they are too clever—though Mr. Landor hints at it in his letter to the Secretary of State."[22] In another letter to the bishop some ten days later, Weld cast his actions in terms that appealed specifically to altruism: "[I]t was necessary in the interests of the protection of the Aborigines, and for the honour of the public service, that I should act decisively . . . and in defending myself, I am defending the weak against oppression, which is far more important than myself."[23]

Writing to his patron and friend William Monsell, latterly parliamentary under-secretary of state for the colonies, Weld implied that the tolerance of murder was built into the functioning of the law and the Colonial Office, but—wisely, as far as his own interests were concerned—he concluded that the fault ultimately lay with the colonists and not with the imperial authorities:

> [A]s I shall never get so clear a case against a magistrate again I fear that equal justice for all classes will never be enforced till the whole social character of this Colony is changed, & that future Governors will be inclined to

pass over things, as I myself was plainly given to understand on my arrival that it was far the wisest course to do with regard to the outrages on natives by men of position—to which stipendiary magistrates in some cases have simply shut their eyes.[24]

Commenting more generally on his reputation within the colony (and, clearly, attempting to smooth the way for a promotion), Weld allowed himself to bare his fangs a little, noting that it was "a small clique who wish to rule the country by backstairs influence, a few ex-convict editors, and those who think that 'gentlemen' ought to be allowed to shoot natives & take their wives," who bitterly opposed him.[25] Weld wrote again to Monsell nearly a year later, perhaps with the looming appointment of a governor to Tasmania on his mind, with further self-justification: "I think I can hardly have been wrong. indeed my own conscience & common sense would tell me *that*."[26] These letters show that Weld was keen to fortify his reputation for kindness with his most influential patrons, but his plaintive words cut little ice in official quarters, where his lack of political acumen was dismissed as indicative of an adolescent sensibility. R. G. W. Herbert, then permanent under-secretary (the position James Stephen formerly held), wrote at the end of 1874 that "Mr Weld's mind and literary style are those of a promising lad of fifteen; and I fear that he is now too old to have much prospect of developing into a statesman."[27] Nevertheless he received an imperial honor, and the desired promotion to Tasmania.

Amidst the determination of officials in Western Australia and in England to exonerate the colonists, Weld's main concern was that he be seen as having acted fairly. Just how important this was to him is indicated not only by the letters quoted above, but by events of a year earlier. Weld's credibility and authority in the colony had been undone after he was ordered by London to apologize to two colonists, after the colonial secretary in Perth, F. P. Barlee, had referred to them as former convicts.[28] During the kerfuffle that ensued, Weld sought to defend himself (as many governors did) by writing privately to an influential friend—in this case, Monsell—who he thought might put his case to the political head of the Colonial Office (then Lord Kimberley). After appropriate salutations and apologies for presuming on their relationship—indeed, urging Monsell to burn the letter if he found it inappropriate—Weld noted: "I have now received so grave a rebuke from Lord Kimberley that I cannot but think that some misconception has been the cause of it."[29] Weld's plaintive letter to Monsell was four times the length of his epistle to the same recipient pertaining to the Burges/Landor case, and, by comparison, its tone verges on hysterical. Weld supported Barlee's actions by painting a vividly derogatory portrait of his critics in the colony, before mounting an impassioned self-defense:

The former of these men . . . is a clergyman who was sentenced to life trans-portation commuted to 15 years for forgery & his colleague was sent out for robbery with violence & using a weapon both . . . men of bad character (I do not mean thieves) & gain their livelihood by a system of literary terrorism. Governor Hampton & Acting Governor Bruce were before me the objects of their violence abuse & vilification, and when they found that I was insen-sible to their gross adulation at the expense of my predecessors, & that I was not inclined to buy them but steadily went on doing my duty, they publicly warned me that they would write me down . . . *many fear them.* . . .

No man takes more interest & trouble about convicts than I do, many a one I help and many a one do I speak a kind word to when ill or dying in the hospital, many a time do I encourage those who are trying to reform & earn an honest living by respectable means, this is not the case of either Mr Beres-ford or Pearce I am sorry to say.—if it were I should be the first to help them especially Beresford, as there are the remains of a gentleman about him.[30]

Such animation, exceptional in the Weld correspondence, demonstrates that when his competence was questioned, Weld would cite benign purpose to jus-tify his actions, as he would later do in the Burges/Landor case—and be satis-fied when this aspect of his reputation was upheld. As he concluded to Monsell, in the wake of the first controversy, "I have had very satisfactory private letters from Lord Kimberley & Mr Herbert I see I can rely on a fair hearing & if after that I am shewn to be wrong in any matter I am quite willing to be told so, *as long as I get credit for honesty of purpose.*"[31]

These contrasting examples demonstrate that Weld was, at the most per-sonal level, much better able to withstand controversy in a case in which his rep-utation for benevolence was being upheld rather than impugned: writing in pri-vate about the murder case, he is much less agitated than during the controversy prompted by those whom he derided as conmen and bullies. In this context, it is worth asking whether belief in his own benevolence was always so central to Weld's identity. To examine this question, I want to return to the subject of his career prior to entering imperial service, focusing in particular on Weld's views of indigenous peoples. The trajectory of Weld's life is usefully outlined in the eulogy delivered at his funeral in 1891, an account that accorded well with his own sense of his self and values as being shaped always and primarily by his identification as a devout Catholic:

Frederick Aloysius Weld, late governor of the Straits Settlements, and Knight of the Grand Cross of the Order of St. Michael and St. George, and Knight of the Order of Pius IX, was descended from one of the oldest and staunchest Catholic families in England. . . . Whether we contemplate him as a boy at College, or as a young man going forth to the distant shores of New Zealand, there to win fame and fortune; or as interesting himself in the political welfare of his adopted country, first as member of the first Ministry, and later on as Premier, we shall be equally in admiration of his honesty of purpose, and his extraordinary sense of justice, on account of which he sometimes incurred violent, though temporary, obloquy—as, for instance, when defending the natives of Western Australia from the lawlessness of certain Europeans, and when claiming an equal justice for the black man as for the white.[32]

As this praise of his endeavors might lead us to expect, Weld is to the fore in those accounts of New Zealand's colonial history that pay particular attention to politics or pastoralism, while in general histories he appears, with his partner in pastoralism Charles Clifford, as an emblematic figure of colonial enterprise.[33] Writing for the *Oxford History of New Zealand,* Raewyn Dalziel calls him "a prominent, highly respected Roman Catholic pastoralist," while the pen-sketch in William Hosking Oliver's *Story of New Zealand* is typical:

> While the better sort of colonist had his [social] diversions, at other times he was likely to be hard at work on the real business of colonisation. . . . Once out of the towns the most graceful adornment of the drawing-room might prove the hardest of workers. Such a one was Frederick Weld, later to be premier of New Zealand and Governor of West Australia, Tasmania and the Straits Settlements, who followed his sheep first to the Wairarapa then to the Wairau and eventually to Canterbury.[34]

Such stories about "the real business of colonization" not only naturalize invasion and dispossession, they also (and importantly) presume a white reader. This reader is positioned as the heir to the work of good men like Frederick Weld, entirely approving of the process of colonization because its beneficiary.

The Australian colonies provided breeding stock for the partners of the Clifford-Weld venture and, just as importantly, a model for the appropriation of land. Indeed, Australia is very often cited as the ideal model, where colonists and imperial representatives alike presumed the desirability of dispossession and extermination of indigenous peoples. As the *Oxford History of New Zealand* puts it,

> The first wave of New Zealand squatters . . . saw that inexperience and *legal prohibition had been no barrier* to sheep-grazing in the Australian outback, and would not be in New Zealand. They did their own exploring, *bargained with Maori chiefs for illegal leases,* and shipped Merinos from Australia. In 1844 they drove their first flocks by difficult and devious routes out from Port Nicholson to the Wairarapa. A few years later these pioneers—C. R. Bidwill, Frederick Weld, Charles Clifford, and others—were being deferred to as experts in a highly profitable field.[35]

This passage implies a certain disapproval of the ease of transition from "outlaw to lawmaker," hinted at in the reference to "difficult and devious routes" taken by the sheep and their drovers.

The largest of the Clifford-Weld holdings was Flaxbourne in the South Island of New Zealand, the sheer size of which demonstrates the ways Weld's ambitions as a pastoralist were materialized: at 78,000 acres, it dwarfed the family holdings in England.[36] The rate of increase of flocks was such that Weld, at a relatively young age, was fairly quickly able to establish very considerable wealth and security, although a large family would leave him with constant concerns about money in later life. It is hardly surprising that Weld, in possession of such assets at such a young age, should write to his father in a somewhat self-satisfied tone, "I am convinced that if God places a man in a position [in the wilderness] which deprives him of religious succour . . . He thereby binds himself in a manner to afford proportionate graces and assistance."[37] As Weld saw it, the extraordinary wealth derived from his labors in the antipodes was some kind of compensation for his exclusion from the daily life of the church. More specifically, the apparent abundance and richness of resources was part of a kind of divine plan for the advancement of the white race.

Weld and Clifford's response to sighting vistas of potential grazing land was, in their own words, "overwhelmingly enthusiastic": "'The magnificent expanse of undulating grassland made beautiful by the deep shades and curling mists of morning'" was, as Weld's biographer notes, "doubtless made all the more attractive by a mental vision of hundreds of sheep upon it."[38] Jeanine Graham's interpretation of this moment introduces a trope that is central to the literature, fictional and nonfictional, of pastoralism: what I want to call, adapting a term from Mary Louise Pratt, "agricultural reverie." Pratt's "industrial reverie," a mode she associates with a period—the 1820s and 1830s—in which those traversing Empire were in search of suitable projects for European venture capital, tended not to mystify or aggrandize Europe's expansion, but rather to thematize it, "indeed, consecrate" it in a "modernizing extractive vision."[39] In colonialist histories, by way of contrast, "agricultural reverie," perhaps a mood as much as a trope, takes as its source of energy not modernization but fertility; not extraction, but reproduction; and it does similar work in fantasizing a complete absence of indigenous peoples. Yet it was not through mere fantasy, but through violence and theft, that Weld was able to transform a vision of the unfettered and accelerated reproduction of his sheep into the reality, acquiring previously unthinkable wealth. Nevertheless, reverie—with all its connotations of unfettered imagination—beautifully captures the mode of Weld's musing (and perhaps of Rutherford's interviewee).

A second element of "agricultural reverie" is the emphasis that is placed on the "unlimitedness" of the resources available to the colonist, a strategy with which any reader of Australian narratives of colonization is familiar.[40] While the trope might have been used by Weld in describing New Zealand because he was aware to some degree of the ways in which the (competitor) Australia colonies were being written, a more likely explanation is that it is crucial to the way colonization was imagined: as occurring in places so vast that competition for land was negligible. Having noted the availability of "unexhaustible pasturage combined with that shelter from wind and weather, and dryness of soil, so essential to that class of animals to which the sheep belongs," Weld suggests that the entire South Island of New Zealand, "with the exception of the great block of the Kaiko[u]ra mountains, is one vast tract of pastoral country," available for seizure by the "first" white man who surveys it: "Standing on any summit of the offspurs of the Kaikoras, or of the inland range that runs down the centre of the island, the eye wanders over an apparently interminable waste of grass land, sometimes level, sometimes heaving in a wavy outline like a sea, whilst here and there it is attracted by the gleam of rivers and streamlets, or rests on the landward peaks of snow that look down on the wide prairie."[41] The panoramic view becomes not only a metaphor for appropriation but also a promise of material wealth. And as Weld puts it, "No one can have traversed the undulating downs and grassy plains so characteristic of the Middle [South] Island, or the rich open valleys that invite the grazier in many parts of the North Island, without being struck with their peculiar fitness for stock-farming, and in many cases *for that only*."[42]

In Weld's rhetoric, the material work of colonization—taking over the land, "civilizing" or eradicating or evicting the indigenous inhabitants—becomes the accepting of an invitation not merely from the ruler of Empire, but from God, whose creative powers have been co-opted to the provision of pastoral resources. Colonization, naturalized as pastoralism, comes to constitute a benevolent and beneficent project. Notwithstanding divine assistance, Weld wrote to his mother admitting that there was active resistance to his occupation of Maori land. He confesses, "[W]e were in hourly uncertainty as to the continuation of the friendly dispositions of the natives with individuals of whom we were constantly obliged to differ & occasionally to ~~fight~~ use our fists to maintain our rights & the respect due to us."[43] Graham notes that in his diaries, "Weld recorded a number of occasions during March when his tenure was challenged";[44] another letter records a recollection of threats to burn down his house.[45] Yet at this time Weld was able to write positively of justice to individual Maoris. In the same letter to his mother, he declared,

[T]he wretched European who committed a most infamous murder at Auckland . . . has been hanged & the execution has done an infinite of good amongst the Natives who would hardly believe that we would hang a white man—There is at present a European in gaol for a brutal attack on a Native—& if the native dies he will be undoubtedly hanged—and will well deserve it this is *the first* case of European outrage against a Native that I have ever heard of and public feeling is very strong against him.[46]

Weld's condemnation of the murder of a Maori man and his expression of pleasure that a white person has been brought to justice in some important respects anticipates his actions in Western Australia—but they sit in stark contrast to his own role in occupying Maori land and defending that occupation with (an admittedly more moderate form of) violence.

When they had applied to the New Zealand Company for confirmation of their tenure, Weld and Clifford were unable to secure all the land they had initially claimed.[47] In closing his *Hints to Intending Sheep Farmers,* a handbook for British readers contemplating emigration to the colonies, Weld suggests that the colonist's only serious impediment to rapid financial advancement is the uncertainty of tenure; however, it is not Maori resistance but imperial and colonial policy that Weld cites as the danger:

I would not advise any intending flockmaster to enter upon a New Zealand career . . . were I not aware that the pastoral interest is now growing so powerful in the country—that its welfare is so intimately connected with the interests of every section of the community, and its demands so moderate and just—that I believe that the government, which has neglected it in its infancy, cannot now continue to refuse to listen to its demands.[48]

Agitation for self-government and participation in government were integral to consolidating the legitimacy of illegal squatters such as Weld—part of the transformation of colonization from an illegal into a "beneficial" process. And perhaps as a consequence of his own disappointments Weld was one of many in Australia and in New Zealand "with a vested interest in pastoral regulations [who consequently] became involved with the question of settler participation in the running of colonial affairs—or, self-government."[49]

Faith in benevolence could have a remarkable flexibility: so committed to his benignity was Weld that he could convince himself that Maori were most hurt by those who extended them charity. Writing to fellow colonist John Robert Godley in 1860, as the wars between the colonists and the Maori moved into perhaps their most heated phase,[50] he opined: "I really feel for the natives— they have been ruined by a maudlin pseudo philanthropy. Had they been treated with firmness and justice combined, they might have been saved but they have been undone by their friends. At all events the Colonists are innocent of this. The Native blood lies at the door of Exeter Hall."[51] "Exeter Hall" was the headquarters of the Aborigines Protection Society, thence a frequently used but pejorative shorthand for those with benevolent attitudes toward indigenous peoples (but, the implication was, lacking "colonial experience").[52] Significantly, notwithstanding the fact that he was speaking frankly in defense of colonial interests, Weld felt it necessary to claim a position validated by "true" benignity. He did this when he implied that a *genuine* kindness lies in "firmness and justice"; amazingly, he could thereby claim that the violence was the fault of those whites who sought justice for Maori people, not those doing the killing.

Weld's frank admission of Maori resistance to his "leases" in New Zealand, set against his behavior in the Burges/Landor case, seems to imply a contradiction that is explicable in terms of self-interest: as an imperial representative he allowed the "benevolent" aspect of his views to gain the upper hand, whereas as a colonist Weld was prepared to fight to hold his land, justifying his actions in a language that valued "true" over "false" benevolence. Certainly he was anomalous in seeming to move from the expression of a "colonial" to an "imperial" position. But the implication of expediency does not sit well with Weld's actions in Western Australia, and it also sets aside the deep religious commitment that seems to have ensured that, throughout his life, even his strongest critics spoke in admiring terms of Weld's determination always to act in good faith. So while part of the explanation for Weld's change of mind is certainly, as Graham argues, his changed institutional position, we might add that this was a change that implied a redefinition of the notion of benevolence. What remained constant in Weld was the desire to *see himself* as good. That this needed public as well as private reinforcement can be inferred from his letters, which so often make recourse to plaintive statement of his kind intentions.

Such a position makes it necessary for Weld to distance himself from extreme violence, notwithstanding the fact that that violence was intrinsic to the colonizing process in which he took such an energetic part, and from which he derived such substantial profit. That there *was* extreme violence—a point much in dispute in modern Australia[53]—was emphasized by Weld himself, in an 1874 letter to Monsell, now Baron Emly, in which he reviewed the context and the outcomes of the Burges/Landor case:

> [In Western Australia] public opinion allowed natives to be shot, & did not allow magistrates to do their duty when leading settlers & influential men were concerned. It was my duty at all risks to my future career (which the enemies I have made boast now that they have ruined at the Colonial Of-

fice) to strike a blow that would be decisive. . . . However I have my reward in knowing that since my action, *though colonization has been much extended* amongst wild natives in inland districts, there has been no outrage either on the part of whites or blacks.[54]

Weld glumly acknowledged Colonial Office toleration of the situation when he concluded by remarking, "Lord Kimberley ended by Knighting the Chief Justice. If I am promoted to Tasmania which will be vacant shortly I suppose I shall be considered as whitewashed as well as the Chief Justice."[55]

In an effort to substantiate his claims about violence toward Aboriginals, Weld directed Monsell to a letter published recently in the *Sydney Morning Herald* newspaper: "[H]eaded 'Whites and blacks in Queensland' signed by (as I am informed) a most respectable and trustworthy gentleman a Colonist that letter unfolds a state of things with regard to the treatment of the Australian blacks that is almost inconceivable but that every body says is true. . . . Do read that letter and if it does not make your hair stand on end & astonish you I do not know what will."[56]

The author of the article (which was actually titled "Black and White in Queensland"), Chas. G. Heydon, himself took up a *Herald* story of a month earlier, a report "purporting to be written by one of the Queensland Government Expedition to the North."[57] Heydon was trenchantly critical of the account of an Aboriginal stealing a flag, particularly of the lament that members of the expedition failed to shoot the thief:

> This paragraph deserves serious attention from all your readers, and from all residents in Queensland who think that blacks are human beings and not some mere vermin formed by some unaccountable freak of nature in the shape of men. Let them notice the utter want on the part of the writer and his companions of the slightest hesitation or sense of wrong in putting a native to death.
>
> This party on board the Leichardt [*sic*] had gone to establish a settlement at the Endeavour River. . . . Might we not expect that at such a time, the intruding, *civilized,* Christian, and immeasurably stronger race, would show some small desire to do good to the other, would at least wish to be friends with it? Is it at this time of day, in this nineteenth century of progress and humanity, that Englishmen, upon their settlement among an inferior race, are to despise the slightest attempt to conciliate or improve it, but to begin at once to war upon it and (for that is what such a war means) to exterminate it, for such paltry offences as that mentioned above?[58]

Heydon recounted his experiences, in his journey to the northern parts of Australia, of hearing "white men talk openly of the share they had taken in slaughtering whole camps, not only of men but of women and children": "One murder of a black woman was mentioned to me in seriousness as the sort of thing which justified any reprisals. When taken prisoner after a fight, or rather butchery of her tribe, she spat in the face of her captor."[59] Heydon's account of the "butchery," and the subsequent murder of a survivor that was justified on the grounds that she had spat at the murderers, shows the way in which a radically incommensurate response is justified by the claim to believe that murder is not a criminal act, whereas spitting is.

Heydon's argument presumes that the distinctive quality of this period in history—what he calls "this nineteenth century of progress and humanity"—should ensure justice for Aboriginal people. Whereas later interpreters presume that justice will not prevail because of the times, Heydon, writing *in that time,* presumes that *because of the time* some notion of justice should prevail. If the Burges/Landor incident calls into question the claim that "They didn't have courts like we do now," Weld's and Heydon's correspondence equally calls into question the view that the ultimate outcome of the Burges/Landor controversy—as Weld put it, a "whitewash"—is explicable simply in terms of the particular conjunction of time and place.

The violence in Western Australia was committed by colonists, but also condoned by the Colonial Office. This is surely evident in Jeanine Williams's assessment of the views of the parliamentary under-secretary of state for the colonies in 1872, Sir Edward Hugessen Knatchbull-Hugessen, on the Burges/Landor case. Summarizing Hugessen's reaction to Weld's initial dispatch, she writes, "it was clear that Weld had been carried away with his ideas of protecting the Aboriginal against 'white' oppression."[60] The scare quotes used to enclose "white" imply the impossibility of oppression: exoneration by virtue of skin color. In his own words, Hugessen's view was that "white settlers should know that in casting their lot in a British Colony . . . they are not to be subjected to the despotic power of a Governor"—that "despotism" being Weld's "interference" in judicial proceedings in an attempt to see that a charge of murder was laid.[61]

Interpretations of causality that rely on the power of convention give the lie to the complexity and volatility of individual positions within specific debates. They also inevitably perpetuate that toleration of and habituation to colonial violence built into official and unofficial policy, a particular kind of blindness that allows white perpetrators of even the worst atrocities to retain their fundamental goodness. One newspaper account of the trial of the perpetrators of the Myall Creek massacre, in which some thirty Aboriginal people were shot, mutilated, and burned, records that the judge shed tears as he passed sentence upon them—lamenting it seems (from the press account) not the massacre, but the punishment of its perpetrators.[62] Being white seems sufficient and unchallengeable proof of capacity for human feeling. Thus even Heydon describes one of the white officers of the native police as follows: "he gave me the impression of being a man animated by intense hatred for the native, and positively craving for opportunities of killing them" yet "naturally, as I really believe, *kind-hearted, and undoubtedly very pleasing in his manners.*"[63] The belief that good manners and a kind heart can be coupled with a "craving" for murder is a demonstration of the extraordinary tensile strength of belief in the inherent goodness of those who enjoy that "exclusive privilege" of calling themselves "Anglo-Saxon."

What makes the example of Frederick Weld important is that claims to benevolent intention in relation to indigenous peoples still mask racism in post-colonial societies. Rather than distinguishing between "true" and "false" forms of goodwill—although this strategy is certainly retained when considering modern cases—contemporary forms of colonialist rhetoric open up a space for the toleration of violence by claiming that colonization occurred *in another time,* thereby implying that its impact is restricted to that time. By opening up a gap between "then" and "now," a speaker can disavow responsibility for violence by claiming that ethical standards of the past were different, that violence was not regarded as problematic. It is a history that Jennifer Rutherford's One Nation interviewee reclaims, but expresses a wistful distance from: he is both the approving inheritor, and the nostalgic orphan, of an *imagined* past in which racist violence did not endure the scrutiny (let alone the condemnation) of any public institution. By looking at the history of Frederick Weld, we can know that "they" *did* "have courts like we do now," but we can also see that "[f]ar from [being] a moral absolute, the use of violence is rendered more or less justifiable, necessary, painful, or reasonable according to circumstances. The use of 'legitimate force' in 'our' society is a moral imperative in response to the use of 'violence' by 'others.'"[64] That the most significant attempt in his life to give effect to his rhetoric of benevolence met with attacks on Weld's credibility and competence from colonists *and* his imperial superiors is perhaps not comforting proof that racism is confined to another time and place, but rather suggests that the contours and outcomes of the Burges/Landor dispute are depressingly familiar to modern readers.

NOTES

1. Frederick Weld, letter to Gore Browne, quoted in Jeanine Graham, *Frederick Weld* (Auckland: Auckland University Press, 1983), p. 106. Where possible I have listed published sources for letters: among these, Graham is better than the 1914 biography by Lady Alice Lovat, *The Life of Sir Frederick Weld, G.C.M.G.: A Pioneer of Empire* (London: John Murray), the author of which is sometimes listed as Alice Mary Fraser. Al-

though Lovat reprints much of Weld's correspondence, many silent changes have been made; some other scholars also "smooth" out Weld's "hasty" style.

2. Tim Collins, "This Is a Mess of Our Own Making," *Guardian Weekly,* September 23–29, 2005, p. 16.

3. Two enduring sources of conflict were the number of imperial troops committed to the colonies and, relatedly, the level of financial support given to them.

4. Right Hon. Sir James Stephen, *Addresses of Sir James Stephen on British Colonies and Colonization* [and the Right Hon. J. Napier on *Jurisprudence and Amendment of the Laws*] (London: 1858), p. 3.

5. Ibid., p. 7.

6. Jennifer Rutherford, *The Gauche Intruder: Freud, Lacan, and the White Australian Fantasy* (Melbourne: Melbourne University Press, 2000), p. 7.

7. The One Nation party rose to prominence in the 1996 Australian federal election and a subsequent election in the state of Queensland. The headline-grabbing claims of leader Pauline Hanson about the threats to Australia posed by Aborigines and illegal immigrants, notably in her maiden speech to Federal Parliament, allowed the equally toxic but more carefully "reasoned" claims of then Prime Minister John Howard to go largely unchallenged.

8. One Nation supporter, quoted in Rutherford, *The Gauche Intruder,* p. 8.

9. Weld, letter to William Monsell, April 26, 1870, Letters from Sir Frederick Weld to Rt. Hon. J. Monsell (Under Secretary for Colonies), with some brief notes on Christian doctrine, 1869–74, Battye Library, Perth, Priv. Arch. Stack, ACC 1031A. Unless otherwise stated, references to Weld's letters refer to those held in this archive, which contains manuscripts of his correspondence pertaining to Western Australia. Monsell's correct name was William, not "J.," and his position was actually parliamentary under-secretary of state for the colonies.

10. The most detailed account of these events is Jeanine Williams's essay "Governor Weld and the Landor–Burges Affair: A Consideration," *Anthropological Forum* 3, no. 2 (1972): 157–79, some of which is reused in the briefer account given in the chapter "Western Australia," pp. 118–45 in her book *Frederick Weld,* published under the name of Jeanine Graham. See also George Russo, "Religion, Politics and W. A. Aborigines in the 1870s: Bishop Salvado and Governor Weld," *Twentieth Century* 29 (October 1974): 5–19, esp. pp. 8–10.

11. In his own defense, Landor claimed that "his insistence alone had prevented the case from being summarily dismissed." See Williams, "Governor Weld," p. 164.

12. Williams, "Governor Weld," p. 161; Graham, *Frederick Weld,* p. 137.

13. On the reinstatement see Williams, "Governor Weld," pp. 167–69; and Graham, *Frederick Weld,* p. 138.

14. Williams, "Governor Weld," pp. 172–74; Graham, *Frederick Weld,* p. 139.

15. Williams, "Governor Weld," pp. 163–74; Graham, *Frederick Weld,* pp. 137–40.

16. Williams, "Governor Weld," p. 162; Graham, *Frederick Weld,* p. 137.

17. Williams, "Governor Weld," p. 161.

18. This is mentioned in the Williams essay, but not in the biography. See ibid., p. 176.

19. *Frederick Weld,* p. 136.

20. Weld, letter to Lord Kimberley, July 18, 1872, quoted in Williams, "Governor Weld," pp. 168–69. Gipps was governor of New South Wales from 1838 until 1846.

21. On the cases *R. v. Kilmeister (No. 1)* and *(No. 2)*, 1838, both of which pertain to the Myall Creek massacre, see Division of Law, Macquarie University, "Decisions of the Superior Courts of New South Wales, 1788–1899," http://www.law.mq.edu.au/scnsw/Cases1838–39/html/r_v_kilmeister__no_1___1838.htm (accessed October 3, 2005); and http://www.law.mq.edu.au/scnsw/Cases1838–39/html/r_v_kilmeister__no_2___1838.htm (accessed October 3, 2005).

22. Weld to Bishop Salvado, June 27, 1872, quoted in Williams, "Governor Weld," p. 166; see also Russo, "Religion, Politics and W. A. Aborigines," p. 9. Early in their acquaintance Weld had described Salvado thus: "a very good man deficient perhaps in ~~princip~~ talent. though

of that I am not sure." Weld, letter to Monsell, March 3, 1870.

23. Weld, letter to Salvado, July 8, 1872, quoted in Russo, "Religion, Politics and W. A. Aborigines," p. 9.

24. Weld, letter to Monsell, November 1872. A slightly different version of this quotation is printed in Williams, "Governor Weld," p. 170.

25. Weld, quoted in Williams, "Governor Weld," p. 170.

26. Weld, letter to Monsell, August 20, 1873.

27. R. G. W. Herbert, quoted in Graham, *Frederick Weld,* p. 143.

28. Graham, *Frederick Weld,* p. 130.

29. Weld, letter to Monsell, June 15, 1871.

30. Ibid.

31. Weld, letter to Monsell, August 11, 1871 (emphasis added).

32. John S. Vaughan, *In Memoriam: Words Spoken at the Funeral of Sir Frederick A. Weld, G.C.M.G. by the Rev. John S. Vaughan, July 24th, 1891* (London: Westminster Press, 1891), pp. 5–6.

33. For the former, see George William Rusden, *History of New Zealand in Three Volumes,* vol. 2 (Melbourne: Melville, Mullen, and Slade, 1895); for the latter, see Alfred Hamish Reed, *The Story of New Zealand* (Wellington: A. H. and A. W. Reed, 1959); Angus John Harrop, *England and New Zealand: From Tasman to the Taranaki War* (London: Methuen, 1926); and Johannes Stephanus Marais, *The Colonisation of New Zealand* (1927; London: Dawsons, 1968).

34. Raewyn Dalziel, "The Politics of Settlement," in *The Oxford History of New Zealand,* ed. William Hosking Oliver with B. R. Williams (Wellington: Oxford University Press, 1981), p. 101; William Hosking Oliver, *The Story of New Zealand* (London: Faber, 1960), p. 75.

35. W. J. Gardner, "A Colonial Economy," in Oliver and Williams, *Oxford History of New Zealand,* p. 63 (emphasis added).

36. Graham, *Frederick Weld,* p. 24.

37. Weld, letter to his father, quoted in Graham, *Frederick Weld,* p. 17.

38. Graham, *Frederick Weld,* p. 19.

39. Mary Louise Pratt, *Imperial Eyes: Travel Writing and Transculturation* (London: Routledge, 1992), p. 148.

40. Kevin Frawley, "Evolving Visions: Environmental Management and Nature Conservation in Australia," in *Australian Environmental History: Essays and Cases,* ed. Stephen Dovers (Oxford: Oxford University Press, 1994), p. 63.

41. Frederick Aloysius Weld, *Hints to Intending Sheep-farmers in New Zealand* (London: Trelawney Saunders, 1851), p. 3.

42. Ibid., p. 3 (emphasis added).

43. Weld, letter to his mother, [September?] 1848 (emphasis added). The date is implied by a postscript dated October 3, 1848.

44. Graham, *Frederick Weld*, p. 13.

45. Weld, letter to his mother, [September?] 1848; see also Lovat, *Life of Sir Frederick Weld*, p. 75.

46. Weld, letter to his mother, [September?] 1848.

47. "Runs were allocated [to whites] on a first-come first-served basis and Clifford and Weld were allocated a licence to depasture 78,000 acres only." Graham, *Frederick Weld*, p. 24.

48. Weld, *Hints*, p. 12.

49. Graham, *Frederick Weld*, p. 37.

50. For an influential discussion of the wars see James Belich, *The New Zealand Wars and the Victorian Interpretation of Racial Conflict* (1986; Auckland: Penguin, 1988).

51. Weld, letter to J. R. Godley, [May?] 1860, quoted in Graham, *Frederick Weld*, p. 70.

52. Graham interprets Weld's hostility as reflecting his "religious prejudice": "only if the doctrines of Exeter Hall . . . had been Catholic-inspired could he have upheld the orthodox humanitarian ideal." *Frederick Weld*, p. 5; see also p. 70.

53. See Judith Wright, *Generations of Men* (Melbourne: Oxford University Press, 1959); William Edward Hanley Stanner, *After the Dreaming: Black and White Australians: An Anthropologist's View* (Sydney: A.B.C., 1969); George Shaw, ed., *1988 and All That: New Views of Australia's Past* (St. Lucia: University of Queensland Press, 1988); Henry Reynolds, *Why Weren't We Told: A Personal Search for the Truth about Our History* (Melbourne: Viking, 1999); Robert Manne, ed., *Whitewash: On Keith Windschuttle's* Fabrication of Aboriginal History (Melbourne: Black Inc. Agenda, 2003); Bain Atwood and Stephen Glynn Foster, *Frontier Conflict: The Australian Experience* (Canberra: National Museum of Australia, 2003); Stuart McIntyre and Anna Clark, eds., *The History Wars* (Carlton: Melbourne University Press, 2003); Stuart McIntyre, ed., *The Historian's Conscience: Australian Historians on the Ethics of History* (Carlton: Melbourne University Press, 2004); Bain Atwood, *Telling the Truth about Aboriginal History* (Crows Nest: Allen and Unwin, 2005). For provocative rejections of these academic accounts see Keith Windschuttle, *The Fabrication of Aboriginal History* (Sydney: Macleay, 2003); and John Dawson, *Washout: On the Academic Response to* The Fabrication of Aboriginal History (Sydney: Macleay, 2004).

54. Weld, letter to Baron Emly [Monsell], April 23, 1874 (emphasis added). A slightly different version of this quotation is printed in Williams, "Governor Weld," p. 177.

55. Ibid.

56. Ibid.

57. For an account of race relations in colonial Queensland (in which Heydon is briefly mentioned) see Raymond Evans, Kay Saunders, and Kathryn Cronin, "'The Nigger Shall Disappear,'" part 1 of *Race Relations in Colonial Queensland: A History of Exclusion, Exploitation and Extermination* (1975; St Lucia: University of Queensland Press, 1988), pp. 25–145.

58. Chas. G. Heydon, "Black and White in Queensland," Letter to the Editor, *Sydney Morning Herald*, February 2, 1874, p. 3.

59. Ibid.

60. Williams, "Governor Weld," p. 167.

61. Sir Edward Hugessen, quoted in Williams, "Governor Weld," p. 167.

62. Press accounts of the trial record the impediments placed in the way of those investigating the crime, and the court itself; it was perhaps significant that all of those hanged were former convicts, although the judge seems to hint strongly at the involvement of at least one landowner, Henry Dangar. See Division of Law, Macquarie University, *R. v. Kilmeister (No.2)*.

63. Heydon, "Black and White in Queensland," p. 3 (emphasis added).

64. Gillian Cowlishaw, *Blackfellas, Whitefellas, and the Hidden Injuries of Race* (Malden, Mass.: Blackwell, 2004), p. 141, citing David Riches, ed., *The Anthropology of Violence* (Oxford: Blackwell, 1986), pp. 3, 4.

7 Women, Philanthropy, and Imperialism in Early Nineteenth-Century Britain

Sarah Richardson

The lives of middle-class women in nineteenth-century Britain were intimately bound up with philanthropic activities. Charity, it is argued, was the one arena in the public sphere open to middle-class women, and indeed was their mission or calling, one for which they were particularly suited.[1] It has been claimed that women, excluded from all other areas of public and political life, colonized charities, organized missionary and evangelical campaigns, and adopted moral causes as an alternative to or as a distraction from their otherwise home-based lives.[2] Indeed, the very application of women's domestic experience to charitable activities has been considered one of the distinctive features of nineteenth-century philanthropy. For some commentators, women utilized philanthropy as a form of moral superiority, to impose middle-class values upon the hapless members of the poor whom they sought to reform,[3] although others have contested that charity transcended class.[4] For others, as Peter Mandler has recently asserted, "philanthropy provided an ideal theatre for the play of personal ambition."[5] Frank Prochaska, the most influential and perhaps most cited author on women and philanthropy, outlines a number of reasons why benevolent activities were "most compelling" to leisured women of the middle class: such activities utilized their supposed "skills" in caring for the young, the sick, and the elderly; appealed to the mission to reform the morals of the wider industrial society; became an extension of women's domestic role; and registered the influence on the female mind of the Bible's doctrine of self-sacrifice and giving.[6]

Historians have widely appreciated the contribution middle-class women made to social welfare through their philanthropic actions, both within Britain and in the wider world. The literature abounds with case studies of individual women philanthropists or examples of female local and national committees. However, these interpretations accentuate women's informal, auxiliary, and largely apolitical role in the huge expansion of philanthropic activity in the period. This is contrasted with male approaches, which are considered theoretical and which supplement practical deeds with policy initiatives. The focus on female practical acts of charity emphasizes the notion of the individual heroine tackling poverty and deprivation by direct action and underplays the intellectual and political contexts in which these women were operating. These stereotypical models do little to appreciate the varied intentions underpinning the charitable actions of both men and women in the nineteenth century.

This essay argues that middle-class women were not merely practitioners of philanthropy, but that they also made a critical contribution to the intellectual arguments that prompted and sustained such work. Middle-class women were uniquely placed in British society to participate in the theoretical debates on the role of the state and the treatment of the poor. They used both their practical experiences in the field and their identification with the philosophy of "woman's mission" to assume intellectual authority in such discussions. Women's writing in this area was widely disseminated and reviewed by contemporaries but has largely been overlooked by historians. In certain areas, for example on political economy, their work outsold that of their male contemporaries, and women played a key role in popularizing the ideas of classic theorists such as David Ricardo and Thomas Malthus.[7] Middle-class women utilized a range of literary tools to promote their political ideas for the alleviation of poverty. These included novels, poems, periodical articles, pamphlets, conduct manuals, and handbooks, which enabled them to reach both elite and popular audiences in order to maximize the appeal of their message. In these works, the language employed is complex and often contradictory. For example, middle-class women frequently sought to differentiate themselves from those they viewed as the objects of their charity. The poor are usually regarded as the uncivilized, non-Christian Other. Occasionally, writers also attempted to identify with the suffering of the underprivileged and dispossessed, regarding their powerlessness as akin to the civil and legal disabilities faced by all women in this period. This was particularly perceptible in female writing on antislavery, where there was an attempt to empathize with female slaves as oppressed women.[8]

Many treatises, pamphlets, and discussion papers on the issue of women and philanthropy were infused throughout with the language of cultural, social, racial, and ethnic superiority. The conservative educationalist Sarah Trimmer's approach is typical in this regard. Her early conduct manual, *The Oeconomy of Charity* (1787), intended to provide models for female philanthropy in the area of Sunday schools and charity schools. She encouraged women to visit the poor in their cottages in spite of their seeming "little better than savages or barbarians, with whom any familiar discourse would be degrading . . . if not dangerous."[9] The more radical Quaker commentator Elizabeth Heyrick of Leicester also depicted the poor as a different category in order to emphasize her argument of an ever-increasing gulf between the rich and poor: "at present, the resemblance between the higher and lower orders is too faint to excite sympathy; the rich and the poor appearing not so much of different *orders,* as of different *species.*"[10] Although these two writers advocate very different solutions for the problem of poverty and deprivation—Trimmer promoting the cultivation of religious principles amongst the poor in order to engender a sense of gratitude and obedience toward their social superiors and Heyrick advancing the notion of state intervention to protect the rights and standards of living of the poor—both women utilize an imperialist, racist, and hierarchical discourse when describing the underprivileged and destitute to their readership. They employ terms such as "savage" and "species" to encourage sympathy for the subjects of their philanthropic methods but also to emphasize their own distance from the poor (viewing this in either a positive or negative light). This rhetoric has been extensively analyzed in studies of the female contributions to the antislavery movement,[11] while recent scholarship by Clare Midgley and Alison Twells has explored how women utilized philanthropy more directly in order to assert their imperial personae in their missionary and campaigning activities at a point that Twells terms "a formative moment in the construction of British class and national identities."[12]

The complex relationship between gender, philanthropy, and imperialism may be further explored by considering the interventions by English women in debates about the treatment of the poor in Ireland. Contemporary intellectual reflections on the role of the state, of the church, and of the responsibilities of Empire were significantly enriched by these contributions. The complicated relationships between colonizer and colonized, elite Protestant English women and poor Catholic Irish men and women, and middle-class women and the governing establishment demonstrate that a simplistic model to explain the motives for middle-class female benevolence is unsustainable in such a context. Women philanthropists intervened rigorously in debates on the causes and treatment of poverty in the imperial as well as the national arena. Their philanthropic objectives in countries as diverse as Sierra Leone, India, and Ireland were supplemented by a desire to bolster the Empire and "civilize" the subject peoples.

There was considerable ignorance about Ireland and the Irish in early nineteenth-century England. The country that had been brought into the Union in 1800 was deemed by many as alien and remote as colonies in Australia or Africa, incapable of nationhood. Thus, the learned and politically astute English visitor Charlotte Elizabeth Phelan (née Browne, later Tonna, but widely known under her pen name, Charlotte Elizabeth) could write in her autobiography: "To be sure I hated Ireland most cordially; I had never seen it, and as a matter of choice would have preferred New South Wales, so completely was I influenced by the prevailing prejudice against that land of barbarism. . . . Ireland had no antiquities, nothing to distinguish her from other barbarous lands, except that her people ate potatoes, made blunders, and went to mass. I felt it a sort of degradation to have an Irish name."[13] Charlotte Elizabeth was the daughter of a Norwich clergyman, well-educated and widely read. She moved in political circles in Norwich, and Clara Lucas Balfour describes her as growing up "a Protestant, a Patriot, and a Tory."[14] She was further politicized by her experience of both radicalism and patriotism in Norwich during the Napoleonic wars. In her early twenties, she married an army officer, Captain George Phelan. After accompanying him to Nova Scotia, she traveled with him to Ireland, where he wished to reclaim his estates. The marriage was abusive and unhappy, and Charlotte Elizabeth was virtually deserted by Phelan in Ireland; she lived in rural Kilkenny whilst he resided in Dublin. However, during her visit to Ireland, she began what would be a highly successful and extensive literary career, writing Protestant religious pamphlets for the Dublin Tract Society. Charlotte Elizabeth's preconceptions of Ireland as an uncivilized, uncultured territory were supplemented by her fervent belief in "ultra" Protestant Evangelicalism, which manifested itself in a bigoted and venomous anti-Catholicism. Her intemperate and extreme anti-Catholic views perhaps explain the neglect of her work by historians, but her views were by no means exceptional in the early nineteenth century.[15]

Margracia Loudon, who moved in Rational Dissenting circles in Leamington and London, had a similar approach to the Roman Catholic Church in Ireland. She wrote a wide-ranging work on philanthropy and political reform in the 1830s and summed up her section on alleviating poverty in Ireland by calling for "relief from the oppressions of the Church of Rathcormac, with its widows' houses steeped in blood for its altars; its widows' sons, slain on their mother's hearths for human sacrifices; its dragoons for ministering high priests, and the eternal fast it imposes on the poor, to furnish forth an everlasting feast, of pomps and vanities for the rich."[16]

The vehemence of anti-Catholic writing in this period was heightened by political events. In the 1820s rural Ireland was in the grip of an outbreak of violence and terrorization known as the Rockite movement. Disputes about the legitimacy of the landownership of the mainly Protestant gentry and the payment of tithes by a largely Catholic population to the clergy of the Church of Ireland were compounded by a millenarian movement which dated the end of Protestantism to the year 1825. Therefore, the sporadic acts of violence, intimidation, and sabotage were accompanied by localized campaigns to convert Protestants to Catholicism in order to save them from the coming apocalypse.[17] Charlotte Elizabeth experienced this herself during her residence in Kilkenny in the early 1820s when her Catholic neighbors sent a nun to try to effect her conversion.[18] Whilst the Rockite movement was unsystematic and not centrally organized, it did aid in the politicization of the rural Catholic population. The issues it raised about land ownership and the role of the Church of Ireland would be later exploited by politicians such as Daniel O'Connell. The isolation and paranoia of the Protestant gentry was further compounded by the Catholic Emancipation Act of 1829, which enfranchised eligible Catholic men, giving rise to fears that the Protestant electorate would be swamped by uneducated, uncouth voters owing their primary allegiance to Rome rather than London.[19] Writers such as Loudon and Charlotte Elizabeth directly attributed the widespread poverty of the Irish population to their Catholicism. The Catholic Church diverted resources away from the poor and encouraged ignorance and superstitious practices. For example, Charlotte Elizabeth surmised, "I am equally sure that the most ample supply of all their [the Irish] temporal need will be alike inefficacious, while their minds remain under the baneful influence of Popery."[20] For many English Protestants of all hues, Catholicism was not just a threat to the welfare of the Irish people but also an assault on their status as subject peoples, thus endangering the stability of the British Empire.[21]

While the anti-Catholic rhetoric of Loudon and Charlotte Elizabeth is abhorrent and was indeed considered too extreme by some of their contemporaries,[22] this should not obscure the intellectual and practical contributions that they, and other female philanthropists, made to the ongoing debate about the alleviation of poverty and suffering in Ireland. Although Charlotte Elizabeth's views of Catholicism were not modified by her visit to Ireland and perhaps became more extreme, she did revise her impressions of the Irish people. In her autobiography she wrote: "Unfounded prejudice was succeeded by an attachment based on close acquaintance with those among whom I had dwelt; contempt by respect, and dislike by the warmest, most grateful affection. . . . [T]he guilt of my country's responsibility lay heavily on my heart."[23] While she still argued that any continuing adherence to Catholicism would prevent many advances for the Irish people, she did admit that the major cause of suffering was the "*culpable neglect of the poor.*"[24] She became a staunch advocate for the Irish people, defending them against charges of indolence and apathy and placing the responsibility for social and educational reform with the British government. On her return to England, she undertook extensive charitable work in the London parish of St. Giles, where a large number of Irish immigrants lived in squalor and poverty, and she supported the promotion and extension of the Irish language (arguing it should not be the preserve of "Romish priests"). She also spearheaded a movement to establish an Irish Anglican church in the parish, in which services were conducted in Irish.[25]

Charlotte Elizabeth's industrial novels, particularly *Helen Fleetwood* (serialized in *The Christian Lady's Magazine*, 1839–1840) and *The Wrongs of Woman* (serialized 1843–1844),[26] were pioneering in the emergent field of social reform novels because of the use they made of government reports, official committees, and witness statements recorded in parliamentary blue books.[27] Her novels were therefore devices to educate her largely female middle-class English readership about the deprivation and hardship facing the newly industrialized districts of England. She employed similar tactics in her work on Ireland. In her 1833 novel, *Derry: A Tale of the Revolution,* she noted in her dedication that she had "faithfully adhered to the historical data afforded by authentic writers."[28] Her *Letters from Ireland* (1838) contained references to reports of the Poor Law Commissioners on Ireland, and an appendix gave detailed summaries from committees of the House of Lords. She considered that her purpose was "simply, to read Ireland as [she] read an important book: to receive no text without a careful examination of context; and on every occasion to refer to first principles."[29] Therefore, her earlier knee-jerk stereotyping of Ireland and the Irish people was replaced by a more reflective and informed consideration of the difficulties facing any mitigation of their suffering.

The main social and theoretical debate about Ireland at this time focused on the question of whether the classical principles of political economy that dominated political ideology in England could be applied in the Irish context. More specifically, should there be legislation akin to the Poor Law Amendment Act (1834) for Ireland? The British government had made a series of attempts to investigate the causes of poverty in Ireland and to provide some legislative solutions. There had been a succession of parliamentary select committees in 1804, 1819, 1823, and 1830, as well as over one hundred royal commissions and scores of special committees of enquiry between 1800 and 1840. None had produced any concrete results, although there had been a series of recommendations, including land improvement schemes, public works projects, improved education, development of the fishing, farming, and manufacturing industries, and emigration schemes. However, the Protestant Irish gentry, whose political interests were well represented in Parliament, resisted the introduction of any of these schemes. In addition, intellectual resistance came from many English and Irish political economists, who argued that the specific economic challenges in Ireland—the peasant economy and the imbalance between population and capital—would impede the successful operation of many of the fundamental principles of political economy that they were so enthusiastically advocating in England, Scotland, and Wales.[30]

Although in *Helen Fleetwood* Charlotte Elizabeth had bitterly attacked the implementation of the Poor Law Amendment Act in England, she was equally critical of the inability of the British government to implement *any* legislative provision for Ireland, arguing "that one remedy alone can reach the seat of disease, a competent provision for that neglected class. . . . [W]ithout a permanent, legalized, sufficient provision, on the plan of a poor-law enactment, nothing whatever will be done to improve the state of Ireland."[31] She also attacked the notion that the theories of the political economist could have any relevance for the Irish context. Other female writers also participated in these debates, using their practical experiences of poor relief in addition to intellectual arguments. For example, Elizabeth Heyrick, who wrote more than twenty pamphlets on a range of social, humanitarian, and economic issues, used the example of Ireland in her assault on the classic political economists. In her *Enquiry into the Consequences of the Present Depreciated Value of Human Labour,* she argued that Malthusian theories on population were essentially defective: "Ireland, which has made no legal provision for her poor, is suffering still more than England from the competition for labour, and her apparently disproportioned population to the means of subsistence."[32] Heyrick was dismissive of the role of private charity, arguing that the effort of individuals was both unproductive and demeaning. In all her economic writings, she prioritized the "*claims* or *rights of the poor*" and called for legislative intervention. She argued that the needs of the laboring classes were more pressing even than reform of Parliament. Her rejection of the work of classical political economists led her to advocate what she termed "Christian economy," which would put the emphasis on humanity and give workers a minimum wage rate. Again, in her pamphlet *On the Advantages of a High Remunerating Price for Labour,* she turned to the example of Ireland to justify this argument: "Have the *low* wages of the people of Ireland, Poland, and Hindostan, made them industrious? [O]r the *high* wages of the Americans, the English, and the Hollanders made them lazy, riotous, and profligate? Just the contrary."[33] Heyrick's work on wage theory was viewed by contemporaries as her most innovative intervention in the debate about social welfare policies in early-nineteenth-century Britain.[34] Her contribution to the debate, which was informed by her experience of the suffering of the Leicester handloom weavers, influenced local working-class political activists.[35]

Like Charlotte Elizabeth, Margracia Loudon drew on an extensive corpus of parliamentary reports, periodical articles, scientific surveys, statistical material, and theoretical works to write her book on philanthropy and political economy. In addition, her knowledge of Ireland was supplemented by the experiences of her landowning family in Limerick. In *Philanthropic Economy or, the Philosophy of Happiness, Practically Applied to the Social, Political, and Commercial Relations of Great Britain* (1835), Loudon too called for legislative intervention. She argued that political economy should be made subservient to "philanthropic economy": a form of active benevolence to all members of society, based on the principle of equality. Active benevolence, in her view, should be a key principle governing state intervention as well as private charitable actions; therefore Loudon's work calls for a whole host of legislative reforms including the abolition of the House of Lords and the reorganization of the taxation system. *Philanthropic Economy* was widely read and reviewed favorably in contemporary periodicals and the press. In 1842, Loudon's chapter on the Corn Laws was reprinted by the Anti-Corn Law League, which distributed it along with other relevant publications via the new penny post to nine million electors. Her theoretical works were supplemented by three humorous novels, in which she attempted to apply her ideological principles in a fictional setting. In *Fortune Hunting* (1832),[36] the hero, thwarted in love, turns to the study of political economy. Loudon also discusses the idea of a female parliament. In addition to the baleful influence of the Catholic Church, she assessed Ireland's poverty to be caused by absentee landowners charging high rents, the lack of a manufacturing industry, which enhanced the competition for diminishing land resources, and the absence of educational provision. Loudon too observed a pressing need for poor laws, arguing that the implementation of poor rates to finance relief would compel landlords to remain in Ireland and "look to the welfare of their tenants."[37] In addition, in a chapter entitled "Appropriation of Irish Church Property and Church Reform," she argued that the revenue of the Anglican Church in Ireland should go toward public works for the permanent relief of the poor and to provide employment and a manufacturing industry.[38]

The British government eventually yielded to the increasing pressure to tackle the problem of poverty in Ireland. It dispatched one of the English Poor Law Commissioners, George Nicholls, on a hasty tour of the country and, unsurprisingly, he rejected the recommendations of previous parliamentary commissions and enquiries, proposing that the Irish adopt the English system of poor relief, financed through poor rates and offered only via workhouses. Although there was widespread opposition to the legislation in Ireland, both from landlords, who feared the expense of the proposal, and from tenants, who lobbied for outdoor relief schemes rather than the degrading and inhumane workhouse, the Irish Poor Law Act was passed by the English Parliament in 1838. The workhouses that were established by the act were almost immediately overwhelmed by the Great Famine. This catastrophic event inspired further interventions in Ireland by a new generation of English female philanthropists.

Some of the most prolific and extensive contributions came from Angela Burdett-Coutts. In 1837, she had inherited almost two million pounds from her family, who had a major financial interest in Coutts bank. Almost immediately, she embarked on an impressive and varied series of philanthropic projects, including establishing refuges for prostitutes, endowing ragged schools, improving sanitation in slum areas, and promoting schemes to encourage alternative employment for the population of the East End of London.

As with Charlotte Elizabeth, Burdett-Coutts's dedication to the Church of England informed much of her philanthropic work. Indeed, William Howitt referred to her as the "nursing mother of the Church of England."[39] She supported colonial expansion, particularly via the mechanism of the Anglican Church. Her adherence to imperialism resulted in the endowment of bishoprics in South Africa, Australia, and British Columbia, modeled on the English diocesan system. In Ireland, she assisted with the foundation of St. Columba's College, a school developed in County Meath in 1843 to advance Anglican Church education. She was not as overtly anti-Catholic as either Charlotte Elizabeth or Loudon and saw the plight of the Irish connected less to religious practices or beliefs than to the particular traits of the country and its inhabitants: an "indescribable lassitude appears to hang over all—children, peat, crops, goats, men and women, animate and inanimate nature. The country seems to be perishing from itself."[40]

Coutts provided practical assistance for the Irish people, particularly those living on the southwest coast. She opened stores in the area to sell basic food at a minimum cost and to distribute food and blankets. She also established schools and basic education facilities to equip local men and women with new skills so that they could find alternative employment to potato farming. In addition, she tried to create a demand for Irish embroidery in England, sent out a flock of sheep to offer another source of income for the rural population, and revived the fishing industry by providing loans for boats and a Fishery Training School in Baltimore. She also funded emigration programs to Canada. Her work in Ireland was largely undertaken by others, directed by her and using her resources, but her male friends in the English political establishment discouraged even this intervention. The Duke of Wellington criticized her views on Ireland, which would, he alleged, encourage beggars. In spite of this opposition, Burdett-Coutts was effective at lobbying for government initiatives to supplement her own private charity. In the 1860s, she commissioned W. H. Wills, a subeditor for Charles Dickens's *Household Words*, to visit Ireland and write a report on the conditions he found. She sent copies of Wills's findings to Sir Robert Peel (Jr.), the chief secretary to the lord lieutenant of Ireland, and to William Gladstone, who was chancellor of the Exchequer at that time. Although Peel continued to criticize the native population of Ireland for not availing themselves of the workhouses, he did provide some outdoor relief and foodstuffs.[41] In the 1880s, Burdett-Coutts's offer of £250,000 of aid again shamed the British government into providing aid and assistance to the area.

Angela Burdett-Coutts's biographers usually depict the recipients of her aid as universally grateful and adoring. However, although it is difficult to find the authentic voice of the poor Irish beneficiaries of Burdett-Coutts's largesse, there are signs that her insistence on providing aid that was not just material but morally improving met with some resistance. For example, Duchess Teck wrote of the "ignorance" of the people of Hare Island where Burdett-Coutts had proposed building some model dwellings. They had objected to the designated sites of the cottages, claiming one was haunted, another was too close to a "Killeen," or burial place of children dying unbaptized, and yet another "crossed the ridge" or ran at right angles to the furrows, which was considered unlucky.[42] Many of these residents were later "encouraged" to emigrate to Canada. Those who defaulted on installments to Burdett-Coutts for fishing boats were also dealt with summarily, often by measures including public naming and shaming before their local congregations.[43] The Irish persisted in utilizing aid they received from female philanthropists in the nineteenth century for their own purposes and would not obediently conform to schemes for their improvement, however well meant.

It is important to understand the complex and contradictory relationships between gender, imperialism, and philanthropy in the nineteenth century. English women theorists of the concept of benevolence and female practitioners of charity alike were observers of poverty in Ireland that was on an incomprehensible scale and that was not replicated elsewhere in Britain. These cultural signals often had conflicting and paradoxical consequences. Middle-class women were forced to set aside their deeply held, hierarchical, and bigoted attitudes in order to take direct action, often confronting the political establishment in the process. In so doing, they were challenging existing interpretations of the public role of middle-class women and asserting their authority to comment on and to shape policy in the area of poor relief. This authority was supported both by their intellectual contributions to debates and by their direct lobbying of influential male politicians. Frequently, their interventions in the area helped them to construct relationships across class, ethnic, and gender divides. The Irish ceased to be an abstract category of "savages," "barbarians," and "heathens," partly because commentators such as Charlotte Elizabeth and Margracia Loudon encouraged their readership to take a more empathetic, reflective, and compassionate view of the problems of poverty in Ireland. But frequently these very actions were effective in reinforcing English, Protestant hierarchies, and women writers legitimized their policies by emphasizing their difference and distance from those they wished to assist. It seems, then, that English women used their assumed cultural superiority and authority to enable them to intercede in a colonial context that contrasted with the restrictions they faced on such interventions at home. Philanthropic activities should not therefore be simply interpreted as either reinforcing or diminishing gender, racial, and hierarchical divisions. The ways in which middle-class women sought to understand contemporary positions on imperialism, class, and gender resulted in inconsistent and multifaceted responses. While women's intellectual and political contributions to debates about philanthropy—particularly those concerning the colonial context—have often been overlooked in favor of their more practical responses, female benevolence should be understood as much more than merely a strategy for middle-class women to participate in public affairs.

NOTES

1. Alex Tyrrell, "'Woman's Mission' and Pressure Group Politics (1825–1860)," *Bulletin of the John Rylands Library* 63, no. 1 (1980): 194–230.

2. Leonore Davidoff and Catherine Hall, *Family Fortunes: Men and Women of the English Middle Class, 1780–1850* (London: Hutchinson, 1987), esp. chapters 1–3.

3. Gareth Stedman Jones, *Outcast London: A Study in the Relationship between Classes in Victorian Society* (Oxford: Clarendon Press, 1971); John Foster, *Class Struggle in the Industrial Revolution: Early Industrial Capitalism in Three English Towns* (London: Weidenfield and Nicolson, 1974).

4. Frank Prochaska, "Philanthropy," in *The Cambridge Social History of Britain, 1750–1950*, vol. 3, ed. Francis Michael Longstreth Thompson (Cambridge: Cambridge University Press, 1990), pp. 357–93; Brian Harrison, *Peaceable Kingdom: Stability and Change in Modern Britain* (Oxford: Clarendon Press, 1982); Alan Kidd, "Philanthropy and the Social History Paradigm," *Social History* 21, no. 2 (1996): 180–92.

5. Peter Mandler, "From Almack's to Willis's: Aristocratic Women and Politics, 1815–1867," in *Women, Privilege and Power: British Politics, 1750 to the Present,* ed. Amanda Vickery (Palo Alto, Calif.: Stanford University Press, 2001), p. 164.

6. Frank Prochaska, *Women and Philanthropy in Nineteenth-Century England* (Oxford: Clarendon Press, 1980), chapter 1.

7. See particularly Jane Marcet, *Conversations on Political Economy,* 3rd ed. (London: Longman, Hurst, Rees, Orme, and Brown, 1819); and Harriet Martineau, *Illustrations of Political Economy,* 9 vols. (London: Charles Fox, 1832–34).

8. Vron Ware, *Beyond the Pale: White Women, Racism and History* (London: Verso, 1992), pp. 59–61.

9. Sarah Trimmer, quoted in David Owen, *English Philanthropy, 1660–1960* (Oxford: Oxford University Press, 1965), p. 99.

10. [Elizabeth Heyrick], *Enquiry into the Consequences of the Present Depreciated Value of Human Labour, &c. &c. in Letters to Thomas Fowell Buxton, esq.* (London: Longman, 1819), pp. 29–30.

11. See Ware, *Beyond the Pale;* and Clare Midgley, *Women against Slavery: The British Campaigns, 1780–1870* (London: Routledge, 1992).

12. Alison Twells, "Let All Begin Well at Home: Class, Ethnicity and Christian Motherhood," in *Radical Femininity: Women's Self-Representation in the Public Sphere,* ed. Eileen Yeo (Manchester: Manchester University Press, 1998), p. 27. See also Clare Midgley, "From Supporting Missions to Petitioning Parliament: British Women and the Evangelical Campaign against Sati in India, 1813–30," in *Women in British Politics, 1760–1860: The Power of the Petticoat,* ed. Kathryn Gleadle and Sarah Richardson (Basingstoke: Palgrave Macmillan, 2000), pp. 74–92.

13. Charlotte Elizabeth [Tonna], *Personal Recollections,* 4th ed. (London: Seeleys, 1854), pp. 104–105.

14. Clara Lucas Balfour, *A Sketch of Charlotte Elizabeth [i.e. Charlotte Elizabeth Phelan afterwards Tonna]* (London: W. and F. G. Cash, 1854), p. 12.

15. Ivanka Kovačević and S. Barbara Kanner, "Blue Book into Novel: The Forgotten Industrial Fiction of Charlotte Elizabeth Tonna," *Nineteenth-Century Fiction* 25, no. 2 (1970): 152–73.

16. Margracia Loudon, *Philanthropic Economy, or the Philosophy of Happiness Practically Applied to the Social, Political, and Commercial Relations of Great Britain* (London: E. Churton, 1835), p. 269.

17. James S. Donnelly Jr., "Pastorini and Captain Rock: Millenarianism and Sectarianism in the Rockite Movement of 1821–4," in *Irish Peasants: Violence and Political Unrest 1780–1914,* ed. Samuel Clark and James S. Donnelly Jr. (Madison, Wisc.: University of Wisconsin Press, 1983), pp. 102–39.

18. Charlotte Elizabeth [Tonna], *Letters from Ireland* (London: R. B. Seeley and W. Burnside, 1838); Charlotte Elizabeth [Tonna], *Personal Recollections.*

19. Brian Jenkins, *Era of Emancipation: British Government of Ireland, 1812 to 1830* (Montreal: McGill-Queen's University Press, 1988).

20. Charlotte Elizabeth [Tonna], *Letters from Ireland,* pp. 32–33.

21. Susan Griffin, *Anti-Catholicism and Nineteenth-Century Fiction* (Cambridge: Cambridge University Press, 2004).

22. Kovačević and Kanner, "Blue Book into Novel," p. 155.

23. Charlotte Elizabeth [Tonna], *Personal Recollections,* pp. 220–21.

24. Charlotte Elizabeth [Tonna], *Letters from Ireland,* p. 32.

25. Ibid., p. 119.

26. Charlotte Elizabeth [Tonna], *Helen Fleetwood* (London: Seeleys, 1848); Charlotte Elizabeth [Tonna], *The Wrongs of Woman* (New York: W. M. Dodd, 1852).

27. Kovačević and Kanner, "Blue Book into Novel," p. 164.

28. Charlotte Elizabeth [Tonna], *Derry, a Tale of the Revolution* (London: James Nisbet, 1833).

29. Charlotte Elizabeth [Tonna], *Letters from Ireland,* pp. 27–28.

30. Thomas A. Boylan and Timothy P. Foley, "A Nation Perishing of Political Economy," in *Fearful Realities: New Perspectives on the Famine,* ed. Chris Morash and Richard Hayes (Blackrock: Irish Academic Press, 1996), pp. 138–50.

31. Charlotte Elizabeth [Tonna], *Letters from Ireland,* pp. 32–33.

32. [Elizabeth Heyrick], *Enquiry into the Consequences,* p. 73.

33. [Elizabeth Heyrick], *On the Advantages of a High Remunerating Price for Labour* (Leicester: Albert Cockshaw, 1825), p. 6.

34. James Smith (Manchester), letter to Samuel Coltman (Bakewell), November 16, 1831, Leicester Record Office, Coltman MSS 15D57/218.

35. Noel Thompson, *The Real Rights of Man: Political Economies of the Working Class 1775–1850* (London: Pluto, 1999), chapter 4.

36. Margracia Loudon, *Fortune Hunting* (London: Colburn and Bentley, 1832).

37. Loudon, *Philanthropic Economy*, p. 269.

38. Ibid., 274.

39. William Howitt, quoted in Clara Burdett Patterson, *Angela Burdett-Coutts and the Victorians* (London: Murray, 1953), p. 217.

40. Angela Georgina Burdett-Coutts, *Baroness Burdett-Coutts: A Sketch of Her Public Life and Work, Prepared for the Lady Managers of the World's Columbian Exposition, by Command of Her Royal Highness, Princess Mary Ann, Duchess of Teck* (Chicago: A. C. McClurg, 1893), pp. 152–53.

41. Diana Orton, *Made of Gold: A Biography of Angela Burdett-Coutts* (London: H. Hamilton, 1980), p. 184.

42. Burdett-Coutts, *A Sketch of Her Public Life*, p. 138.

43. Ibid, p. 150.

8 Blixen's Africa: Wonderland of the Self

Kirsten Holst Petersen

What a dictionary definition of benevolence ("a wish to do good") does not convey is the problematic fact that benevolence presupposes asymmetry. It is rarely conceived—or practiced—as a reciprocal relationship, but relies on hierarchy and is thus not normally possible between equals, on either a personal or a societal level. In societies in which equality is an ideal, if not a reality, the concept is therefore compromised, suspected of harboring ulterior motives, of hiding or glossing greed and various forms of exploitation. On the other hand, in societies that are organized along hierarchical lines, and where inequality is an acknowledged and legitimate feature, benevolence takes on a different value. Here the alternatives are exploitation, cruelty, and a variety of forms of injustice. From this point of view, benevolence is a voluntary, humane, possibly even self-sacrificing sentiment.

The concept of benevolence thus partakes of two opposing value systems, occupying a different place in each system. This need not create difficulties in understanding or assessing the concept, as long as the broad value systems are separated by either time or space. In earlier forms of social organization (for instance, absolute monarchy, as in some European societies in the Middle Ages), benevolence helped to mitigate the effects of the structural and economic asymmetries inherent in the political systems at hand. In democracies, by contrast, it often appears as a self-serving leftover from previous times, as a reluctance to accept the conditions of a democratic worldview. However, when the value systems overlap in time or space, as they did during the era of the late colonial European empires (and still do to a certain extent), benevolence becomes an ambivalent concept, and discussions of it raise uncomfortable questions about the sincerity of the ruling classes' transition from a feudal to a democratic outlook.

One set of such questions concerns racism. In *Imagined Communities: Reflections on the Origin and Spread of Nationalism,* Benedict Anderson sees what he refers to as "official nationalism" as "a response on the part of threatened dynastic and aristocratic groups—upper *classes*—to popular vernacular nationalism," and he views racism as "a major element in that conception of 'Empire.'" He conjures up an image summarized as "capitalism in feudal-aristocratic drag": "the bourgeois gentilhomme speaking poetry against a backcloth of spacious mansions and gardens filled with mimosa and bougainvillea, and a large supporting cast of houseboys, grooms, gardeners, cooks, amahs, maids, washerwomen and, above all, horses."[1] Anderson has no difficulty in describing the attitudes of this class as racist, but they, or some of them, saw themselves as benevolent, and there is a section of mainly popular culture today that likewise still sees the builders and upholders of the Empire as essentially devoted to doing good for humanity at large. The time-warp aspect, the creation of a feudalistic society by aristocratic or would-be aristocratic refugees from modernism's onslaught on inherited privileges, is what makes it possible to describe the same actions and attitudes as both racist and benevolent.

Danish writer Karen Blixen has been the subject of a heated debate about exactly this topic. Blixen owned and ran a coffee farm in Kenya from 1914 until 1931, when she went bankrupt and had to sell the farm and return to Denmark, where she subsequently wrote *Out of Africa* (1937) and, much later, *Shadows on the Grass* (1960).[2] The controversy about Blixen's perspectives on Africans is based on the evidence of those books, but in this discussion I will also draw on her letters written back to Denmark while she was in Africa, as well as interviews in the Danish press.

If Blixen, who died in 1962, can still create controversy it is because of the nature of her writing. Her fame, especially in America, rests largely on her literary technique: a unique blend of highly evocative, lyrical prose and fairytale content in a masterful storytelling style that brings to mind both Hans Christian Andersen and Argentinean writer Jorge Luis Borges. Her views of Africans are thus embedded in a metaphorically charged language, and this creates a special kind of difficulty in analyzing and assessing them. Blixen spins Africa and its landscape, people, and animals into a cocoon of luminous words, creating at times an enchanted world that is very seductive. The magic of this universe overwhelms the reader and blunts more sober, critical attitudes to the work. Such criticism somehow comes to seem pedantic, small-minded, and philistine, qualities that Blixen mocked in her writing and that she associated with the bourgeoisie, whom she despised.

Karen Blixen was born at Rungstedlund, a small estate north of Copenhagen, in 1885. Her mother came from a solid bourgeois background with strict

Victorian ideas about the education and comportment of girls, which included not going to school but being taught at home; this may account for some of her dislike of bourgeois values later in life. Her father, by contrast, was a colorful and adventurous figure who fought in several wars in Europe, lived for two years among Indian tribes in America, and also became a member of the Danish Parliament. Danish writer and critic Georg Brandes describes him in an essay as "a dreamer in broad daylight."[3] In 1895, when Blixen was ten years old, her father committed suicide. Blixen admired him and subscribed to his Rousseauesque view of nature and natives. In 1958, she gave a talk on the Danish radio, revealing her esteem for him: "He turned away from Europe and its civilization and lived for three years among Indians in North America without seeing another white man. He was a skilful and successful trapper, but he spent the money he earned on his Indian friends."[4] Because her father's family had connections through marriage with the Danish aristocracy, Blixen was able to spend summer holidays on a large estate in Jutland, and here she experienced the aristocratic lifestyle that she later described in glowing terms and contrasted to the dull, unimaginative, duty-bound, bourgeois tenor of her everyday life. From her fascination with the aristocratic lifestyle, she developed a sense of noblesse oblige as a guideline to her own conduct, and in a light vein she wrote in an essay, "On Mottoes of My Life":

> The great Emperor Otto
> Could never decide on a motto
> He hovered between
> "*L'Etat c'est moi*" and "*Ich dien.*"[5]

This mixture of a premodern belief in absolute power and (pretended) humility became a pattern in her dealings with Africans and a source of the controversy about her and her attitudes toward Africa and Africans.

When Blixen reached adulthood, she attempted to mix in the exclusive circles of the Danish nobility, without having the money to do so and without having a definite place in its hierarchy. She solved this situation by marrying her Swedish cousin, Bror von Blixen-Finecke, who was a baron. Armed with a title, an adventurous spirit, financial backers, and an ideology of ruling and serving their new country (but without any knowledge of farming), Blixen and her husband bought a farm twelve kilometers out of Nairobi and started growing coffee in 1914. Without knowing it, she had arrived at a place where she could live out her fantasies.

The area, now known as Kenya, was settled by English immigrants as a result of the opening up of the country by the Uganda railway, which was finished in 1901. A European plantation agriculture, based on cash crops, was established. The first settlers were big-game hunters and adventurers drawn from the English aristocracy and upper-middle classes. They established a series of large estates, and to run these successfully they needed land and labor. The Land Ordinance in 1902 established reservations for the natives who were not working for the estates and set up a system of squatters who remained on the land, now owned by the white farmers, for whom they had to work for minimal wages. Because of a labor shortage, a hut and poll tax was imposed in 1911 to pressure the natives to earn cash income by working on the estates. In 1920 the kipande (an equivalent to the South African passbook) was introduced, taxes were doubled, and native cattle were culled to stop overgrazing and to further coerce natives into farm labor. Natives and Indians were prohibited from owning land in the highlands, and natives were prohibited from growing cash crops.

Blixen arrived in Kenya when this system had been set up, and in the course of her stay it was strengthened—or worsened, as far as natives were concerned. The settler community, led by Lord Delamere, fought the Colonial Office in London for an independent say in the affairs of the colony. Heavily influenced by the white settler community in South Africa, settlers petitioned for harsh measures to gain strict control over the native population, as well as to keep Indians and Jews out of the white highlands. The Colonial Office resisted strongly in principle; as early as 1904 the governor, Sir Donald Stewart, told the settler representatives that "the primary duty of Great Britain in East Africa [was] the welfare of the native races."[6] This statement was reiterated throughout the period, but not acted upon in any significant way. Incipient African political initiatives were either ignored or thwarted. (The Kikuyu Association—a not very radical group consisting of chiefs and elders—was denied a hearing in negotiations in London in 1923, while the more radical activist, Harry Thuku, was arrested and deported as "dangerous to peace and good order" in 1922.) The tide started to turn with the economic recession in England and Lord Delamere's death in 1931, the year Blixen left Kenya. She thus lived in what even then was a kind of time-warp characterized by brutal repression carried out by a highly educated and very cultured British upper class. They sought to recreate in East Africa the position they had lost back in Britain, and for a brief period they succeeded.

The moment in history, combined with the unique features of the development of settler society in the white highlands, made it possible for colonizers to work closely with Africans, who had limited or no prior knowledge of Western civilization, in an atmosphere tempered by an aristocratic and artistic Western sensibility, disguising the cruelty that underpinned the system. This mix allowed Blixen to create a dream world in which the apparent Otherness of the

Africans could act as a foil to the role she herself wanted to play—the feudal lord, a role denied her in Denmark. In the Kenyan highlands she finds a seemingly feudal society, readymade with serfs and aristocrats, to which she applies the mythic cultural baggage that in the European consciousness accompanies this kind of social structure, thereby constructing a version of it that puts Africans in the role of medieval European serfs and romanticizes the difference that the alien cultural practices of the natives and the exotic landscape add to this otherwise well-known scenario.

Out of Africa opens with a description of the landscape around the farm: "[T]he formation gave to the tall solitary trees a likeness to the palms, or a heroic and romantic air like full-rigged ships with their sails furled. . . . Everything that you saw made for greatness and freedom, and unequalled nobility."[7] The slippage in this passage from description of nature to value judgment ("heroic," "freedom," "nobility") shows what Abdul JanMohamed describes as "a transition from a scientific-empirical to the mythic mode of consciousness."[8] In this mythic setting already imbued with the values of a past and glorious age, Blixen as a medieval lord (or lady) loves the natives: "It is clear by now that the grand passion in my life is my black brother here in Africa. . . . Even Dennis [her aristocratic English lover] carries no weight compared to that."[9] Although this love is all encompassing, it is also an abstract or an ideal, as explained in one of her letters: "I would hate to see an idea or an ideal represented by an individual. Even though I know that my relationship to my black brother is the greatest passion in my life, I also know that there is no individual amongst them whom I could not live without, but that does not significantly change my relationship to them."[10] This strangely cold and abstract passion leaves her free to construct the Africans in her own image. They are at the same time soul brothers and alien Others. As soul brothers, they are lined up with her against the modern Western bourgeoisie, whom she considers pedantic and soulless: "[T]he true aristocracy and the true proletariat of the world are both in understanding with tragedy. To them it is the fundamental principle of God. . . . In this they differ from the bourgeoisie."[11]

Socially, Blixen constructs a symbiotic relationship with the natives, imputing to them desires to fit her own: "The servant needs a master to be himself."[12] She casts herself in the role of the master (that she was, in effect) not just because of her superior economic power but also because the natives seemingly wanted, indeed needed, her to play that role. "Because of their gift for myth," she says, "they can turn you into a symbol. You cannot guard yourself from that."[13] In the same way she establishes herself as God in their eyes. When admitting her shortcomings as a doctor, for instance, she comforts herself by comparing her approach with God's: "[A]mong the qualities that he [the native] will be looking for in a master, or a doctor, or in God, imagination, I believe, comes high up on the list."[14] In this capacity as interpreter of unknown native minds, Blixen does not act as an anthropologist; she aligns herself intuitively with their Otherness, stressing the difference in order to create as much space as possible between herself and modern, industrialized, bourgeois society, which in some sense is the mainly absent protagonist of her fiction. Age, essence, authenticity, unchangeability, and a spiritual contact with nature become the values that ward off the soullessness and pedantry of modern life.

Blixen also creates native "traditions," drawing from her imagination to present what she feels an authentic African world picture should be. The most extreme case of this, I find, is her interpretation of the cruel torture of an African called Kitosch. A settler flogged him severely, tied him up, and left him in his storehouse overnight with a boy to watch him to make sure he did not escape. Kitosch died, but the settler received a very lenient sentence of two years because at some time during the night Kitosch had said to the boy that he wanted to die. The judge decided that he died because he wanted to die, so the settler was guilty of only grievous bodily harm. Blixen interprets this as an instance of native transcendence: "[T]he figure of Kitosch, with his firm will to die . . . stands out with a beauty of its own. In it is embodied the fugitiveness of the wild things who are, in the hour of need, conscious of a refuge somewhere in existence; who go where they like; of whom we can never get hold."[15] Here, Blixen demonstrates both the desire and the power to manufacture Otherness. She does not rage against the injustice; she establishes an ancient nobility of which Africans and wild animals partake, but to which modern man has lost access. At the same time, she aligns herself nostalgically with the Africans as one who has regrettably lost the primal connection with nature but who can see the beauty of it, as opposed to the other settlers, who simply use the boy's confession as an excuse to escape punishment.

Kenyan writer Ngugi wa Thiong'o specifically takes Blixen to task for the ways in which she has fetishized Africa and Africans, in the process disguising racism as benevolence. In an address to the seventieth anniversary of the Danish Library Association in 1982 he outlines three different images of Africa in the Western European mind, and after mentioning the businessman's Africa and the tourist's Africa, he continues: "[B]ut there is a third Africa—and for me a most dangerous Africa—beloved by both the hunter for profit and the hunter for pleasure. This is the Africa in European fiction."[16] Ngugi then singles out *Out of Africa* as "one of the most dangerous books ever written about Africa," and he gives as his reason "precisely because this Danish writer was obviously gifted with words and dreams. The racism in the book is catching, because it is persuasively put forward as love."[17] He goes on to quote two instances of racism in the book that particularly enrage him, each illustrating Blixen's tendency to equate animals (wild and tame) with Africans. The first evokes a kind of noble savagery: "What I learned from the game of the country was useful to me in my dealings with the native people."[18] The second, and more damning instance, is Blixen's description of being offered some Kikuyu food by her cook: "even as a civilised dog who has lived for a long time with people will place a bone on the floor before you as a present."[19]

Ngugi acknowledges the fact that these sentiments were expressed in the 1930s and that this should be taken into account—"they were the views of a young ignorant lady of an aristocracy in decline"[20]—but he finds further evidence of Blixen's pervasive racism in her later book about Africa, *Shadows on the Grass,* which was published in 1960: "The dark nations of Africa, strikingly precocious as young children, seemed to come to a standstill in their mental growth at different ages. The Kikuyu, Kawirondo and Wakambo ... stopped quite suddenly at a stage corresponding to that of a European child of nine. The Somalis had gone further and had all the mentality of boys of our own race at the age 13–17."[21] In Ngugi's opinion, Blixen has been constructed as "a literary saint" who surreptitiously "embodies the great racist myth at the heart of the Western bourgeois civilisation." In this capacity, she has become "the authority on Africa."[22] Apart from his political and literary reasons, Ngugi has a special reason for singling out Blixen as a particularly pernicious representative of European views on Africa: her farm occupied land alienated, or stolen, from his group of people. His father was a tenant laborer on what used to be his own land, but was usurped by a white farmer, like Blixen.

The Zimbabwean writer Yvonne Vera has also attacked Blixen's portrayal of Africans. Her speech, "A Voyeur's Paradise," delivered at the Images of Africa festival in Copenhagen in 1996, critiques a specific image in *Out of Africa* that likens Africans to ants: "When we really did break into the natives' existence, they behaved like ants, when you poke a stick into their ant-hill; they wiped out the damage with unwearied energy, swiftly and silently—as if obliterating an unseemly action."[23] Vera sees "the construction of primary images of Africans" as "one of the most urgent tasks" in addressing (European) biases and misconceptions. She argues that Blixen creates "a myth of Africanness captured in the words 'swiftly and silently,'" which renders Africans "without communication ... for like the ants, they are not heard to speak. ... The anthill image removes from the Africans the possibility of language and grants them instead, a telepathic effort." Vera particularly objects to the image of "obliterating" because it allows for neither reflection nor remembering, which she sees as "essential to any recovery."[24] Ngugi and Vera conduct their critiques in very different ways; Ngugi is a social realist writer and Vera a modernist writer whose style is not dissimilar to Blixen's, and this is reflected in their objections to Blixen's work. Ngugi pounces on straightforwardly racist passages, while Vera teases racist implications out of an extended metaphor of precisely the kind that has given Blixen a large and devoted readership in America and Europe.

A major problem in assessing or understanding Blixen's view of Africans is the fact that her writings are not consistent but instead shot through with doubts and contradictions. This is the case with the Kitosch story. Blixen was asked by the editor to leave it out of *Out of Africa*, but she refused and made its inclusion a condition of publishing the book, which in turn helped to establish her as an African rights activist. Ngugi's accusation that *Out of Africa* was a racist book unleashed a torrent of furious refutations from the Danish literary establishment, and Tove Rasmussen, a Blixen scholar, released a previously unpublished manuscript, *Bogens Verden,* in which Blixen writes that she had not many times in her life been as shaken or upset by an event as she had been by Kitosch's death.[25] It seems that she acted in a socially committed way by insisting on the inclusion of the Kitosch story, but she nevertheless wrote up a highly romanticized version in her published book.

Blixen's somewhat bewildering mixture of racist, romantic, and benevolent attitudes is demonstrated in various ways. She describes her arrival at her farm with her husband after having been married in Mombassa in 1914 in terms that hint of distaste: "[T]here was a surprise for me; all the 1000 boys were lined up in rows and with a truly deafening noise they followed the car up to the house and surrounded us when we got out and insisted on touching us. All those black heads right in your face was rather overwhelming."[26] As *Out of Africa* progresses, she builds a fantasy world peopled with wise and spiritual Africans; yet in her letters home she complained about Africans lying and being unreliable. This is what makes the controversy possible. In this respect, *Out of Africa* resembles Joseph Conrad's equally controversial novel, *Heart of Darkness,* even though the two writers arrive at very different insights as a result of their meeting with Africa.

At the bottom line, Blixen's comparisons of Africans with animals and children and her gross generalizations align her with the settler community, as when she writes: "All natives have in them a strong strain of malice, a shrill delight of things going wrong, which in itself is hurting and revolting to Europeans."[27] She reveals her frustration in terms that demean native tribes: "[S]ometimes one can get absolutely furious with the natives. The Kikuyu really are a slave race—but then there is also something touching about them."[28] And she again resorts to animal analogies to disavow fear: "By the way, one is never afraid of the natives, or not more than one would be of one of one's own savage dogs."[29] At times, her proprietary attitude is even suggestive of slave ownership:

"I have taken over a Somali from Dennis,"[30] she explains in one letter. In another, after describing a lively, but very vain, little girl helping in her house, she writes: "I have given her as a present to Dennis. He has bought her shoes and a scarf."[31]

Despite this, Blixen had a reputation among the British settlers for being "pro-native," and she disassociates herself strongly from settler complaints about the natives. In *Out of Africa,* she betrays no interest in politics—although she mentions the introduction of the kipande, it is only as an administrative nuisance[32]—but in her letters she expresses strong political opinions that do set her apart from the majority of settlers. On the very sensitive subject of barring natives from growing cash crops, her views must have appeared downright treacherous to the settler community. In October 1922, she asserts that "the future of the country, to a much larger extent than now, must build on native production. In Uganda natives produce . . . and export large quantities of cotton, sim sim and coffee, and the tribes here could probably be taught many things."[33] In a letter to her brother in February 1926, she devotes a paragraph to a very angry denunciation of settler politics: "I am so furious with the English because they want to increase the poll tax on natives. . . . If only people at home knew that this country is strangely outside the rule of law and justice. . . . Natives are going to die of starvation and the Governor builds a Government House for £80.000, and the champagne flows. . . . Lord Delamere had a dinner in Nakuru where they drank 600 bottles."[34] These opinions earn her the respect of the otherwise very angry critic, JanMohamed. "Dinesen [Blixen's pseudonym] is a major exception to the . . . pattern of conquest and irresponsible exploitation," he argues, citing as further proof her efforts at giving medical care to Africans and starting a school for them on her farm (traditional outlets for benevolence).[35]

However, Blixen's attitude to the school and native education as such is, in fact, vacillating. In March 1923, she writes home that she "would very much like to start a school on the farm" but has doubts about its utility: "I actually don't know if it wouldn't be better if the natives could be kept at their primitive stage, but I consider that to be out of the question. . . . [C]ivilisation would get hold of them in some form or another, and I think one should try to make it the best possible way."[36] In a letter in May 1926, she is ready to give up the school: "My school isn't going very well . . . I don't think the natives are ripe for that sort of development yet."[37]

Back in Denmark she gives contradictory reports of her pupils to the newspaper *Politikken* in 1937, three days before *Out of Africa* was released. One the one hand, she claims, "I taught them school. And they were excellent at arithmetic and maths," then on the other, she asserts limits to African educability: "If you set an army of clever business people on them, teaching them all kind of technical things they will perish. They must be kept back, like the Greenlanders. They can easily learn to drive a car and fly an aeroplane, but the real love of technology takes centuries to build up."[38] A week later she tells *Ugejournalen:* "But it is wrong when we want them to wear European clothes; an African in a pair of khaki trousers easily becomes shifty, a bit spoilt. The traditional Africans were wonderful."[39] This reads as reluctant acceptance of the inevitable, however regrettable, and if there is any greatness to be found in Blixen's dealing with Africans, this acceptance is perhaps it, because the emergence of the educated, Westernized African is precisely the feature that will topple the fantasy world she managed to build.

Benevolence (medical care, food handouts, schooling) is part of that world, but educated Africans with no need of, or even wish for, benevolence puncture the fairytale bubble of Blixen's magical Africa. In notes for a lecture given in February 1938, she writes: "I loved the natives. In a way the strongest and most incalculable emotion I have known in my life. Did they love me? No. But they relied on me. . . . A stupendous obligation. One would die for them. They took that quite for granted."[40] Blixen was in love with the Africans' trust in her, bestowing on her feudal power, but she also realized that they consciously maintained a strategic distance: "I reconciled myself to the fact that while I should never quite know or understand them, they knew me through and through."[41] I do not agree with Abdulrazak Gurnah when he argues that "[t]he central yearning in *Out of Africa* is to find the true self in the other, and then to expel the other by representing its otherness."[42] Blixen both (re)presents the Other and draws back from it. In the make-believe world inhabited only by her and "her" natives, this touch of distance and mysticism enhances the attraction, whereas when she steps out of that world and into the world of "reality," she often reverts to racist stereotypes. The many contradictions in her relationship with Africans stem from the fact that she finds it difficult to keep the two worlds apart.

An added complication is her own, somewhat contradictory, insistence on the literal truth of her writing about Africa. In an interview with the Danish newspaper *Berlingske Aftenavis* in December 1935, while she was writing *Out of Africa*, she states:

> I think it would be a good thing if we here in Europe gained some real knowledge about Africa and the Negroes amongst whom I have lived for so many years and whom I love dearly. I think it would be important, particularly if it was a truthful account. I want to write a book in which everything is true, in which everything that is written, *actually happened.* I want it to be

the truth about the blacks as I have experienced it myself. The descriptions I have read of Africa have all built on *approved opinions*. . . . I don't want approved opinions, but the truth as I have felt and seen it, without embellishments, without being influenced by received opinions.[43]

Blixen insists on having presented nothing but a truthful account in several other interviews, particularly one with the women's magazine *Hus og Frue* on October 8, 1937, two days after the book was released: "To me Africa was not, as it is to so many others, an adventure, an exciting hunting adventure, no, to me it was a life, a busy everyday life."[44]

When Europeans (and Americans) even today are fascinated by Blixen's African world, they are responding to the seductions of what Ngugi referred to as "an aristocracy in decline." Blixen sets herself up (co-opting Africans in the process) as a European aristocratic Other, so that her readers (who by virtue of their modern lives represent the bourgeoisie she rejects), ironically accept her as their spokesperson. In doing this they also unconsciously accept an unacknowledged view of themselves. If you align yourself emotionally with Blixen, her writing allows you to transcend aspects of your own, usually acknowledged, modernity. You accept her version of the Africans in order to gain access to her version of what you yourself cannot be by virtue of your democratic, intellectual, ethical standards. They effectively bar you from the possibility of being benevolent. Instead, Blixen allows you to become savior, benefactor, spiritual sister, god. The literary quality of her work both obscures and legitimizes a battery of forbidden desires, making her writing popular—and dangerous.

Clearly, in Blixen's authorship racism and benevolence coexisted, and therefore it is also possible to cast her as either racist or benevolent. Either interpretation is dictated by the needs of the readers. The Africans' need to critique her racism is self-evident, but the Western need to rescue her from accusations of racism and praise her for her benevolence raises worrying questions about our present view of Africa and Africans.

NOTES

1. Benedict Anderson, *Imagined Communities: Reflections on the Origin and Spread of Nationalism* (London: Verso, 1992), pp. 150–51.

2. Karen Blixen, *Out of Africa* (1937; Hamondsworth: Penguin, 2001); *Shadows on the Grass* (1960; New York: Vintage, 1974).

3. Georg Brandes, quoted in Donald Hannah, *Isak Dinesen and Karen Blixen: The Mask and the Reality* (New York: Random House, 1971), p. 14.

4. Blixen, quoted in Hannah, *Isak Dinesen and Karen Blixen,* p. 13.

5. Blixen, quoted in Hannah, *Isak Dinesen and Karen Blixen,* p. 34.

6. Sir Donald Stewart, quoted in Vincent Harlow and E. M. Chilver, eds., *History of East Africa*, vol. 2 (Oxford: Clarendon Press, 1965), p. 275.

7. Blixen, *Out of Africa*, p. 13.

8. Abdul JanMohamed, "Out of Africa: The Generation of Mythic Consciousness," in *Isak Dinesen: Critical Views*, ed. Olga Anastasia Pelensky (Athens, Ohio: Ohio University Press, 1993), p. 142.

9. Blixen, *Breve fra Afrika*, sec. 2 (Copenhagen: Gyldendal Paperbacks, 1996), p. 210. All quotations from the letters are translated by Kirsten Holst Petersen.

10. Ibid., p. 193.

11. Blixen, *Out of Africa*, p. 177.

12. Blixen, *Shadows*, p. 6.

13. Blixen, *Out of Africa*, p. 98.

14. Ibid., p. 30.

15. Ibid., p. 243.

16. Ngugi wa Thiong'o, *Moving the Centre: The Struggle for Cultural Freedom* (London: James Currey, 1993), p. 133.

17. Ibid.

18. Blixen, *Out of Africa*, p. 24, quoted in Ngugi, *Moving the Centre*, p. 134.

19. Blixen, *Out of Africa*, p. 43, quoted in Ngugi, *Moving the Centre*, p. 134.

20. Ngugi, *Moving the Centre*, p. 134.

21. Blixen, *Shadows*, p. 12, quoted in Ngugi, *Moving the Centre*, p. 134.

22. Ngugi, *Moving the Centre*, p. 135.

23. Blixen, *Out of Africa*, p. 26, quoted in Yvonne Vera, "A Voyeur's Paradise," in *Encounter Images in the Meeting between Africa and Europe*, ed. Mai Palmberg (Uppsala: Nordic Africa Institute, 2001), p. 115.

24. Vera, "A Voyeur's Paradise," pp. 115–16.

25. Blixen, *Bogens Verden, Tidsskrift for Kultur og Litteratur* no. 6, (1983): 16.

26. Blixen, *Out of Africa*, p. 32.

27. Ibid., p. 38.

28. Blixen, *Breve*, sec. 1, p. 192.

29. Ibid., p. 41.

30. Ibid., p. 102.

31. Ibid., p. 173.

32. Blixen, *Out of Africa*, p. 121.

33. Blixen, *Breve*, sec. 1, p. 177.

34. Ibid., sec. 2, p. 20.

35. JanMohamed, "Out of Africa," p. 146.

36. Blixen, *Breve*, sec. 1, p. 195.

37. Ibid., sec. 2, p. 35.

38. Blixen, "Giv dette folk endnu to hundrede års fred," interview by Haagen Falkenfleth, *Politikken*, October 3, 1937, in *Samtaler med Karen Blixen*, ed. Else Brundbjerg (Copenhagen: Gyldendal, 2000), p. 52.

39. Blixen, "18 fantastiske år som kaffefarmer i Afrika," interview by Otto Gelsted, *Ugejournalen*, October 10, 1937, in Brundbjerg, *Samtaler med Karen Blixen*, p. 60.

40. Blixen, quoted in Hannah, *Isak Dinesen and Karen Blixen*, p. 34.

41. Blixen, *Out of Africa*, p. 27.

42. Abdulrazak Gurnah, "Settler Writing in Kenya," in *Modernism and Empire,* ed. Howard J. Booth and Nigel Rigby (Manchester: Manchester University Press, 2000), p. 286.

43. Blixen, interview by Tage Tanning, *Berlingske Aftenavis,* December 3, 1935, in Brundbjerg, *Samtaler med Karen Blixen,* p. 42.

44. Blixen, "Hvorfor er folk så bekymrede? Hvorfor denne angst for livet?," interview by Gunver Federspiel, *Hus og Frue,* October 8, 1937, in Brundbjerg, *Samtaler med Karen Blixen,* p. 55.

Part 2
Contemporary Benefits?

9 From Benevolence to Partnership: The Persistence of Colonial Legacies in Aotearoa–New Zealand

Chris Prentice

Since the 1980s, Aotearoa–New Zealand has increasingly sought to articulate itself in terms of a biculturalism founded on the articles and terms of the Treaty of Waitangi, the document that established New Zealand as a Crown colony in 1840.[1] Treaty biculturalism has been statutory since the Treaty of Waitangi Amendment Act (1985) empowered the Waitangi Tribunal to hear claims under the treaty dating back to 1840. Postcolonial biculturalism comprises practical and symbolic measures at state, institutional, and personal levels.[2] While neither practical nor symbolic measures are uncontested or uncontroversial, practical measures include claims and restitution relating to land, fisheries, and other resources, and to cultural properties argued to be guaranteed under the articles and principles of the treaty. They also include measures toward equity in socioeconomic and citizenship domains. Symbolic dimensions constitute much of the "image" of postcolonial biculturalism. In 1987, the Maori Language Act made Maori one of the two official languages of New Zealand, and now state and institutional names and titles commonly have Maori counterparts. The naming of the country itself testifies to a bicultural sensibility: "Aotearoa" is sometimes hyphenated with the colonial designation "New Zealand," and historically displaced Maori place names are increasingly replacing or being partnered with the British names (such as Aoraki–Mt. Cook). Maori greetings are commonly heard in a wide range of contexts, and ceremonial welcomes and other rituals and protocols of encounter frequently begin institutional and cultural occasions. Both practical and symbolic dimensions of biculturalism suggest that Aotearoa–New Zealand has attained what Simon During identified as the postcolonial desire of ex-colonies "for an identity granted not in terms of the colonial power but in terms of themselves," and that "New Zealand is inevitably coming to know itself in Maori terms."[3]

The "benevolence" of colonization by way of the treaty rather than direct conquest may be seen as underpinning the contemporary focus on partnership and the agency this implies for the colonized Maori. To this extent, the treaty has come to be situated as the basis and instrument for an "enlightened" postcolonialism, enacted as the partnership of two peoples, in contrast to hierarchies characterized by either disregard or denial of the indigenous people's status and rights, and to colonialism's paternalistic benevolence toward a protected, subjected minority. At one extreme, such biculturalism maintains that Maori do or should live according to "Maori culture," and Pakeha according to "Pakeha culture."[4] The other extreme envisages Maori and Pakeha as both being as fluent in each others' cultures as their own. However, both in these and in the more modulated versions between, bicultural partnership implies two "parallel positivities,"[5] whether partners stay within their own spheres, presumably linked by some transcendent bridge between them, or else cross between one delineated sphere and the other, possibly generating hybrid blends as evidence of the *accommodation* of one to the other. In aligning particular positively rendered cultures to particular peoples, these cultural essentialisms are clearly shadowed by the disavowed discourse of "race."[6]

Moreover, there are aspects of the ways the nation both does and does not conform to the ideal image of treaty biculturalism that suggest the problematic implication of contemporary discourses of postcolonial cultural politics (partnership, Maori self-determination or *tino rangatiratanga*) in the very terms to which they oppose themselves (paternalism, assimilation, discrimination). The problems reach back to the ambivalence of benevolence itself, both in principle and in practice, as well as to how its legacies inform the bases of bicultural partnership and agency. It may be an outcome of statutory biculturalism that cultural debate in Aotearoa–New Zealand tends to lock into binarized positions. It is therefore a considerable challenge to offer a critique that denounces the physical and epistemic violences of colonialism, historical injustice, and oppressive power relations, and yet that critically interrogates the terms that have come to represent the political and sociocultural expression of such denunciation. Certainly there are critics of biculturalism who reject its acknowledgement only of Maori and Pakeha/European, excluding New Zealanders of Pacific Island, Asian, or other British descent, or who advocate a unified "New Zealand" identification. More complex concerns about biculturalism, to the extent that it implies the coexistence of two culturally distinct peoples, point either to the constitutive hybridity of Maori and Pakeha identities emerging from a history of cultural encounter and engagement, or conversely to the insinuation of one shared set of goals and aspirations.[7] Both register anxiety about cultural difference; the former can lead to political objections to the social and legislative effects of differentiation, including affirmative action or positive discrimination, while the latter points to the production of a neo-assimilative politics of "difference." I contend that this neo-assimilative politics of difference is equally an outcome of benevolent colonialism by way of treaty and the "civilizing mission," transformed into contemporary discourses of "development."

Cultural discourse in Aotearoa–New Zealand instantiates the paradoxical hybridity of terms—Maori and Pakeha—that constitute the two parties to a bicultural ideal, despite discursive practices and spaces focused on maintaining the distinctiveness of two separate cultures. Hybridity is exemplified in the fact that "Maori," as the ethnic designation of the indigenous people, emerged in the context of colonial contact, to some extent overriding the primacy of *hapu* (subtribal), *iwi* (tribal), or *waka* (ancestral canoe descent-group) designation to effect a necessary new unity. Indeed, it appears that the Treaty of Waitangi was the first official document to designate the native people of New Zealand in this way.[8] Similarly, the common designation of the majority British-descended population by the term "Pakeha" demonstrates the hybridity of a nation "coming to know itself in Maori terms,"[9] and is often contested for just this reason. Further, "Aotearoa" was not the term by which Maori designated the islands of New Zealand, but has come to signify a Maori naming, a means of attaching (to) a *postcolonial* indigeneity, available to *both* Maori and Pakeha.[10] Nevertheless, regionally delimited subtribal and tribal identifications were never fully displaced by the cultural politics of colonialism and nationhood (or Maori nationalism), and have actually been reanimated, albeit redefined—hybridized—by the deliberations of the Waitangi Tribunal, in the period following the official ideology of assimilation and the urban drift of Maori from ancestral lands to towns and cities after World War Two.[11] Most claims brought to the tribunal have been specific iwi claims to particular lands and coastal regions and resources, though "cultural" claims involving language and means of language promotion such as access to broadcasting rights constitute an exception to this, and are articulated as Maori.[12]

One problem for a Maori political platform of "cultural difference," implied in biculturalism, is that cultural difference is threatened with collapse as Pakeha assert their "indigenized" postcolonial identity and belonging.[13] At the same time, just as Pakeha are coming to know themselves in Maori terms, Maori can also be shown to have come to know themselves in Western terms. These terms relate to the ideological foundations of benevolence, and the specific institutional supports that shape the position of Maori as treaty partners. In the following discussion, I argue neither for the collapse of the terms of the cultural binary into a new syncretic whole, nor for their discrete coexistence in the relativistic indifference of "separate spheres." Instead, I argue that a living cultural *relation* implies (mutual) encounter, challenge, and transformative engagement of the terms of "culture" and "identity" themselves, a process that cannot take place if both cultures are committed to their "identities," or if in fact they have already become one totalizing monoculture. The theoretical stakes in such a proposition relate to culture's ability to retain its symbolic power to issue challenges to the orders of truth and political power, and their institutionalized machineries of production. The Other, constituted within a discourse of truth and power (as the object, the marginalized, the oppressed), remains either within or complicit with such a discourse to the extent that it believes in its history and its identity within these terms. It reneges on its very strength, which is the symbolic challenge to social forms, structures, and edifices.[14] Consequently there is a need to scrutinize the meanings and uses of "culture" in the present managerial era of cultural politics and to critically evaluate the current goals and aspirations of Maori agency in those politics as they have come to be articulated around "development." As biculturalism is taken to signify partnership, I suggest that this partnership has involved less a decolonizing benevolence than inhabiting its legacies.

As historian Keith Sorrenson has pointed out, while British treaties with native peoples had not been unusual since the fifteenth century, the 1837 Report of the House of Commons on Aborigines declared treaties "inexpedient" because of their ability too easily to disadvantage Aboriginal peoples through "the ambiguity of language" and the "superior sagacity" of Europeans in treaty matters.[15] At least the former of these concerns would come to be crucial to the instability of the Treaty of Waitangi as an agreement between Maori and the Crown.[16] Nevertheless, Claudia Orange proposes the development and later decline of discourses of benevolence, beginning largely in the 1830s, as an important background to the advent of the Treaty of Waitangi. During this decade missionaries, with the support of the humanitarian lobby in London,[17] often expressed concern to protect native races from the egregious effects of the colonial expansion of the British Empire that had already been witnessed, for example in Australia. In the case of New Zealand, Maori trade with sealers and whalers, shore traders, and the few settlers—and, problematically, with some missionaries themselves—had seen the destructive spread of muskets, alcohol, and tobacco.

Any account of discourses of humanitarianism and benevolence informing the treaty process in the early to mid-nineteenth century must acknowledge that Maori had long been active participants in trade and the economic and political calculation of interests for a diverse range of ends. Coastal Maori, particularly, could not be seen as unfamiliar with economic, and even currency, transactions.[18] Ranginui Walker points to the mutual interests served by early trade with missionaries: "[T]he missionaries were dependent on the Maori for food, which they traded for iron tools and muskets," while Hongi Hika extended his protective *mana* over a second mission at Kerikeri in 1819 in the hope that "their presence would attract more ships to the Bay of Islands, thereby increasing his chances for trade."[19] Although such trade is not necessarily incompatible with Maori deployment of European objects in the pursuit of Maori social and political ends, the intersections of Maori and missionary interests had destructive long-term implications for Maori physical and cultural survival. Most missionaries were concerned about the effects of such trade, of settler lawlessness, of bad land deals and disputes, *and* of aspects of Maori social and cultural life and customs they believed were contributing to increasing disease and degradation among Maori.[20] They predicted depopulation and eventual extinction, unless the condition of Maori was ameliorated by "civilization." The benevolence of this amelioration—both in temporal measures relating to health and education and through Christian conversion—was ambivalent in the sense that, as Walker argues, "[u]nlike the traders, who were motivated only by commercial gain, the missionaries were the cutting edge of colonisation. Their mission was to convert the Maori from heathenism to Christianity and from barbarism to civilisation. Underlying this mission were ethnocentric attitudes of racial and cultural superiority."[21] The "good" of benevolence is, in other words, always produced and bestowed from a particular cultural or ideological perspective, straining any notion of cultural difference supported or protected by benevolence.

Orange suggests that the new humanitarian policy toward "native races," informed by the strength of the humanitarian movement in the 1830s, was to some extent also designed to "redeem the British record."[22] In this way, "protection" and "salvation" would pave a smoother way to extensive settlement, as traditional Maori society would be dismantled and the Maori people amalgamated with the settler community. Not only was salvation "not intended to preserve traditional Maori society but ultimately to destroy it and amalgamate Maori with the settler community,"[23] but "British traders and travellers likewise hoped that good treatment of the Maori people by officialdom would oblige them to reciprocate. . . . The Crown, therefore, turned a benevolent face to the Maori people."[24] Thus benevolence was implicated in imperial expansion. In fact, while the 1835 Declaration of Independence of the United Tribes of New Zealand, acknowledged by the Crown in 1836, might suggest the treaty, formulated four years later, could be properly understood as one between two sovereign parties, the declaration had been promoted by British government–appointed Resident James Busby for expediency in preventing intertribal warfare, for trade, and to secure the territory against other external interests. Busby called a meeting of thirty-four chiefs and persuaded them to sign a Declaration of Independence "asking King William IV 'to be the parent of their infant state . . . its protector from all attempts upon its independence.'"[25] This declaration made New Zealand "a dependency of the British Empire in everything but the name."[26] Busby, concerned about "the 'miserable condition' of the Maori people, especially the high mortality rate," referred in 1837 to "the 'present humane policy' towards native peoples in British colonies,"[27] implying its contingent and political nature. The policy's constitutive ambivalence is captured in Orange's account of how, as an introduction to the treaty, Lord Normanby of the Colonial Office wrote a "lengthy dissertation [that] amounted to an apology for British intervention":

> It reflects Colonial Office difficulty in reconciling conflicting principles and in accommodating the interests of opposing pressure groups. Normanby had to recognise Maori independence, even a sovereignty of sorts, but he also had to negate it; he had to allow for British colonisation and investment in New Zealand, yet regret its inevitability; and he had to show that justice was being done the Maori people by British intervention, even while admitting that such intervention was nevertheless unjust.[28]

A similar ambivalence informs the directions given to consul William Hobson for setting up a British Crown Colony, as Orange explains:

> Incorporated in the instructions were provisions for Maori welfare. A Protector would be appointed to safeguard Maori interests in land negotiations; mission work would receive the moral and financial support of government, and schools would be established; with the exception of "savage practices," such as human sacrifice and cannibalism (which were to be forcibly suppressed), Maori custom was to be tolerated until Maori could be "brought within the pale of civilized life."[29]

Notably, "Maori custom" would be tolerated *until* the progressive process of "civilization" rendered it obsolete. Perhaps "Maori interests in land" were considered relatively unproblematic in a context where mission work and schooling would convert Maori into individualized subjects within a legal and economic system predicated on the possession of private property, more amenable to

Western economic constructions of land and other alienable goods than to traditional, *whakapapa*-based cultural attachment to ancestral land. Orange recounts how during treaty negotiations around the country later in 1840, at Pukitea, local Maori claimed they "had been 'betrayed', that if the government wanted the land, it would have been better to take it openly, for then they would 'know how to act,'"[30] suggesting cultural as well as economic alienation.

Many of the suppressed practices and cultural forms, from those indicated above to those targeted in the 1907 Suppression of Tohunga Act (which outlawed traditional and/or spiritual practices by Maori priest healers) and the banning of *tangihanga* (mourning and burial rites), referred to a Maori relation of symbolic exchange between the living and the dead, itself indicative of a cyclical conception of time.[31] As the energies of industrial modernity gathered force in Britain, "civilization" would become implicated in an economic demarcation of life and death, privileging the productivity of life against the abjection or waste of time and the body identified with death. Nicholas Thomas describes how Protestant missionaries in Fiji predicated their work on "the criteria of degradation and progress, the techniques of salvation and reform, the grand narrative of conversion, [and] the place of industry," indeed "how their benevolence and will to control were indissociable."[32] Thus they were parties to ideologies and processes of development, modernization, and progress, suppressing a cyclical conception of time in favor of the linearity of productive time in the accumulation of economic value. Missionary benevolence was complicit in the assimilation of the Maori world, in life and in the afterlife, while it also served to secure agreement to a treaty that would presage the displacement of Maori from majority to minority status in the emergent colony.

The presentation of the treaty to the assembled chiefs at Waitangi in February 1840, and subsequently around the rest of the country, emphasized rights and benefits over losses and responsibilities. Between the first and second day of the Waitangi meeting, the missionary Henry Williams, who had described the treaty as "an act of love towards [the Maori] on the part of the Queen who desired to secure to them their property, rights, and privileges,"[33] told the chiefs that "the question was for their own benefit, to preserve them as a people,"[34] a claim more evocative of paternalistic benevolence than agency or partnership. However, by the 1850s, the political climate of humanitarianism was declining,[35] and Maori found it difficult to "reconcile government actions with official statements about the Treaty's good intent."[36] In 1856, Alexander Macdonald, in an address to the Wellington Philosophical Society, quoted the superintendent of the Province of Wellington as expressing the views of the influential colonists: "A barbarous and coloured race must inevitably die out by mere contact with the civilised white; our business, therefore, and all we can do is to smooth the pillow of the dying Maori race."[37] This sentiment echoed through the rest of the nineteenth century, as its social Darwinism was seemingly vindicated by the absolute decline in the Maori population, and the relative decline brought about by the increase in settler numbers. It also suggests the flexibility of the benevolent attitude, able to encompass both protection/preservation and the amelioration of inevitable death.

As Maori increasingly resisted growing British numerical and political supremacy through the 1850s into the 1860s, "the tone of official statements shifted from acknowledgement of the treaty's humanitarian concern, to an insistence on the Maori people's moral obligation to uphold the treaty and to accept the rights it conferred on the government."[38] The *Bay of Islands Observer* referred to "this cloak of benevolence" as covering "the greatest hypocrisy, to obtain possession of the country."[39] The 1860s was the decade of the Land Wars between Maori and Pakeha/government, and after the 1870s, by which time the settler population outnumbered the Maori, the treaty faded from Pakeha consciousness. Orange suggests that "[t]he prospect of a country with only a few Maori survivors no doubt encouraged the view that the Treaty had served its purpose."[40] Nevertheless, both Orange and Walker recount continuous Maori engagement with the treaty—insisting on ratification, presenting grievances, and seeking social transformation—throughout the nineteenth and twentieth centuries. The reemergence of the treaty into *national* consciousness around the middle of the twentieth century occurred in terms of its value for the ideology of "one nation" from the "partnership of two races,"[41] though still with strong assimilationist values and policies, especially evident in land legislation. Both the 1953 Maori Affairs Act and the 1967 Amendment, "disregarded traditional Maori values and aimed at economic rationalization" and a utilitarian conception of land usage.[42]

Colonialism's civilizing mission was informed by both the humanitarian concerns of missionaries and the belief in universal (and the universalization of) European values of progress and modernity. The pursuit of assimilation was one expression of this mission, while conversely the treaty appeared to promise the protection of Maori culture in the Article Two guarantee of "full and undisturbed possession of Lands and Estates and . . . other properties." In addition to the problems of intercultural translation and interpretation in calling on the treaty for the (re)affirmation of cultural difference, the legacies of the treaty as a benevolent (paternalistic) as well as an assimilative (Westernizing) basis for "enlightened" postcolonial biculturalism include its effects as an instrument of European political rationality through which "Maori" are constituted as signatory-subject(s) in an economy of subjectivity predicated on Western constructions of the individual and the collective. Alan Ward has pointed to the problem of reliance on treaties for negotiating intercultural relationships and processes of social change, "because both parties may still be attempting to regulate complex human situations through legalism, codification, dogma and ideology, rather than opening up a process which enables the common ground to be pursued."[43] Yet I argue that the process of codification whereby Maori are required to argue for and enact "culture" as property in the name of legally abstracted and politically corporatized identities means there is little *other* than that common ground: a political economy predicated on individual identity and private property articulated through institutions of representational democracy—all hallmarks of the modern West.[44] Ward's point that the value of a treaty lies in its function "as a political compact, a broad undertaking to collaborate, to share with mutual respect the common tasks of modernity,"[45] begs the question of whether it is possible to have a (modern) treaty between fundamentally different cultures that preserves the difference(s) of those cultures with respect to modernity. Indeed, Australian magistrate and advocate of civil and Aboriginal rights Pat O'Shane has argued against a treaty with indigenous Australians, claiming that the wrongs suffered by Aboriginals will not be rectified "by trying to define ourselves in the very same terms as those which the lawyers used to define us out of existence. After all, the concept of sovereignty belongs in the same bag with the concept of nation and *terra nullius*."[46] In Aotearoa–New Zealand, treaty biculturalism has specifically called on the concept of sovereignty in the name of "Maori," the colonially produced indigenous subject-position fully inhabited as identity defined by culture. Acknowledging Gayatri Spivak's notion of the deconstructive position of the postcolonial subject who cannot *not* want to "exchange, to establish sociality" by way of "access to the so-called culture of imperialism," to "a structure that one critiques yet inhabits intimately,"[47] I suggest the element of critique has been deterred by the hegemony of (economic, cultural) participation under the sign of "agency." If colonial benevolence smothers agency, then agency emerges as a sign of decolonization; however, the intertwined economic and cultural discourses through which Maori agency is articulated indicates the need for further critique of the decolonization of benevolence and its civilizing mission.

The secular expression of the colonial civilizing mission has been "development," a concept and process that Trinh Minh-ha associates with the "White Cancer" of deculturation and with "the well-meant intention of equating the unequal." She argues that "the invention of 'needs' and the mission to 'help' the needy always blossom together."[48] Similarly, critic of development Serge Latouche emphasizes its deculturating violence, "uprooting" those cultures that have been subject to it, including Fourth World indigenous cultures of colonized territories.[49] He argues that "[t]he key concepts of (natural) need, scarcity (meanness of nature), work (transformation of nature to satisfy natural needs), production, income, consumption . . . really have nothing obvious about them . . . and the hold that they have over reality is largely particular to our culture."[50] By "our culture," he refers to the modern West, and describing development as the "Westernisation of the world," he states that "not only is the economic not complementary to culture but, in the West, it is tending to become a substitute for culture, by absorbing all expressions of culture into itself."[51] Thus development predicated on (or predicating) cultural identity/difference is a contradiction: development is unidimensional, devouring rather than fostering difference.[52] In the light of Latouche's argument, it is important to examine some of the discourses and processes of Maori development, its transformation from the paternalistic colonial civilizing mission, through its implication in assimilative social and administrative policies in the mid-twentieth century, to its current expression as self-determination articulated through partnership in treaty biculturalism.

The translators of Latouche's *In the Wake of the Affluent Society* point out that while in no way minimizing the effects of material exploitation, he insists that "[t]he West's primary domination lies in the very terms by which value is conceived, and in its domination of the basic institutions that codify social life."[53] Against the notion that it is possible to confine development to the economic sphere, leaving culture undisturbed—as though the economy itself were not a cultural phenomenon—the translators encapsulate Latouche's argument that for a culture to "become developed," and a fortiori to seek to develop itself, spells its annihilation as a distinct culture, in becoming acculturated to Occidental values,[54] and they suggest that development's avowed concern for cultural difference amounts largely to "respects paid *postmortem*."[55] Deculturation is evident precisely to the extent that a culture expresses its "predicaments and aspirations in terms of the 'developmentalist' categories of the invading culture."[56]

Latouche traces a trajectory from the political decolonizations of the 1960s that saw the "acceptance of the *rights of all peoples to self-determination*" to the expectation that "prosperity for all and the *right to development* were next in line."[57] The political and cultural activists of the 1970s and 1980s Maori renaissance predicated their concerns and demands on the notions of visibility and voice following years of assimilated invisibility and silence as *subjects* of cultural identity. Yet while Maori are now more visible in the political, commercial, and cultural spheres, even those run "by Maori, for Maori" function more as signs of inclusion and participation in, rather than difference from or challenge to, the fundamental structures and values of Western techno-bureaucracy. Walker discusses the gains won in the last few decades: "[M]onocultural Pakeha power structures were not immune to Maori pressure. . . . They were capable of being modified to incorporate Maori values and the concept of biculturalism."[58] In addressing the empowerment of the Waitangi Tribunal to hear claims dating back to 1840, he concludes that "the change cast New Zealand firmly into the post-colonial era in which resort to ideology to sustain Pakeha dominance is now untenable."[59] But perhaps there is little need to resort to an ideology of Pakeha dominance when the driving economic values of Pakeha society are hegemonic, inclusive of Maori (albeit with "winners" and "losers" as generated by that system). Indeed, while crediting the patience and efforts of Maori in persisting with the treaty, Walker notes that the challenge to Pakeha domination "would not have occurred without a responsive government and Pakeha supporters within bureaucratic systems who could see advantages for their concerns accruing from the incorporation of the Treaty in their statutes."[60]

Development is no longer imposed by colonial missionaries, administrators, or policy makers; instead its values and assumptions are articulated in the overall vision, as well as specific projects, of Maori development as expressions of agency, consistently seeking differentiation from "the imposition by the Crown of a paternalistic relationship with Maori,"[61] and from "the old days of paternalism," declared "long gone."[62] In 1984, a Maori Economic Summit "highlighted the under-utilisation and under-development of Maori resources, including land, people and culture. It also noted that the gap between Maori and non-Maori rates of achievement by all socio-economic indicators was widening."[63] The summit led to the establishment of the Maori Economic Development Commission that same year, and in 1987 the Maori Economic Development Corporation was established. Two reports were produced out of the Royal Commission on Social Policy, entitled *Partnership Perspectives* (1988) and *Partnership Response* (1988),[64] and the subsequent Ministry of Maori Development (1991) emphasized "the concept of involving Maori much more closely in identifying their own needs, designing their own strategies and implementing them."[65] Economic and bureaucratic discourses of Maori development are evident in programs of "identifying needs," "designing strategies," and "implementing actions" for "outcomes."[66] Specifying self-sufficiency, social equity, and cultural affirmation as the goals of the 1984 summit, Mason Durie cites the advent of Maori corporate and tribal commercial organizations as part of the attendant economic devolution and mainstreaming. He points both to future Maori participation *as citizens* in society and in the economy and to "the development of Maori people *as Maori*."[67] Adding that "[d]evelopment must be responsive to the notion of adding value to Maori lives, Maori society, and Maori knowledge,"[68] Durie links "cultural affirmation" to commercial principles and operations, as the latter are definitive and productive of value: culture furthers economic ends, and economic means further cultural goals—a closed circuit between culture and economics, or political economy.

Paternalistic benevolence has been replaced by partnership and agency within the late capitalist economy and the bureaucratization of social, cultural, and political life. "Culture" increasingly circulates as signs of difference (diversity) within a larger (Western) economy of signification, rather than challenging that economy's fundamental values. The Treaty of Waitangi was underpinned by a humanitarian policy of benevolence toward native peoples, and Maori have called on the treaty in asserting their understanding of its promise of self-determination, seeking to turn an instrument of colonization into one of decolonization. Nevertheless, agency and partnership are cast in terms of isomorphic treaty subjectivities, attached to modern notions of identity and property. Maori "development" is simply a current expression of this long historical process. However, Latouche points to the increasing evidence that the dream of development is unsustainable—even for the West—prompting the question of why another culture would wish to invest so fully in it. He concludes that "what remains most vibrant in decultured societies, and irreducible to the Western metaphysics is the relationship with nature. People feel that they are the servants and children of nature, not the masters."[69] This familiar proposition of the Fourth World as offering a "vision of the world which can be humanity's saving grace as an alternative to productivism"[70] has been cogently critiqued for its romanticization of indigenous cultures in a self-serving displacement of authenticity on to Others while the West continues to reap and consume the wealth from the world's material resources. However, it is worth considering the extent to which, in their own attachment to specifically Western values of life and well-being as quantitative and materially based rather than cultural, such critiques fail to take seriously enough those indigenous expressions of dissent from the exploitative relation with nature.

Development depends on the consumption of resources, but the notion of limitless resources and non-zero-sum development is in visible crisis. This era of Maori development coincides with postindustrial late capitalism, where resources are often human, social, and cultural. If what is being developed is culture (or identity—"Maori as Maori"), is it any less dangerous to presume such resources are limitless, or that, if they are endlessly supplied, they have not entered the realms of the hyper-real "Xerox-degree" of culture?[71]

This discussion has offered a critique of partnership under treaty biculturalism as constituting a legacy of colonial benevolence while asserting its refutation under the sign of agency. I have sought to displace biculturalism—and the partnership of two positivized cultures—as two essentialisms, no matter how complex each term of the partnership may be. I have wished just as emphatically to critique a monoculturalism of two races, the soft assimilation of hegemony, in which the economic assumptions and imperatives of development reduce culture to tokenistic signs of difference that diversify, rather than challenge or transform, the structures and values of the (post)colonial West against which such difference is asserted. Essentialism and assimilation have been two contradictory outcomes of benevolent colonization by way of a treaty, and articulations of biculturalism forged through these ideological underpinnings either attach supposedly bounded cultures to hereditary genetic or ethnic identities or render culture a simulation over monocultural in-difference. To overcome this impasse will require a radical interrogation of terms currently regarded as "givens" within the debates about biculturalism in Aotearoa–New Zealand.

NOTES

1. After a preamble, the English text of the three articles of the Treaty of Waitangi reads:

I. The Chiefs of the Confederation of the United Tribes of New Zealand and the separate and independent Chiefs who have not become members of the Confederation cede to Her Majesty the Queen of England absolutely and without reservation all the rights and powers of Sovereignty which the said Confederation or Individual Chiefs respectively exercise or possess, or may be supposed to exercise or possess over their respective Territories as the sole sovereigns thereof.

II. Her Majesty the Queen of England confirms and guarantees to the Chiefs and Tribes of New Zealand and to the respective families and individuals thereof the full exclusive and undisturbed possession of their Lands and Estates Forests Fisheries and other properties which they may collectively or individually possess so long as it is their wish and desire to retain the same in their possession: but the Chiefs of the United Tribes and the individual Chiefs yield to Her Majesty the exclusive right of Preemption over such lands as the proprietors thereof may be disposed to alienate at such prices as may be agreed upon between the respective Proprietors and persons appointed by Her Majesty to treat with them in that behalf.

III. In consideration thereof Her Majesty the Queen of England extends to the Natives of New Zealand Her royal protection and imparts to them all the Rights and Privileges of British Subjects.

The text of the Treaty of Waitangi (Maori and English versions) may be found in Appendix 2: "Te Tiriti o Waitangi; The Treaty of Waitangi (1840)," in Claudia Orange, *The Treaty of Waitangi* (Wellington: Allen and Unwin; Port Nicholson Press, 1987), pp. 257–59.

2. See James Ritchie, *Becoming Bicultural* (Wellington: Huia Publishers; Daphne Brasell Associates Press, 1992); and Andrew Sharp, "Why Be Bicultural?," in *Justice and Identity: Antipodean Practices,* ed. Margaret Wilson and Anna Yeatman (Wellington: Bridget Williams Books, 1995), pp. 116–33. In differentiating between practical and symbolic measures, I am invoking a distinction similar to that which has been applied to Australia's reconciliation processes; see Michelle Grattan, ed., *Reconciliation: Essays on Australian Reconciliation* (Melbourne: Bookman Press, 2000).

3. Simon During, "Postmodernism or Postcolonialism," *Landfall* 39, no. 3 (1985): 369, 370.

4. "Pakeha culture" means the British-derived but locally adapted culture of the majority white settler population.

5. Victoria Grace, *Baudrillard's Challenge: A Feminist Reading* (London: Routledge, 2000), p. 23.

6. See Etienne Balibar, "Is There a 'Neo-Racism'?" in *Race, Nation, Class: Ambiguous Identities,* ed. Etienne Balibar and Immanuel Wallerstein (London: Verso, 1991), pp. 17–28; and Walter Benn Michaels, "Race into Culture: A Critical Genealogy of Cultural Identity," *Critical Inquiry* 18, no. 4 (1992): 655–85.

7. For example, major Maori writer Witi Ihimaera is apparently uninterested in "a society where two cultures reach 'a common destination.'" For Ihimaera, biculturalism is "about different cultures—'two treasures'—strong and independent"; quoted in Tim Watkin, "The Homecoming," *New Zealand Listener,* June 26, 2004, p. 22.

8. Ranginui Walker, *Ka Whawhai Tonu Matou: Struggle without End* (Auckland: Penguin, 1990), p. 94. Claudia Orange points out that by the 1820s, a sense of "Maoriness" existed in contrast to other races, but the term itself was not widely used until the mid-nineteenth century. The territorial concept of "Nui Tireni" emerged at this time to express a similar unity; Orange, *Treaty of Waitangi,* p. 23.

9. See Paul Spoonley, "Constructing Ourselves: The Post-colonial Politics of Pakeha," in Wilson and Yeatman, *Justice and Identity,* pp. 96–115; and Avril Bell, "'Halfcastes' and 'White Natives': The Politics of Maori-Pakeha Hybrid Identities," in *Cultural Studies in New Zealand: Identity, Space and Place,* ed. Claudia Bell and Steve Matthewman (Melbourne: Oxford University Press, 2004), pp. 121–38.

10. Nevertheless, proponents of biculturalism increasingly (re)invoke the Maori legendary narrative of the demi-god Maui fishing up the islands of New Zealand, referring to the North Island as Te Ika a Maui (Maui's fish) and the South Island as Te Waka a Maui (Maui's canoe), or Te Waipounamu (Greenstone Island), with Stewart Island in the far south named Rakiura.

11. In "(De)Constructing the Politics of Indigeneity," in *Political Theory and the Rights of Indigenous Peoples,* ed. Duncan Ivison, Paul Patton, and Will Sanders (Cambridge: Cambridge University Press, 2000), pp. 137–51, Manuhuia Barcham has argued, though, that "iwi-isation" has been a product of postcolonial history itself, and at least in its current form does not represent the traditional or precolonial basis of organization and decision making.

12. See also Hauraki Greenland, "Maori Ethnicity as Ideology," in *Nga Take: Ethnic Relations and Racism in Aotearoa/New Zealand,* ed. Paul Spoonley, David Pearson, and Cluny McPherson (Palmerston North: Dunmore Press, 1991), pp. 90–107, for an account of contemporary Maori ethnicity as "ideology."

13. For instance, poet and keen fisherman Brian Turner insists "there is a relentless presumptuousness about the way in which non-Maori feelings for land and water are dismissed as less heartfelt, less sensitive, less spiritual." "Mine or Ours? A Response to the Recent Open Letter from Ranginui Walker," *New Zealand Listener,* November 29, 2003, p. 34.

14. See Jean Baudrillard, *Seduction,* trans. Brian Singer (New York: St Martin's Press, 1990), pp. 6–8.

15. Keith M. P. Sorrenson, "Treaties in British Colonial Policy," in *Sovereignty and Indigenous Rights: The Treaty of Waitangi in International Contexts,* ed. William Renwick (Wellington: Victoria University Press, 1991), p. 15.

16. Orange, *Treaty of Waitangi,* pp. 39–45; Walker, *Ka Whawhai Tonu Matou,* pp. 90–97.

17. Orange, *Treaty of Waitangi,* p. 2; Richard Mulgan, *Maori, Pakeha and Democracy* (Auckland: Oxford University Press, 1989), p. 91.

18. Orange, *Treaty of Waitangi,* pp. 6–7, 9–11; Walker, *Ka Whawhai Tonu Matou,* pp. 78–90, 98–102; Alan Ward, "Land and Law in the Making of National Community," in Renwick, *Sovereignty and Indigenous Rights,* p. 129.

19. Walker, *Ka Whawhai Tonu Matou,* p. 81.

20. Orange, *Treaty of Waitangi,* p. 2; Walker, *Ka Whawhai Tonu Matou,* pp. 84–87.

21. Walker, *Ka Whawhai Tonu Matou,* p. 86. Walker further links this conversion to missionary involvement in teaching literacy, carpentry, agriculture, and domestic skills.

22. Orange, *Treaty of Waitangi,* p. 2.

23. Ibid.

24. Ibid., pp. 9–10.

25. Ibid., p. 21.

26. Ibid., pp. 19–22.

27. Ibid., p. 25.

28. Ibid., p. 30.

29. Ibid.

30. Ibid., p. 94.

31. See Jean Baudrillard, *Symbolic Exchange and Death,* trans. Iain Hamilton Grant (London: Sage, 1993).

32. Nicholas Thomas, *Colonialism's Culture: Anthropology, Travel and Government* (Melbourne: Melbourne University Press, 1994), p. 61. Thomas is clear that an important distinction between the Fijian and Australian (and New Zealand) colonialisms lay in the imperative in the latter cases to create spaces for settlement by displacing native peoples (p. 124, see also p. 157). Nevertheless, the "grand narrative of conversion" is likely to have informed missionary work in both the Fijian and the New Zealand contexts, whatever the secular colonial concern.

33. Henry Williams, quoted in Orange, *Treaty of Waitangi,* p. 45.

34. Ibid., p. 51. The "question" at issue here is not specified as such in the original; however, it seems to imply "the matter under discussion."

35. Ibid., p. 138.

36. Ibid., p. 136.

37. Alexander Macdonald, quoted in Harry Orsman and Jan Moore, eds., *The Heinemann Dictionary of New Zealand Quotations* (Auckland: Heinemann, 1988), p. 258.

38. Orange, *Treaty of Waitangi*, p. 136.

39. *Bay of Islands Observer,* quoted in Orange, *Treaty of Waitangi,* p. 91.

40. Ibid., p. 185.

41. Ibid., p. 242.

42. Ibid. In such rationalizations, there is little space for non-utilitarian concepts such as, for instance, *whenua,* which means both "land" and "placenta" and which points to a relation other than land as commodity/possession.

43. Ward, "Land and Law," p. 126.

44. See also Barcham, "(De)Constructing the Politics"; and Sharp, "Why Be Bicultural?" pp. 116–33, for discussions of problems in constituting and defining treaty partners for contemporary politics.

45. Ward, "Land and Law," p. 127.

46. Pat O'Shane, "A Treaty for Australians?" in Renwick, *Sovereignty and Indigenous Rights,* p. 155.

47. Gayatri Spivak, "Theory in the Margin: Coetzee's *Foe* Reading Defoe's *Crusoe/ Roxana,*" in *The Consequences of Theory,* ed. Jonathan Arac and Barbara Johnson (Baltimore: Johns Hopkins University Press, 1991), p. 42.

48. Trinh T. Minh-ha, *Woman, Native, Other: Writing Postcoloniality and Feminism* (Bloomington: Indiana University Press, 1989), p. 54.

49. Serge Latouche, *In the Wake of the Affluent Society: An Exploration of Post-Development,* trans. Martin O'Connor and Rosemary Arnoux (London: Zed Books, 1993), p. 160.

50. Ibid., p. 137.

51. Ibid., p. 25.

52. Ibid., p. 158.

53. Martin O'Connor and Rosemary Arnoux, Introduction to Latouche, *In the Wake,* p. 10.

54. Ibid., pp. 7–9. Here O'Connor and Arnoux nevertheless bear in mind Latouche's point that the West has already decultured itself, and one cannot acculturate to a non-culture. See Victoria Grace, *Baudrillard's Challenge: A Feminist Reading* (London: Routledge, 2000), p. 95.

55. O'Connor and Arnoux, Introduction, p. 11.

56. Ibid., p. 10.

57. Latouche, *In the Wake,* p. 39.

58. Walker, *Ka Whawhai Tonu Matou,* p. 250.

59. Ibid., p. 254.

60. Ibid., p. 266.

61. Mason Durie, *Kahui Pou: Launching Maori Futures* (Wellington: Huia, 2003), p. 89.

62. Doug Kidd, quoted in Denese Henare, "The *Ka Awatea* Report: Reflections on its Process and Vision," in Wilson and Yeatman, *Justice and Identity,* p. 57.

63. Ibid., p. 54.

64. See also Kaye Turner, "The *April Report* of the Royal Commission on Social Policy: Treaty Partnership as a Framework for a Politics of Difference?" in Wilson and Yeatman, *Justice and Identity,* pp. 78–95 for discussion of the commission's focus on treaty partnership, and the problems and possibilities of partnership for a politics of cultural difference.

65. Henare, "The *Ka Awatea* Report," p. 57.

66. See Durie, *Kahui Pou,* p. 87.

67. Ibid., p. 96 (emphasis added).

68. Ibid., p. 102.

69. Latouche, *In the Wake,* p. 230.

70. Jean-Jacques Gouget, quoted in Latouche, *In the Wake,* p. 125.

71. See Jean Baudrillard, *The Transparency of Evil: Essays on Extreme Phenomena,* trans. James Benedict (London: Verso, 1993), p. 9.

10 Refusing Benevolence: Gandhi, Nehru, and the Ethics of Postcolonial Relations

Rajeswari Sunder Rajan

In our critical endeavors to discriminate among forms of benevolence, is it possible to identify a position outside the usual questions posed of its authenticity versus its dissimulation? Such "radical" benevolence would have to lie, moreover, entirely outside the motivations, contexts, and conditions in which benevolence is usually viewed. It would not emerge, for instance, from a mere superfluity of possessions, nor would it be caught up in the circuits of exchange (cf. Jacques Derrida: "the gift must remain aneconomic"[1]); and furthermore, unlike most acts of philanthropy or charity, it would have to be free of moral calculation.

I seek such radical "relations" (of giving) in (a certain) postcolonial ethics. For anticolonial intellectuals the *ethical* could become and often was developed as an explicit agenda. Gandhi's emergence as a "mahatma" in the Indian nationalist struggle is of course the most widely known instance of such purposiveness, but in other parts of the colonial world too, visions were articulated and practices were initiated whose terms were those of the ethical. One need not seek far for the reasons. Alongside their insistence that colonialism's mission was unconscionable, colonized people claimed the moral high ground of the injured. Righteousness functioned as a compensation for the lack of material power, allowing them to go beyond the abjectness of victims, or the rage and *ressentiment* of the vanquished. Postcolonial ethical discourse has been most resounding when it has held up the colonizer's civilization to its own best values, as in Fanon's challenge to European humanism. When anticolonial struggles were launched, they threw up leaders marked by individual "greatness." Many found the rhetoric of moral rightness as much as political rights of strategic use in mass mobilization.

But in this essay I want to emphasize instead a quite different "use" of the ethical, directed not *at* the colonizer, but inward, as a mode of self-fashioning that was both individual and communal.[2] In anticolonial struggles—and following their culmination in political independence, in nation-building projects—the "social" and the "national" as forms of community had to be forged across existing, indeed deeply entrenched, divides of class, gender, caste, religion, language. In these enterprises nationalist leaders had to be creative in finding ways to relate to the "people" that would avoid replicating not only colonial authoritarianism but, equally, colonialist benevolence. Finding ways of being "one with the people" was not always easy, since relations of power have a tendency to assume similar forms across different contexts. The distance and divide between native elites and the masses was reflected in the reformist drive, the pedagogical rhetoric, and the performance of sacrifice and service that often characterized the leadership exercised by the elites. The attempt to transcend the limits of such authoritarian benevolence led, I argue, to the self-conscious development of a kind of indigenous ethicality, with varying degrees of success. The question of benevolence is, therefore, central to postcolonial politics and its forms and practices: in India specifically as a politics that relates to the function, and the functioning, of democracy.

The ethico-political mode of identification explored in this essay will be limited to the idioms and practices of "giving," insofar as it constitutes the basic structural—and performative—component of benevolence. In India these moral positions are identified by the names of the two most prominent nationalist leaders of the time: Mohandas K. Gandhi and Jawaharlal Nehru. Gandhi gave us the political morality and way of life that we call tautologically—since they appear so entirely sui generis—Gandhianism; while Nehru exemplified and urged a relationship of intimacy and responsibility between nation and people, and *among* the people, for which the word "patriotism" will serve as shorthand. In different but related ways they responded to the liberalism, and liberality, of colonialism by conceptualizing a *benevolence without giving* or, more radically, a *giving without benevolence:* this, as both an ethics and a political agenda. I shall invoke Gandhi at the origin of the concept of a specific technology of self that I name *dissemination* and Nehru as the author of a concept of postcolonial responsibility that resembles noblesse oblige.

Gandhi named his morality as a series of "experiments with truth." It was a set of successive, lifelong exercises, physical and spiritual, that he first of all performed on himself, then persuaded his family and friends to follow, and sooner or later brought to the attention of a larger public through his articles, letters, and speeches—as confession (if he failed), or exhortation (if he succeeded).

Gandhian experiments with truth resemble nothing so much as the "technologies of self" practiced in classical Greece and early Christian Rome that Foucault has expounded for us,[3] though with the crucial difference that they were incorporated into an active political life. The most well known and comprehensive of these moral truths is *ahimsa,* or nonviolence. Gandhi's different technologies of self cohered into a single doctrine, *satyagraha,* or soul-force, which he put to use in the Indian freedom struggle and, before that, in South Africa.[4] Voluntary poverty was central to achieving satyagraha, the first "necessity" that Gandhi says he recognized as essential for a life in politics.[5]

Gandhi came late and by stages to the spectacular nakedness that made him "the greatest exponent of voluntary poverty in the world."[6] We can follow the stages in his autobiography. In the account of his student years in London, Gandhi describes his initial comic extravagances of dress and social life, which he begins to check as soon as he realizes that his family's means will not support such a lifestyle. The changes he consequently makes in his life—moving to cheaper rooms, walking instead of taking public transport, cooking his own meals—are described with his characteristic gusto for such "experiments" in living: "Let not the reader think that this living made my life by any means a dreary affair. On the contrary the changes harmonized my inward and outward life . . . and my soul knew no bounds of joy."[7] But as yet it was only necessity and a principled wish to live within his means that drove him to thus construct the simple life.

It was at the peak of his successful career as a barrister in South Africa in 1906 that he began to be "agitated" by a need to find ways of "further simplifying [his] life and of doing some concrete act of service to [his] fellow men," as he put it in the chapter of the *Autobiography* titled "Spirit of Service."[8] It is significant that Gandhi began to regard the simple life and service to others as going hand in hand—the discipline of the body in his view had to be simultaneously self- and other-directed. No doubt he felt that simplicity by itself would have appeared eccentric or obsessive, and service alone would be hypocritical if he continued to lead the life of the conventional householder. But when combined, each legitimized and strengthened the ethical value of the other. The thought came to him that nothing less than "giving up the desire for children and wealth and living the life of a *vanaprastha*—of one retired from household cares" was required if he was to devote himself completely to a life of public service.[9]

His first steps in the life of public service were marked, however, by dissatisfaction, trial, and error. He tells us of taking into his home a leper, tending his sores and looking after him at first, but then deciding to send him off to the Government Hospital. Though the reasons he gives for abandoning this project (and the leper) are practical ones, the admission "I lacked the will to keep him always with me" makes it clear that the experience was coded in a spiritual (specifically Christian) symbolic register, as abjectness and singularity of contact, that was not congenial to his needs at this time. He was casting around instead for "some humanitarian work of a permanent nature," seeking a larger field of operation.[10] In these years from 1893 to 1906, he successively served as a part-time medical dispenser, volunteered his services as a stretcher-bearer in an ambulance corps in the Boer war, and nursed wounded Zulus in the so-called Zulu rebellion. The troubled reflections during the early years in South Africa led to his setting up the Phoenix ashram. His crucial exposure to Ruskin's *Unto this Last,* described in terms of religious conversion, was the prelude to this decision: "I could not get any sleep that night. I determined to change my life in accordance with the ideals of the book. . . . I arose with the dawn, ready to reduce these principles to practice."[11] In the middle of his endeavors during the Zulu rebellion he took his vow of *brahmacharya,* or celibacy, which was the "preliminary as it were to Satyagraha."[12] He regarded the remainder of his life in South Africa (which he left in 1915) to be in the nature of an experiment, using satyagraha as a political instrument. This life, we must note, was not to be primarily humanitarian in focus but broadly *political* as he emerged as a leader of the Indian community in their struggle for their rights.

In what follows I examine the implications of Gandhi's ideology and practice of voluntary poverty and his doctrine of service separately for analytic purposes. But their logics were actually deeply imbricated in a unique public life, one that was not free of contradictions. Let me begin with an episode that he narrates in the *Autobiography* that will serve as a parable about the attitude to possessions that he had adopted. When traveling to India by ship in 1914, in the company of his Phoenix ashram friend Kallenbach, Gandhi began to nag Kallenbach about a pair of costly binoculars that the other owned. "Rather than allow those to be a bone of contention between us, why not throw them into the sea and be done with them?" he prompted; whereupon Kallenbach replied, "Certainly throw the wretched things away." "And forthwith," writes Gandhi, "I flung them into the sea."[13]

What the episode shows us is that voluntary poverty was for Gandhi less an act of *giving* than of *ridding oneself of things.* When he came to write at length about it, it is in these terms of self-dispossession that he primarily described it: "I must *discard* all wealth, all possessions."[14] He goes on to use other terms similar to "discard"—"give up . . . things" (note: not "give away"), "things slipped away from me," "I threw overboard things which I used to consider as mine," "a great burden fell off my shoulders." And he comes to the conclusion: "Possession seems to me to be a crime."[15]

Gandhi's position, if taken to its extreme logical conclusion—as he does, its extremity provoking Charles Freer Andrews to compare Gandhi to Savonarola![16] —raises some obvious issues, of which he has anticipated and addressed several as moral dilemmas. I shall identify the most significant of these as they relate to the following: the conditions of possibility of a life of voluntary poverty that include living on charity; the consequent issues of dependency, debt, and gratitude; the problem of "real," that is, involuntary, poverty; and reflections on the status of the physical body.

Gandhi is aware that the man without possessions must still find a means of subsistence, and for this "[y]ou have got then to live purely on the charity of the world."[17] To be a recipient of charity under these circumstances is a different matter from being a "real" beggar. About beggary and dependency he expresses a fairly conventional view, quite unlike the radical defense of the case of the voluntarily poor man (himself) living on charity: "The grinding poverty and starvation with which our country is afflicted is such that it drives more and more men every year into the ranks of the beggars, whose desperate struggle for bread renders them insensible to all feelings of decency and self-respect. And our philanthropists, instead of providing work for them and assisting them on their working for bread, give them alms."[18] Alms-taking and -giving must, it seems, be restricted only to those who are voluntarily poor like himself. In this Gandhi is able to build upon Hindu and Buddhist religious practices that enjoined giving to *sanyasi*s or *bhikhu*s (religious mendicants, renunciants), men who have rendered themselves voluntarily poor (and are consequently allowed to live *only* on charity), within a closed and self-serving system of donors and donees. The novelty of Gandhi's chosen poverty was that he was not a religious sanyasi, but one who was, on the contrary, active in secular public life. Such activity would be felt to be incumbent upon a nonreligious person living on charity if he was not to exist as a parasite on society. Living on charity is a contingent, chancy affair that entails subsisting literally from hand to mouth, from day to day. As he became established in national public life, Gandhi's life of poverty naturally became less risky in this sense.[19] Nor was his poverty projected as a matter of dependency—it became an emblem, rather, of agential self-sufficiency.[20] These differences, however, did not prevent Gandhi from embracing the identity of a "poor man" wholeheartedly—a comment not to be viewed as an accusation of hypocrisy but as an acknowledgement of a constitutive contradiction in the unique position he constructed for himself, as simultaneously poor man (subject) and public figure (object of universal charity).

As in the matter of living on charity, Gandhi was unflinching when it came to handling debt and the accusation of ingratitude. Having taken out an insurance policy for his family at a time of financial insecurity, Gandhi experienced a great crisis of conscience: did it not betray a lack of confidence in God, in his brother who had always supported the larger family, and even in the self-reliance of his wife and children? He could breathe easily only when he finally brought himself to cancel the policy. As in the case of charity, dependency had to be accepted with humility; and once again a form of living contingently, on the brink, was the ethical demand of poverty to which he felt obliged to respond. In the same breath he wrote to inform his older brother Lakshmidas that his vow of poverty meant that "henceforth he should expect nothing from me."[21] Having lived on the resources provided by this brother during his student years in London, Gandhi had been expected to take on the responsibilities of the larger family once he was able. His abdication led to a rift between the brothers. As Arun Gandhi explains it in his memoir of Kasturba: "His [Gandhi's] ingratitude was a cruel blow, a humiliation for the whole family."[22] Gandhi argued that he was in fact supporting his family—only, "the meaning of 'family' had but to be slightly widened and the wisdom of [his] step would become clear."[23] Gandhi's unilateral cancellation of the debt replaces the obligation of repayment by a different obligation—that of service to a different (wider) set of recipients. Rather than confine the debt/gift—the gift that is always implicitly a loan—within the intimate closure of return and reciprocity, he sets it in motion on a different and dispersed trajectory.

The trickiest aspect of advocating voluntary poverty is of course the existence and prevalence of *involuntary* poverty. Gandhi is quick to refuse any idealization or compensatory view of poverty as such: "I would not go among my fellows who starve and talk of voluntary poverty; I do not tell them how blessed they would be if they changed that involuntary poverty into voluntary . . . these men have first of all to have the necessities of life before I can talk to them of voluntary poverty."[24] There is therefore a profound paradox that lies at the heart of Gandhi's position: in order to *become* poor, one cannot be poor to begin with. It is choice, not lack, that is the key ethical aspect of voluntary poverty. And since Gandhi was able to determine and dictate an ideal measure of needs and wants, he recast poverty in absolute rather than relative terms, that is, in terms of a universally acceptable standard of sufficiency.

Gandhian voluntary poverty is not a new idea. Gandhi himself alluded to the number of sources, Hindu and Christian, indigenous and foreign, from which he drew with characteristic eclecticism: Christ's teachings, Ruskin, Tolstoy, Thoreau, the Vaishnava saints, the *Bhagavad Gita*, Dadabhai Naoroji, Raychandbhai.[25] But neither was it exactly like any of these other sources and examples. Nowhere do we see in him any desire to store up merit through good deeds; there are no overtones of Christian otherworldliness or of Christian idealization of (natural, involuntary) poverty; nor is it a version of Hindu asceticism.[26]

Gandhi distinguished his credo from socialism;[27] it was more than only a choice of the simple life,[28] and he rarely spoke of sacrifice except in the sense of renunciation.[29]

What remains may be called a kind of ethical self-centeredness. This chosen poverty's justification is its practitioner's *own* "happiness, the bliss, the ability that it gives one," without any reference to the good it might do to others.[30] "Benevolence," he believed, should have no "taste of favour about it." "To serve without desire is to favour not others, but ourselves."[31] Voluntary poverty is not charity, and it is not a redistributive project (hence his advocacy of trusteeship rather than communism);[32] it is not about sharing one's wealth but about sharing the other's poverty; not a giving *to* but a giving *up*. Its practice, as he repeatedly emphasized, results not in (personal) deprivation but (universal) self-sufficiency, which is why he never described it as sacrificial. His poverty would act like a "dissemination": a going forth (casting, broadcasting) without return, but also without recipients (or only accidental recipients). Through dissemination one does not seek to forge a relationship with a designated "other," one loses one's self.

The word "dissemination" is an echo but not an invocation of Derrida. The invocation would be legitimate, nevertheless, authorized by the heterogeneous sources Gandhi himself drew on to enunciate his practical philosophy, but also by Derrida's own repeated returns to the question of (the impossibility of) the gift, which come close to capturing Gandhi's endeavors. In one place Derrida succinctly describes what I have labored to convey through my exposition: the gift is "that which one does not have."[33] Why is this such a crucial ethical project, this giving without expectation of return, and why is it also "impossible?" As Derrida explains the gift/gifting in *Glas*, "when *someone* gives *something* to *someone*, one is already long within calculating dialectics and speculative idealization."[34] The contamination of even the "pure" gift is inescapable. "At the limit, the gift as gift ought not to appear as gift: either to the donee or to the donor. . . . If the other perceives or receives it, if he or she keeps it as gift, the gift is annulled."[35] The gift "puts the other in debt, with the result that giving amounts to hurting, to doing harm."[36] Derrida might be speaking on Gandhi's behalf, in the matter of Gandhi's unilateral cancellation of his debt to his brother, when he insists that the true (impossible) gift requires that "the donee not give back. . . . The donee owes it *to himself* even not to give back, he *ought* not *owe*."[37]

It is this care about refraining from gift/ing or returning the debt, but despite it entering the *circuit* of the gift—which is nothing less than the social itself—that Gandhi "impossibly" managed in his life's experiments.[38]

Tracking the philosophy and practice of voluntary poverty further in Gandhi's life, we can see that it changes—grows stricter, more absolute—from 1915 onward, when he began his political life in India. From being a lifestyle of simplicity adopted primarily as a matter of integrity in public life, poverty in India became for Gandhi a *political* issue and then an issue of nationalist politics. It was Dadabhai Naoroji's *Poverty and Un-British Rule in India* (1901)[39] that gave him, he writes, his "first acquaintance with the extent of Indian poverty."[40] Poverty, in other words, ceased to be simply the tautological condition of the poor, but was, if not newly, certainly acutely, perceived as a consequence of the immiseration of the people caused by colonial rule and capitalist exploitation.[41] Gandhi's attempt to reconcile his structural understanding of poverty with its existential and ethical aspects produced contradictions that became particularly acute in his public/political life.

There could be no question that involuntary poverty must be alleviated wherever it was found, but how could the project of alleviation be effected, or how would it be even affected, by a political leader's example of self-chosen poverty? The life of poverty was an essential condition, in Gandhi's view, for a leader of the Indian masses (though it was not merely a strategy as some analysts have reductively suggested). Gandhi adopted (some would say usurped) the very identity of the poor as well as the untouchable and, on occasion, the female; he sought nothing less than to *become* the figure of the oppressed through identification. Identification with the poor came to mean for Gandhi, as political leader, adopting a number of symbolic outward marks of poverty, the most famous being his dress (the homespun loincloth),[42] his diet (vegetarian: fruit, nuts, and goat's milk), his dwelling (the ashram), his program of spinning (*khadi*), and his favored modes of transportation (walking and third-class train travel), all of which have been extensively analyzed for their meanings and their efficacy, not least by himself.[43]

The public, performative aspect of voluntary poverty was achieved through the precise modalities of *exemplarity* and *service*. The simple life not only would allow him to live in the midst of the masses and gain credibility among them, it also would serve as an inspiration and bring hope to the poor: "They would say: 'He is happy though he possesses nothing; how is it?' I do not need to argue with them; they begin to argue for themselves."[44] He impresses by simply *being* (i.e., by authenticity, or the noncontradiction between practice and preaching).Gandhi's remarks indicate, in addition, that he is not poor as the "poor" are poor: he simultaneously fashions himself as an exemplary model of the condition he embraces.[45] He often urges, for instance, that simple cleanliness and contentment will make poverty tolerable as well as virtuous.

Under most circumstances the authenticity of being (poor) should have absolved Gandhi of any obligation to act. He surely had no need to exert himself any further in acts of service, especially when service, like exemplarity, was bound to intrude the differences of status and power, whereas through identification he sought sameness with the people. But in Gandhi's case as we saw there was a compulsion to serve, closely allied with the ethical imperative of voluntary poverty and indeed instigated by it.

Physical service by means of the body's performative labors is the only form of "gifting" left to a donor who has renounced all worldly possessions—and even then it remains ambiguous as a form of giving. When Gandhi confronted the ontological question of the body's relationship to the self, he decided in favor of a separation of the body as such from self. "In order to realize that ideal [of voluntary poverty] in its fullness . . . I must not possess anything on this earth as my property, not even this body, because *this body also is a possession.*"[46] Since one does not own even one's own body, one must treat it, he says, as a "temporary possession," which, while it is at one's disposal, "must be used . . . for service and service the whole of our waking hours."[47] The body has a central place in his schema. It must be worn out like a pair of slippers with continual use, as the proverb has it. It is through the body's performative labors that he offers his service to suffering humanity.

Seva, or service, has recently been theorized by Ajay Skaria as an aspect of a broader Gandhian political philosophy.[48] Skaria presents seva as Gandhi's response to the "incoherence and injustice" of the application of liberalism's ideals of equality to the subaltern. Gandhi, by contrast, would acknowledge and subscribe to the hierarchies of social relations.[49] The religious idioms in which he described the subaltern—*daridranarayan* (the divine poor) and *harijan* (children of God, referring to untouchables)—allowed him to offer them, instead of a false liberal equality, the devotion of seva through physical labors such as spinning.[50]

Seva nevertheless produces an insuperable contradiction when conceptualized—as how can it not be?—in terms of service *to the other.* Though distinct from forms of giving (wealth), the body laboring on behalf of the other (as opposed to indulging itself by using its labors to serve only oneself), comes close to constituting itself as a gift. Whereas voluntary poverty is solipsistic and self-centered (so much so that Gandhi could take a unilateral decision about adopting it as his condition in life), service, like friendship, is tied to the other. Can one unilaterally decide to serve or befriend the other? Is not service predicated on consent, as friendship is on reciprocity? Can service, even, ever be anything more than a *response,* though prompt and unequivocal, to a request framed by the other—unlike friendship, which implies spontaneity followed by mutuality? There is every likelihood that help, proffered without reference to the other's will, will render the other impotent: *help-less.*

We may follow the implications of this a little further as it applies, specifically, to the issue of caste. Gandhi's stand on untouchability has become one of the key issues for understanding the history of caste politics today. Gandhi presented untouchability as uniquely a problem for caste Hindus, and hence called for reform within Hinduism by means of "service" to untouchables and other forms of reparation to be performed by them. (In this matter Gandhi's attitude shows a return to the abject version of service, coded as singularity and contact, which he had rejected in seeking a larger, more impersonal public and political field of action in South Africa.) Gandhi's hegemonic sway over the caste issue did not go unopposed, however. B. R. Ambedkar, the leader of the untouchables, was caustic in his disapproval of the upper-caste Hindu "service" that turned many *dalit*s (untouchables) into "mere recipients of charity."[51] Gandhi's position, as Vijay Prashad has argued, "did not argue for emancipation *from* dalithood, but for reform *within* dalithood."[52] Gandhi's refusal to address untouchability in any except upper-caste Hindu reformist terms, like his refusal to support any attack on private property or its owners, meant that he successfully contained both dalit and peasant politics within the ambit of bourgeois and upper-caste seva. Seva may counter liberal equality, but in doing so it also checks the revolutionary agency of subalterns themselves.

Untouchability *is* undeniably, in one sense at least, a problem uniquely for upper castes. The word itself represents a curious formation: its abstractness seems to suggest that it is a condition from which dalits suffer rather than what it actually is, a taboo practiced by upper castes. Since dalits perform polluting labor, it is natural to assume that this is the "cause" of their untouchable condition—but they are after all not untouchable to any except upper-caste Hindus.[53] Any agitation for its removal should logically therefore be directed only at the latter.

But Gandhi's emphasis on upper-caste seva claimed monopoly over the caste issue, to the extent that he opposed any lower-caste activism such as satyagraha, or political initiatives such as separate electorates, that addressed aspects of caste other than untouchability. Thereby he sought to retain caste within the ambit of reformability. The difference between voluntary poverty as a response to poverty and seva as a response to untouchability lies in caste's immutability. Gandhi undertook the degraded labors of the untouchables, but it could not make him untouchable as voluntary poverty could make him poor; he could only occupy the upper-caste position as seva became reparation.

Gandhi's doctrine of seva, like his economic prescriptions, was evidence equally of his antistatism, reinforced by the autodidacticism of his ethics.[54] His nonrevolutionary praxis, fearing violence, sought to retain the status quo of class, gender, and caste relations, relying instead on a change of heart that would put the onus of transforming social structures on those in possession of power and privilege. This much, by way of limits, is obvious.

What I wish to propose nevertheless is the likelihood that Gandhi was not oblivious to the possibility, and the shape, of the recalcitrant subaltern response to such initiatives. Though seva functions as gift, and although Gandhi was thwarted by the inability to find a moral strategy similar to voluntary poverty in his response to caste, there is nothing in the logic of his positions on either trusteeship or seva that scripts gratitude or acquiescence as the recipient other's only possible response. At any rate he had little to say about his expectations of the recipient of seva, concentrating instead on the behavior expected of those whose duty it is to perform it. We might even say that resistance articulated as "ingratitude," of the kind expressed by many dalits to the program of the Harijan Sevak Sangh, would cancel debt most effectively, restoring seva to the domain of giving without benevolence. Such nonexpectation of return is a key teaching of the *Bhagavad Gita,* one of Gandhi's major intellectual and spiritual resources.[55] Consider also as a variation of this, by way of a more active *expectation of nonreturn,* Emmanuel Levinas's description of the self's transcendent relation to the "other," which requires a "movement without return" of the kind Derrida posits for the gift: "A work conceived in its ultimate nature requires a radical generosity of the same who in the work goes unto the other. It then requires an *ingratitude* of the other."[56] Inherent in the communitarian self-sufficiency and the worker noncooperation that Gandhi so staunchly supported is an intransigent ingratitude that functions as a practical ethics of subaltern response to *benevolence* as much as to injustice.

The political history of India as it changed from colony to independent nation also marked a regime change from Gandhi's leadership and influence to those of Jawaharlal Nehru.[57] The shift in the dominant ethico-political thought, from Gandhi's anticolonial "anarcho-communitarianism" and "nonstatist idiom," to Nehru's idea of a *state*-sustained postcolonial Indian identity[58]—in other words, toward the idea of liberal citizenship—marks a major difference of emphasis.[59] Though there were continuities as well as changes—Nehru had always been Gandhi's disciple and presumptive heir, and deeply affective bonds united them—the demands of defining and leading a hugely diverse and profoundly underdeveloped nation that was to adopt a democratic republican state form, as much as temperamental and ideological differences from Gandhi, led Nehru to chart a distinctively different path. It was a path that led Nehru, as leader of India's postcolonial democracy, to explore the ideal and praxis of *re-*

sponsibility. Whether its expression predominantly in terms of patriotism and noblesse oblige indeed functioned as an alternative to benevolence, or whether it was instead simply its surrogate, is the question that concerns me in this analysis.

Nehru's first speech as leader of free India, delivered to the Constituent Assembly on August 14, 1947, the eve of Independence, acknowledges Gandhi's legacy, but marks at the same time the nuanced departures from it that Nehru's perception of his new role as elected representative of the people required. This famous speech, both stirring and sober, was delivered as a pledge to serve the people: the "responsibility" that comes with "freedom and power," Nehru declared, "rests upon this assembly, a sovereign body representing the sovereign people of India." Nehru goes on to invoke Gandhi movingly in this short address: "The ambition of the greatest man of our generation has been to wipe every tear from every eye." That wish is both honored and reframed thus: "That may be beyond us, but as long as there are tears and suffering, so long our work will not be over."[60] Nehru is scrupulous to mark the difference between Gandhian seva—which he views here in terms that recall Levinas's invocation of Dostovesky's phrase "insatiable compassion" ("he does not say 'inexhaustible compassion'")[61]—and his own more limited but nevertheless onerous responsibility as a political leader of this new nation.[62]

And yet Nehru could not always contain the dutifulness expressed in these carefully constructed terms of political responsibility from overflowing into the language of affect. It is instructive to turn to another of Nehru's writings, his last will and testament, in order to illustrate the overpowering, and complicated, nature of his feelings for his country.

Written as early as 1954, the will was made public at his death ten years later. It has since become a much-admired text, frequently anthologized, for example, in school and college textbooks. This document allows me now to make the move to a different set of problematics, that of national identity, which is closely linked in postcoloniality to the sentiment of patriotism. Patriotism is a relationship to the national body—the land and its people—that is rhetorically coded here as both claim and allegiance.

In its form and content the will is a conventional one: it bequeaths Nehru's property to his heirs, expresses his love for the people and land of India, and leaves instructions about his funeral. Since, unlike Gandhi, Nehru did not adopt voluntary poverty (he both inherited wealth and earned money from his writings), or refuse political office, his commitment to the nation is neither as total nor as disinterested as Gandhi's could be said to have been. Questions of divided loyalties, and of power, can therefore be found reflected in each of these aspects of the will.

Despite Nehru's anxious reiteration that he has few assets and little property to leave because of the distracted public life he has led, he is clearly uneasy about the disposition of his famous ancestral house, Anand Bhawan, as he debates the rival claims of nation and daughter. The large house in Allahabad that his famous nationalist father Motilal Nehru had built was connected intimately with the national struggle for freedom: "[W]ithin its walls great events have happened and great decisions have been reached." Hence it ought to be, he feels, a national property, "more than a private possession." But in the event it is to his daughter Indira and her sons that he leaves it, with the stipulation, however, that "whoever lives in Anand Bhawan must always remember this [i.e., its historical associations] and must not do anything contrary to that tradition." He hastens to add, "This wish of mine [is] not intended to be in any way a restriction on the proprietary rights conferred upon my daughter."[63]

The conflict between the public and private personae of the nationalist figure could not be clearer and more poignant, especially when it is a question of being a "father"—of the people, but also of biological offspring.[64] *Not* leaving Anand Bhawan to the nation then, he turns to the question of how he might, despite this, acknowledge gratitude, debt, and return. "I have received so much love and affection from the Indian people that I have been overwhelmed by it . . . nothing I can do can repay even a small fraction of it. . . . [T]here can [of course] be no repayment of so precious a thing as affection." Nevertheless we can discern in these lines the unspoken assurance that this affection is his due, the return for *his* services and sacrifices during the nationalist struggle. Writing this document in the early years of political office, he can still look forward to deserving the people's love and gratitude with continued service as the nation's prime minister: "I can only express the hope that in the remaining years I may live, I shall not be unworthy of my people and their affection."[65]

It is in the same affective register—love that dissolves debt and return—that he asks that his body be cremated and a handful of his ashes thrown into the Ganges, not because of any religious sentiment, he clarifies, but because of an entirely secular emotional attachment to the great river from childhood, as a symbol of India, like the Himalayas from which it flows. He asks that the rest of the ashes be scattered from a plane "over the fields where the peasants of India toil," so that "they may mingle with the dust and soil of India and become an indistinguishable part of India."[66]

The wish to merge into the largeness of physical India, its rivers, mountains, and fields, is an expression of abjection, while at the same time it assumes an identification between the individual and the nation that amounts almost to a proprietary relationship. The intimate sense of belonging that he felt to India was therefore also, always already, a form of ownership.[67] It is an attitude not unknown among other colonial elites. But what distinguishes Nehru's attitude from colonialist paternalism—though his tortuous prose is arguably inflected by rhetoric of a similar kind—is the inchoate feeling that we call patriotism.

Patriotism is less a matter of "practical morality" than of "sentiment," Anthony Appiah would argue.[68] In Nehru's case we might modify this to describe a morality *inflected by* sentiment. This primordial sense of belonging to the land is one he had detected also in the Indian masses and written about in *The Discovery of India* (1946). At that time he had held it insufficient to ground a new sense of Indian-ness. In a passage that has become well known, he writes of his pedagogic mission to create the sense of a modern Indian identity that located it in the *people,* both individually and in their relations as an "imagined community," rather than in simply an atavistic sense of belonging to the land. At the vast gatherings he addressed all over India, he would ask his audience:

> [W]ho was this Bharat Mata, Mother India . . . ? At last a vigorous Jat, wedded to the soil from immemorial generations, would say that it was the *dharti,* the good earth of India, that they meant. . . . I would endeavour to explain that India was all this that they had thought [mountains, rivers, forests, broad fields] . . . but it was much more. . . . What counted ultimately were the people of India, people like them and me, who were spread out all over this vast land. . . . You are parts of this Bharat Mata, I told them, you are in a manner yourselves Bharat Mata.[69]

Though Nehru speaks here of "people like them and me" in an attempt at finding the democratic leveling essential for forging the nation as community—as Sunil Khilnani has observed, Nehru was no populist but instead someone who promoted the "idea of an abstract, historically durable 'people' or 'nation'"[70]—there can be no doubt that he related to the people from a position that placed him above and apart from them.

Nehru's love of India was essentially that of a cosmopolitan. He represents what Anthony Appiah terms the "cosmopolitan patriot," a type that, as he observes, is familiar among nationalist elites in South Asia and Africa, whose "roots" are local but who are intellectually nourished by "Europe and its Enlightenment."[71] Offering a similar diagnosis, Sunil Khilnani astutely remarks how fitting the title of Nehru's *Discovery of India* is in that, although it reflects India as "indubitable presence," it acknowledges that "it could not be taken for granted by people of Nehru's class and background—its contours had to be actively plotted."[72] It is this acquired and self-conscious love—none the less intense or authentic for that—which marks Nehru's identification with the land (which is also a claim) as being different from that of his interlocutor, the "vigorous Jat." From this same-but-not-quite position he can offer to the people a share in the identity "Indian," the grounds for the nation-as-community and for his own identification with the people. That the implications of such a pedagogic discourse, marked as it is by condescension, paternalism, and self-righteousness, could be problematic from the point of view of a truly egalitarian relationship, hardly needs pointing out.[73] The term "noblesse oblige" helps to capture some of the contradictory aspects of responsibility in this mode.

Noblesse oblige (lit. "nobility obligates") is a dictum derived from European feudalism; "nobility" itself describes a class ("the quality, state, or condition of being noble in respect of rank or birth"[74]), but in course of time it yields to a description of a meritocracy. The English "have no equivalent phrase in English to '*noblesse oblige*,'" Evelyn Waugh held; instead "everything turns on 'the grand old name of gentleman.'"[75] Nancy Mitford, in her famous little book bearing the phrase as its title—essentially a disquisition upon class—described the "aristocrat" thus: "The purpose of the aristocrat is to lead, therefore his functions are military and political." In war, accordingly, English noblemen have fought bravely, and in politics they "have worked hard for no reward and done their best according to their lights."[76] This sums up English noblesse oblige. In America, in 1867, Emerson had eloquently praised the new democratic elite he was addressing as an assembly of "educated, reflecting, successful and powerful persons." He went on to invoke noblesse oblige: "Yours is the part of those who have received much. It is an old legend of just men, Noblesse oblige; or, superior advantages bind you to larger generosity," going on to outline the great responsibilities borne by "good men" in a society such as America's.[77]

Many of these meanings of the term had particular resonance for those leading anticolonial nationalist struggles, for whom political freedom was itself associated with responsibility. In 1921, Sarojini Naidu, poet, prominent Congress nationalist, and one of Gandhi's closest associates, wrote in a letter to her young daughter:

> Only remember that you are an Indian girl and that puts upon you a heavier burden than if you were an English girl born to a heritage of freedom. Remember that you have to help India to be free and the children of tomorrow to be free-born citizens of a free land. Therefore if you're true to your country's need you must recognize the responsibility of your Indian womanhood. . . . You are not free—no one is—in the sense of being a law unto yourself in defiance of all existing tradition in our country—for freedom is the heaviest bondage in one sense—since it entails duties, responsibilities and opportunities from which slaves are immune. . . . *Noblesse oblige*! And the ampler the liberty the narrower the right to do as one pleases. You have in you all the seeds of true greatness: be great my little child . . . but always remembering that you are a symbol of India.[78]

Middle-class Indian children of Nehru's generation (and those belonging to the following generation, "midnight's children"), have heard variations on this exhortation reminding them of obligations of service to the nation. But sometimes there was more: as in Naidu's case, there could also be a feeling of a calling to "greatness."

One need not resort to cynicism to discern how deeply implicated noblesse oblige is in structures of class or privilege, or how it is, apart from the hierarchies it establishes, also inseparable from authoritarianism. In a pseudonymous essay titled "The Rashtrapati," published in the *Modern Review* in 1937, Nehru discovered in himself the "makings of a dictator," stemming from his very assets as a leader: "vast popularity, a strong will directed to a well-defined purpose, energy, pride, organisational capacity, ability, hardness." Nehru castigated himself for "an intolerance of others and a certain contempt for the weak and inefficient," this despite "his love of the crowd." The wish to serve or to lead the people—the difference becomes irrelevant—is reflected in an "overmastering desire to get things done, to sweep away what he dislikes and build anew."[79]

While undeniably perceptive and morally admirable, Nehru is not unique in finding that noblesse oblige both arises from and breeds power, that it can legitimize the quest for power and its exercise. The criticism itself is in some ways banal. The answer cannot lie in a disavowal of privilege and the responsibility that attends it—such a move can be only disingenuous. The ethically complex issue is whether privilege and responsibility can be handled differently, and how. The contrast with colonial benevolence brings out the specific features of postcolonial responsibility: where the former arises from plenitude and certitude, "responsibility" in postcolonial relations is marked by efforts to determine its own ethical limits.

Therefore, to my mind the most interesting part of Nehru's essay lies in his insight that his impatience "will hardly brook for long the slow processes of *democracy*."[80] He was quick to see that democracy, as the rule of the people, must remain forever in conflict with and resistant to the rulership of elites, however benevolent. Any attempt to reconcile the two can be only wishful and dangerous.

The recent influential argument of Fareed Zakaria stands as an instance of the troubling logic of the attempt to resolve the conflict. Zakaria, pitting the "illiberalism" of the masses ("the tyranny of the majority") against liberal democracy, opts for the latter. He is nostalgic for a time when noblesse oblige in America was expressed in the public school credo "to serve is to reign," and its followers believed that "public service was a responsibility that came with power."[81] In the different context of India, Zakaria harks back to the Nehruvian era when democracy was still an elite prerogative—only to yield, to his dismay, in the decades since then to the growing power of new voters, "almost all from poor, rural, lower-caste backgrounds."[82] Therefore he recommends that democracy be (once again) made the responsibility, and entrusted to the leadership, of the elites, "those with immense powers in our societies."[83]

Nehru was very far from seeking a solution to his dilemma conceptualized in terms such as these. On the contrary, the "Nehru era," Khilnani maintains, "was permeated by the rhetoric of democracy and social reform, and indeed Indian democracy was exemplary as a system of government then; parliamentary and party procedures were priggishly followed, there were few scandals, enough Indians voted to give the system legitimacy without overtaxing its capacities."[84] A genuine attempt was made by the national leadership "to pass the burden of reform down to the lowest levels, through 'community development projects' and local democracy, *Panchayati Raj,* or rule by village councils."[85] Where Nehru did seem to be supporting elite hegemony was through his increasing reliance on a powerful bureaucracy and technocrats, chiefly economists and scientists, in promoting the nation's "development."[86] As far as his political style of functioning was concerned, Judith Brown speaks of his failures only in terms of an exacerbated sense of responsibility, but not of any temptation to take away power from the people (as his daughter, Indira Gandhi, was to do through the notorious Emergency): "in the highest political office in the country he developed a vast and unsustainable role for himself. He proved incapable of delegating authority and effectively sharing power among colleagues."[87]

It is tempting to map Weber's distinction between *gesinnungsethik* and *verantwortungsethik* (translated as "absolute ethics" and "ethics of responsibility") on to Gandhi and Nehru respectively.[88] But while "ethics of responsibility" does in a sense capture Nehru's endeavors, it is not by scanting means for ends, as Weber's heroic leader would, that Nehru enacted such a responsibility.[89] As we saw, the fear of dictatorial behavior—and, implicitly, the recognition of the anachronism of noblesse oblige in an age of democracy—informs Nehru's self-criticism in "The Rashtrapati." Nevertheless Weber's posing of the problem as the constitutive conflict of ethics and politics is central to our understanding of Nehru's dilemma. Even if "power" in his case was benevolent rather than "demonic" as in Weber's argument, its inevitable authoritarianism, as he himself realized, was personally corrupting and could, moreover, endanger the idea of democracy.[90]

Democracy is often claimed to be the "gift" of the West to the rest of the world, either through the instrumentality of colonialism or simply through its own benign example. In the postcolonial world, it tends to be perceived as the "gift" of political equality offered to a largely poor and illiterate population by those who (are *elected* to) rule—rulers who often came to power as a result of their service and perceived sacrifices in anticolonial struggles. This sequence mimics, on the stage of history and politics, the dynamics of the gift and its reciprocities. But democracy is not the thing that exists prior to its gifting. Rather, as Derrida repeatedly emphasizes, it is that which comes into being through ceaseless negotiation. Democracy is always a democracy-to-come.[91] In Nehru's pioneering efforts in India to make democracy work—against the grain of his own inherited noblesse oblige, and despite the constraints of postcolonial underdevelopment, both political and economic—we can begin to discern the outlines of an ethics of responsibility that was more difficult than benevolence, and well in excess of the demands of mere political office.

NOTES

1. Jacques Derrida, *Given Time: 1. Counterfeit Money,* trans. Peggy Kamuf (Chicago: University of Chicago Press, 1992), p. 7.

2. Sunil Khilnani explains attempts at such self-fashioning, as reflected for instance in Gandhi's writing of an autobiography, in terms of the crisis produced by modernity: "For Gandhi, as for his fellow intellectuals . . . an insistent challenge was that of how to translate this alien world [of modernity] into one which was comprehensible, a world where it was possible to find one's moral bearings, and over which Indians, collectively and individually, might gain some control and even mastery." Introduction to *An Autobiography: Or, The Story of My Experiments with Truth,* by Mohandas Karachand Gandhi, trans. Mahadev Desai from the original Gujarati (Harmondsworth: Penguin Classics, 2001), p. 5.

3. Michel Foucault, *Essential Works of Foucault, 1954–1984,* vol. 1, *Ethics, Subjectivity and Truth,* trans. Robert Hurley et al., ed. Paul Rabinow (New York: New Press, 1997).

4. *Satyagraha,* translated into civil disobedience and marked by nonviolence, or *ahimsa,* has received extended attention from Gandhian scholars. See, for example, Joan Bondurant, *Conquest of Violence: The Gandhian Philosophy of Conflict* (Princeton, N.J.: Princeton University Press, 1988); and Manfred Steger, *Gandhi's Dilemma: Nonviolent Principles and Nationalist Power* (New York: St. Martin's Press, 2000).

5. Gandhi, "Speech at Guildhouse Church, under the Auspices of the Franciscan Society," in *The Collected Works of Mahatma Gandhi,* vol. 48, *1931–2* (New Delhi: Publications Division, Ministry of Information and Broadcasting, Government of India, 1971), p. 50.

6. Gandhi is quoting Dr. Maud Royden, a "progressive social reformer, who was in the chair" during his speech. Ibid. p. 53.

7. Gandhi, *Autobiography,* p. 66. Typically also, in these endeavors, Gandhi writes that he consulted "books on simple living." An aspect of Gandhi's modern, or at least unorthodox, ways was his willingness and ability to consult do-it-yourself manuals on a variety of matters. This made him very much an autodidact. More particularly it reduced his dependence on servants and service-providers.

8. Ibid., p. 192.

9. Ibid., p. 196.

10. Ibid., p. 192.

11. Ibid., pp. 274–75.

12. Ibid., p. 291.

13. Ibid., pp. 314–15. He had earlier recorded, in a tone half-comical, half-tragical, a much more fraught struggle of wills with his wife over some costly gifts that were given to him: "We had been fast simplifying our life. . . . What was I now to do with the jewellery that had come upon me?" He finally overcomes her resistance and places the gifts in a trust for the community's needs. Ibid., p. 208.

14. Gandhi, "Speech at Guildhouse Church," p. 51 (emphasis added).

15. Ibid., p. 52.

16. The Rev. Charles Freer Andrews, one of Gandhi's closest friends and associates, invokes the comparison while describing Gandhi's *swadeshi* campaign for the boycott of foreign goods in India: "[W]ith his mind aflame at the sufferings of the poor and the luxuries of the rich, [Gandhi] ordered bonfires to be made of foreign clothes and ornaments on the beach at Bombay. . . . Then he mounted the great pile and himself applied the flaming torch at night, while the vast crowd raised shouts that rent the sky." Though he is quick to qualify his criticism—"such puritanical fervour is never the deepest thing about him"—Andrews's insight into Gandhi's fanaticism about the destruction of wealth is to be borne in mind. "The Influence of Mahatma Gandhi," *Comprehensive Gandhi Website*, www.mkgandhi.org/articles/influence.htm (accessed October 15, 2005).

17. Gandhi, "Speech at Guildhouse Church," p. 53.

18. Gandhi, *Autobiography*, p. 391.

19. We can say, without trivializing the real difficulties and sacrifices involved in the life he followed, that the very fact of being a figure in public life, well known and admired as a mahatma, made Gandhi's life of poverty an elegant and reasonably comfortable one. The quip made by Sarojini Naidu is well known: "You will never know how much it costs us to keep that saint, that wonderful old man, in poverty!" Reported by William Shirer, *Gandhi: A Memoir* (Calcutta: Rupa, 1993), p. 38.

20. Gandhi is unashamed also to be engaged in a more modern form of begging, fund-raising. To be a beggar for a cause, as he undertook to be on occasion, is a matter indeed for pride: "I have got this reputation of being one of the best beggars in India. At one time I collected one crore of rupees, some horribly large sum, but I had no difficulty in collecting it," he boasts. "Speech at Guildhouse Church," p. 55. He attributes his success to the "*scientific result* of this vow of non-possession or vow of voluntary poverty." Ibid. (emphasis added).

21. Gandhi, *Autobiography*, p. 245.

22. Arun Gandhi, *Kasturba: A Life* (New Delhi: Penguin Books, 2000), p. 129.

23. Gandhi, *Autobiography*, p. 245.

24. Gandhi, "Speech at Guildhouse Church," p. 57.

25. Raychandbhai, poet, businessman, scholar, and spiritual guide, was the person Gandhi came closest to adopting as his own guru. Gandhi, *Autobiography*, pp. 92–93.

26. In a note to Gope Gurbuxani, March 17, 1945, Gandhi writes: "Asceticism in the English sense is not needed at the present time. But there is all the need for renunciation." "Renunciation, Not Asceticism," in *The Collected Works of Mahatma Gandhi*, vol. 69, *1945* (New Delhi: Publications Division, Ministry of Information and Broadcasting, Government of India, 1980), p. 261.

27. He often compared his program to socialism without the violence of its means. See, for example, Gandhi, "Who Is a Socialist?," in *The Collected Works of Mahatma Gandhi*, vol. 88, *1947* (New Delhi: Publications Division, Ministry of Information and Broadcasting, Government of India, 1983), p. 283.

28. The misapprehension has, however, gained ground—Gandhi is recuperated in the West today mainly as a guru of countercultural, New Age, anticonsumerist, and eco-anarchist movements.

29. Gandhi did quite often enjoin "sacrifice" in the usual sense of giving up something on behalf of others' well-being, but he was quick to warn of the perils of such sacrifice: for instance, expectations of reciprocity that may potentially approximate tyranny. See "Letter to Narandas Gandhi," in *The Collected Works of Mahatma Gandhi*, vol. 44, *1930* (New Delhi: Publications Division, Ministry of Information and Broadcasting, Government of India, 1971), p. 260.

30. Gandhi, "Speech at Guildhouse Church," p. 58.

31. Gandhi, "Letter to Narandas Gandhi," p. 259.

32. Trusteeship meant that those who are given wealth may keep it, but in a spirit of "trusteeship," intending their wealth not for themselves but for others. To "end economic disparity without violence" is the chief justification Gandhi offered for his espousal of trusteeship. Gandhi, "Answers to Questions at Gandhi Seva Sangh Meeting," in *The Collected Works of Mahatma Gandhi*, vol. 69, *1939* (New Delhi: Publications Division, Ministry of Information and Broadcasting, Government of India, 1977), p. 219.

33. Jacques Derrida, *Specters of Marx: The State of the Debt, the Work of Mourning, and the New International*, trans. Peggy Kamuf (London: Routledge, 1994), p. 27.

34. Jacques Derrida, *Glas*, trans. John Leary Jr. and Richard Rand (Lincoln: University of Nebraska Press, 1986), p. 243a.

35. Derrida, *Given Time*, p. 14.

36. Ibid., p. 12.

37. Ibid., p. 13.

38. It is in some ways trivial to point out that if Gandhi was able to be thus theoretically pure in his ideal of voluntary poverty, there were contradictions and limits, as well as costs, to its *practice*. I shall not elaborate here on the most obvious consequences of Gandhi's public life, his failures as a family man. Gandhi's memoir, *Kasturba*, describes the travails of his sons, whom he denied a proper education and on whom he imposed strict rules of poverty.

39. Dadabhai Naoroji, *Poverty and Un-British Rule in India* (London: Swan Sonnenschein, 1901).

40. Gandhi, "The Birth Anniversary of Naoroji," in *The Collected Works of Mahatma Gandhi*, vol. 25, *1924–25,* (New Delhi: Publications Division, Ministry of Information and Broadcasting, Government of India, 1967), p. 103.

41. Imperialism's complex political and economic networks had consequences even in the home country, as Gandhi saw for himself with distress during a visit to England in 1931—he spent three days in the "devastated areas" of the Lancashire mills, lying idle because of the Indian boycott of mill goods. See Shirer, *Gandhi*, p. 152.

42. He explained his reasons for the change to his trademark attire, in 1921, thus: "In order . . . to set the example I propose to discard at least up to the 31st of October my *topi* [cap] and vest, and to content myself with only a loin cloth and a *chaddar* [shawl] whenever found necessary for the protection of the body. . . . I consider the renunciation

to be also necessary for me as a sign of mourning, and a bare head and a bare body is such a sign in my part of the country." Quoted in Susan Bean, "Gandhi and *Khadi*, the Fabric of Indian Independence," in *Cloth and Human Experience,* ed. Annette Weiner and Jane Schneider (Washington, D.C.: Smithsonian Institute Press, 1991), p. 367.

43. For an extensive treatment of *khadi* and Gandhi's dress, see Emma Tarlo, *Clothing Matters: Dress and Identity in India* (Chicago: University of Chicago Press, 1996); on the ashram, see Andrews, *Mahatma Gandhi's Ideas* and Ajay Skaria, "Gandhi's Politics: Liberalism and the Question of the Ashram," *South Atlantic Quarterly* 101, no. 4 (2002): 955–86; on Gandhi and Gandhi's body, with a special focus on his celibacy and diet, see Joseph Alter, *Gandhi's Body: Sex, Diet and the Politics of Nationalism* (Philadelphia: University of Pennsylvania Press, 2000) and Khilnani, Introduction; and on all these, see Gandhi's *Autobiography.*

44. Gandhi, "Speech at Guildhouse Church," p. 57. It is worth noting, at least as a curious footnote, that while Gandhi intended his example of voluntary poverty to reconcile the *poor* to their lot, he does not seem to have expected it to inspire the *wealthy* to emulate him.

45. Where I have been speaking of exemplarity as a matter of performance, Akeel Bilgrami shows how exemplarity is central to Gandhi's moral *philosophy.* The *satyagrahi* privileges conscience over principle. He sets an example to others by his actions, and by doing so he too, like the man of principle, universalizes his choices. But the concept of the exemplar is able to provide an ethical alternative, Bilgrami explains, to the concept of principle in moral philosophy: it makes the "psychology surrounding our morals" a more "tolerant" one. "Gandhi, the Philosopher," *Economic and Political Weekly,* September 27, 2003, pp. 4159–65.

46. Gandhi, "Speech at Guildhouse Church," pp. 53–54 (emphasis added).

47. Ibid., p. 54.

48. See also R. Srivatsan, "Concept of 'Seva' and the 'Sevak' in the Freedom Movement," *Economic and Political Weekly,* February 4, 2006, pp. 427–38. Srivatsan develops "seva" as an important dimension of the politics of the Indian nationalist movement, including Gandhi's Harijan uplift.

49. Skaria constructs two other Gandhian categories: "mitrata" (or friendship), which is the appropriate response to those who are one's equals, and "satyagraha" (or noncooperation) as the response to those in dominance. All three responses thus sidestep the demand for equality. "Gandhi's Politics: Liberalism," pp. 955–86

50. Ibid., pp. 979–81.

51. Vijay Prashad, *Untouchable Freedom: A Social History of a Dalit Community* (Delhi: Oxford University Press, 2000), p. 128.

52. Ibid., p. 117.

53. Gandhi urged Hindus to make the dalits lead "clean lives" and draw them away from their addiction to "bad and filthy habits" such as "beef carrion and liquor." Ibid. pp. 121–22. We see no evidence here of a structural understanding of dirt as a likely product of untouchables' labor or their poverty. But other reformers too, including lower-caste leaders themselves, urged lower castes to adopt measures of hygiene and unmarked ways of dressing and to give up polluting occupations as a way to remove the stigma that attached to these.

54. Gandhi's position, Skaria explains, stems largely from his antistatist prejudice: conflicts of inequality, in his view, would have to be settled between the two parties con-

cerned *without reference to* the liberal state's mechanisms of law and rights. The antistatism of Gandhi's politics is equally evident in his blueprint for a national economy, a far more controversial agenda for independent India than his idiosyncratic personal lifestyle. Gandhian large-scale economics emphasized village *swaraj* (independence or autonomy): "My idea of a village *swaraj* is that it is a complete republic, independent of its neighbours for its own vital wants, and yet interdependent for many others in which dependence is a necessity." "Question Box," in *The Collected Works of Mahatma Gandhi*, vol. 76, *1942* (New Delhi: Publications Division, Ministry of Information and Broadcasting, Government of India, 1979), p. 308. Toward the end of his life he was exhorting Rajendra Prasad, the soon-to-be president of the free republic, that "it is better for us to starve than to import even a single grain of food from outside." "But mine," he mourned, "is a voice in the wilderness." Gandhi, "A Letter," in *The Collected Works of Mahatma Gandhi*, vol. 88, *1947* (New Delhi: Publications Division, Ministry of Information and Broadcasting, Government of India, 1983), p. 159.

55. This is expressed in the well-known injunction that the doer must be detached from the fruits of his labor. *Bhagavad Gita*, trans. Swami Nikhilananda (New York: Ramaknishna-Vivekananda Center, 1944), see esp. chap. 18.

56. Emmanuel Levinas, "Trace of the Other," trans. A. Lingis, in *Deconstruction in Context: Literature and Philosophy*, ed. Mark Taylor (1963; Chicago: University of Chicago Press, 1986), p. 349.

57. Jawaharlal Nehru (1889–1964), India's first prime minister and leader of the ruling Congress party. In the seventeen years of his leadership of the country he formulated and put in place independent India's major economic, political, and social policies: socialism, industrialization, nonalignment, and secularism, broadly the projects of modernity.

58. Khilnani, *The Idea of India* (New Delhi: Penguin, 1998), p. 166.

59. For the line of argument I am following here, Alasdair MacIntyre's contrast between the Stoic and Aristotelian conceptions of morality in ancient Greece can serve as a suggestive heuristic (with obvious necessary qualifications) to illustrate the differences between the values represented by Gandhi and Nehru respectively. The Stoics sought to do "what is right for its own sake," MacIntyre explains. For them "the good man is a citizen of the universe; his relation to all other collectivities, to city, kingdom or empire is secondary and accidental." *After Virtue: A Study in Moral Theory* (London: Duckworth, 1985), p. 169. Aristotle on the other hand developed the notion of the "virtues" essentially in civic and political terms. Ibid., see chapter 12, esp. pp. 148ff.

60. Nehru speaks in the context of the Partition of the subcontinent that attended independence, marked as it was by enormous turmoil—riots, loss of life, and the displacement and migration of millions across the newly drawn borders of India and Pakistan. Gandhi was at the time in riot-torn Bengal, far from the scene of the official celebrations of Independence in Delhi.

61. Levinas, "Trace of the Other," p. 351.

62. Jawaharlal Nehru, "Tryst with Destiny," in *Independence and After: A Collection of the More Important Speeches of Jawaharlal Nehru from September 1946 to May 1949* (Delhi: Government of India, 1949), p. 3.

63. I have been unable to find this opening section of the will in any of the official editions of Nehru's writings and speeches. It is likely to have been dropped because it brings up the vexed question of Anand Bhawan as national property. I have used the

unexpurgated original version, in this instance, as cited in Arvind Ghosh, "Will and Testament of Jawaharlal Nehru," *Sword of Truth* 39 (September 1999), http://www .swordoftruth.com/swordoftruth/archives/byauthor/aghosh/watojn.html (accessed October 13, 2005).

64. The obvious contrast is to Gandhi's *failed* relationship with his children.

65. Nehru, "Last Will," cited in Shashi Tharoor, *India: From Midnight to Millennium* (New York: Arcade, 1997), p. 133.

66. Nehru, "Last Will," cited in Tharoor, p. 134.

67. An outraged response from a present-day Nehru-basher: "No doubt Nehru thought of India and whatever she stood for as his own creation. There was no room for anyone else, other than himself and his family, who had any right to claim the slightest love and ownership to our land." Ghosh, "Will and Testament."

68. Kwame Anthony Appiah, "Cosmopolitan Patriots," *Critical Inquiry* 23, no. 3 (1997): 622.

69. Jawaharlal Nehru, *The Discovery of India* (Bombay: Asia Publishing House, 1946), p. 39.

70. Khilnani, *Idea of India,* p. 41.

71. Appiah, "Cosmopolitan Patriots," p. 636.

72. Khilnani, *Idea of India,* p. 168.

73. Judith Brown's analysis of Nehru's leadership in her recent political biography emphasizes this aspect: "Nehru sought to spread his vision of a new India by means other than his personal lifestyle. He also adopted a pedagogic role, exhorting and teaching Indians. . . . His tone was often one of exasperated paternalism." *Nehru: A Political Life* (New Delhi: Oxford University Press, 2003), p. 192.

74. Definition from *The Shorter Oxford English Dictionary.*

75. Evelyn Waugh, "An Open Letter to the Honble Mrs. Peter Rodd [Nancy Mitford] on a Very Serious Subject," in *Noblesse Oblige: An Enquiry into the Identifiable Characteristics of the English Aristocracy,* ed. Nancy Mitford (London: Hamish Hamilton, 1956), p. 73.

76. Mitford, "The English Aristocracy," in Mitford, *Noblesse Oblige,* pp. 47–48.

77. Ralph Waldo Emerson, "Address Read before the B. K. Society at Cambridge, July 18, 1867," in *The Complete Works of Ralph Waldo Emerson,* vol. 8, *Letters and Social Aims* (London: George Bell and Sons, 1883), p. 235.

78. Sarojini Naidu, *Sarojini Naidu: Selected Letters 1890s to 1940s,* ed. Makarand Paranjape (New Delhi: Kali for Women, 1996), p. 157.

79. Nehru, "The Rashtrapati," in *Selected Works of Jawaharlal Nehru,* first series, vol. 8, ed. S. Gopal (1937; New Delhi: Orient Longman, 1976), p. 522.

80. Nehru, "Rashtrapati," p. 522 (emphasis added).

81. Fareed Zakaria, *The Future of Freedom: Illiberal Democracy at Home and Abroad* (New York: W. W. Norton, 2003), pp. 233–34.

82. Ibid., p. 108.

83. Ibid., p. 256.

84. Khilnani, *Idea of India,* p. 40.

85. Ibid., p. 79.

86. Ibid., p. 81.

87. Brown, *Nehru,* p. 343.

88. Max Weber, *Politik als Beruf* (Berlin: Duncker and Humblot, 1964). The analogies have been noted by Gandhi scholars already. See Steger, *Gandhi's Dilemma,* p. 193; Brown invokes Weber obliquely, in comparing Nehru to Luther, *Nehru,* p. 340.

89. For a defense of Nehru's "deep moral anxiety about politics as a career," see Sunil Khilnani, "Nehru's Faith," *Economic and Political Weekly,* November 30, 2002, pp. 4793–99. Judith Brown also comes to the conclusion that at the end of his life, in the 1960s, Nehru "increasingly turned to many of the Mahatma's teachings when confronted with his own failure to transform party and country as he had wished." *Nehru,* p. 334.

90. For the exposition on Weber I have depended on Johan Verstraeten, "The Tension Between 'Gesinnungsethik' and 'Verantwortungsethik': A Critical Interpretation of the Position of Max Weber in 'Politik als Beruf,'" *Ethical Perspectives* 2, no. 4 (1995): 180–88, esp. 183.

91. Derrida, *Politics of Friendship,* trans. George Collins (London: Verso, 1997), p. 306.

11 Rescuing African Women and Girls from Female Genital Practices: A Benevolent and Civilizing Mission

Wairimū Ngarūiya Njambi

> They were proud to have raised the benighted Africans out of their
> barbarism by gifts of Christianity, education, public health, and
> peace, and they were furious that the Africans were not "grateful."[1]
>
> —ROBERT EDGERTON

Female genital practices have received much attention lately, with numerous texts promoting intervention with the benevolent goal of eradication that aims to rescue endangered women and girls, mainly in Africa. While this essay neither endorses what is often called "Female Genital Mutilation" (FGM) nor disputes the rights of activists to oppose it, I point out troubling aspects of the current campaign and its rhetoric that appear to borrow in striking ways from the civilizing discourse of colonialism.[2] Consider, for instance, some phrases regarding female genital practices employed by eradication advocates that are intended to shock audiences and mobilize activists. Such phrases include "sadistic and unspeakable atrocities";[3] "a mutilation of minors";[4] "barbaric, futile and illogical";[5] "the most obscene form of violence against women";[6] "a form of child abuse";[7] "a persecution";[8] "a brutal and harmful practice";[9] "a cruel tradition";[10] "a direct attack on women's sexuality";[11] and "immoral and unchristian."[12] Such phrases, which motivate the interventions of a variety of institutions, carry the legacies of historical themes from the age of formal empires, which outlawed various cultural practices by reconstituting them textually to appear horrifying to the intended audiences. These discourses imply that Africa is a dangerous place for girls and women due to Africans' tenacious commitment to "barbaric" cultural practices, and that intervention from more "enlightened" external actors is the only hope for change toward civilization. As the epigraph to this essay indicates, the interveners were and are proud to be part of this mission and wonder aloud why any rational person would question their motives and impacts.

Since the height of colonialism, mainly Euro-American voices of the West, with its persistent benevolent vision of civilizing Africa, have dominated both the knowledge about female genital practices and the push for eradication. Depictions of female genital practices as "unspeakable horrors" have led some Africans to perpetuate the same civilizing discourse in their eradication efforts. For example, Olayinka Koso-Thomas, a Nigerian activist, claims that "it is amazing how many African females have no idea what normal genitalia should look like,"[13] which suggests that ignorance explains why practices continue. By contrast, Nahid Toubia, a Sudanese physician, has been critical of imperialist tendencies in the eradication movement as well as the problematic implications of the term FGM, even though she continues to employ this phraseology throughout her work. Nawal El Saadawi, the prominent Egyptian feminist who has written widely about women's roles in Arab societies, adds that European and American feminists' preoccupation with the "savagery" of female circumcision obscures wider social inequities in developing countries as well as the extent to which Western women remain sexually exploited and commoditized. El Saadawi explicitly denounces female circumcision but also opposes as flawed "attempts to deal with such problems in isolation, or to sever their links with the general economic and social pressures to which women everywhere are exposed."[14]

In this essay, I argue that the debate about female genital practices can progress in productive ways only once it dispenses with the discourses of barbarity, sadism, ignorance, and victimhood relentlessly promulgated in much of the literature on the subject. Following Judith Butler's notion of performativity,[15] I employ the alternative term "female genital practices" in order to render problematic the notion of "female genital mutilation" and to undermine the normative sense of "genitalia" that is presumed by eradication advocates to exist independently of its various discursive formations. Genitalia, whether circumcised or not, are partly products of particular cultural, political, and historical performances that continue to give them not only their meanings but also their materiality. Female genital practices are more heterogeneous and complex than eradication activists have acknowledged and need to be analyzed in the full context of their cultural, social, and gendered histories. As is the case with all *cultural practices*, female genital practices are constantly changing, and do not, therefore, constitute an immutable (and thus ineradicable) tradition.

My essay focuses on three prominent feminists from the United States who have played major roles in helping to shape international policies concerning female genital practices: Fran Hosken, Mary Daly, and Alice Walker. As a prelude to that discussion, I will address briefly some of the ways in which feminist rhetorics of benevolence were mobilized by colonizers in earlier periods (through various cultural intervention efforts) in order to justify colonial domination in Kenya and India. Beyond the language of barbarity, the legacies of colonial discourse continue to mark contemporary Western feminism, notably in the assumptions of who gets to intervene and why. While there are multiple and heterogeneous feminisms in the West and many of them have problematized imperialistic representations of Third-World women,[16] much of the scholarship regarding female genital practices remains trapped in these problematic modes of representation,[17] despite widespread cautions about essentialist approaches to understanding biology and sexuality and the related recognition that genital imaginaries are potent carriers of all kinds of social, political, economic, and historical entanglements.

THE BENEVOLENT MISSION OF COLONIAL FEMINISM

Postcolonial studies has shown various ways in which colonizers constructed cultural practices as barbaric and backward in order to justify colonial domination by demarcating a boundary between the civilized European and the primitive Other. Some scholars have also pointed out ways in which Euro-American feminism was appropriated to meet such colonial needs.[18] For example, Leila Ahmed writes: "Even as the Victorian male establishment devised theories to contest the claims of feminism, and derided and rejected the ideas of feminism and the notion of men's oppressing women with respect to itself, it captured the language of feminism and redirected it, in the service of colonialism, toward Other men and the cultures of Other men."[19] This appropriation was apparent in the controversy generated by colonial officials and missionaries in Kenya when they outlawed what they referred to as "female circumcision" in the late 1920s. As I have explained elsewhere, when colonial missionaries arrived in Kenya, they made it apparent that the practice of *irua ria atumia,* or initiation of women (but not *irua ria anake,* or initiation of young men) was incompatible with Christian morality and had to be prevented.[20] As Kershaw points out, they "interpreted Western monogamy and male circumcision as compatible, but polygyny and female circumcision as incompatible, with Christian doctrine."[21] Responding to such incompatibility, colonizers attempted to abolish irua ria atumia by appropriating the feminist rhetoric of rescuing "native" women from the supposedly immoral traditions dictated by men. Their appeal to the language of "primitivity," "barbarity," "immorality," and "harmfulness" is remarkably similar to that of the contemporary eradication activists.[22]

While the colonizers focused their concern on the irua ria atumia, it was not this practice per se that they found immoral and unchristian, but rather the sexual practices that accompanied such initiations, including *ngwiko* (nonpenetrative sexual encounter), multiple sexual activities, and sexually suggestive dances taught to the newly initiated, which the colonial interlopers considered promiscuous and degrading. As Reverend Keith Cole testifies from his missionary station in Limuru, Kenya, "In every case, however, the ceremonies are accompanied by dancing and immorality. As we shall see, the church was compelled to denounce the immoral practice [ngwiko] which accompanied initiation together with female circumcision as injurious to the body and degrading to the soul."[23] *Irua ria atumia na anake* (initiation of women and men) and the teaching of ngwiko and specific dances also took many months to complete, which interfered with the settlers' labor supply.[24] When the "female circumcision controversy" became an important mobilizing force for the anticolonial Gikuyu resisters led by organizations such as Kikuyu Central Association (KCA), the colonial abolition strategies grew even more serious and began to focus more on the status of women's health and rights.[25]

Earlier, in India, British colonizers sought to eradicate the practice of *sati*, or widow burning. Lata Mani writes that "[c]ontrary to the popular notion that the British were compelled to outlaw *Sati* because of its barbarity, the horror of the burning women [carried] a distinctly minor theme."[26] Although the reconstitution of sati under colonial rule was based on debates about women's rights and social status in Indian society, "these debates [were] in some sense not primarily about women but about what constitutes authentic cultural tradition."[27] The discourse on sati did not emerge from nowhere, Mani warns, "nor was it entirely discontinuous with precolonial discourses in India. Rather, it was produced through interaction with select natives, though [as she shows] officials clearly had power over the natives in question."[28] In this manner, Mani sees the discourse on sati as specifically a colonial production that cared less about understanding the practice, let alone the women involved, than about colonial rule itself and thereby casting colonialism as a benevolent and civilizing mission.

Such "colonial feminism," as Ahmed calls it, was also appropriated as "national feminism" (or what Amina Mama refers to as femocracy[29]) by various nationalist governments in Africa immediately following independence, with the leadership of various movements granted primarily to women in privileged classes. In the case of Kenya, for instance, Maendaleo ya Wanawake, a women's development movement that was founded during the latter years of colonialism, was soon after independence adopted as a national women's movement to represent all women in Kenya, though its leaders were the wives of elite male politicians. Embarrassed by "traditions," many easily adopted views that supported the eradication of female genital practices. Here we have elite women and feminists from Third-World contexts and Euro-American mainstream feminists speaking directly to each other, furthering goals and interests that pertain to their visions and welfare while appearing to be speaking on behalf of all women. Judged only in terms of the accomplishments and the failures of these feminists, the activities of subaltern peasants and working-class and minority women become historically and spatially frozen, marginalized, and/or stereotyped.[30]

The discourse on female genital practices that the colonial regime helped to constitute and normalize textually erased other multiple perspectives that contradicted the desired notion of native women's oppression. It also erased women entirely except, of course, as passive victims. Men, on the other hand, were rendered as active agents that either supported or opposed the abolition. The colonizers' and missionaries' rhetoric of civilizing and rescuing has resurged in significant ways in the recent growth of the globalized FGM eradication movement, starting with the second wave of feminism of the 1970s. As Corinne Kratz points out, "[c]urrent feminist campaigns may not recognize the continuities, but their rhetoric depends on arguments and images that were also central to colonial and missionary projects complete with implicit evolutionary scales and notions of 'progress' defined by their own criteria and values."[31]

I focus on the current campaign as pioneered by Hosken, Daly, and Walker in order to demonstrate this indebtedness of present-day eradication discourses to the colonialist rhetoric of benevolence and civilization. These three feminists have generated enormously influential work on the issue, and because of that, they have greatly enhanced the political strategies that have helped shape what has now become the anti-FGM movement. In their representations of so-called FGM, these advocates have not only replicated the terminology of barbarity and primitivity, they have also produced an image of ignorant and male-dominated native women who must be rescued by enlightened Euro-American feminists. All three have implied that understanding the social and historical contexts of female genital practices is irrelevant since all contexts point to similar patriarchal oppression—in fact, contextualization, in this view, would simply cloud the issue, distracting attention from the identification of the root cause of "women's oppression." By erasing the heterogeneous and contradictory ways in which different histories and cultural practices have created particular and specific women's experiences, Hosken, Daly, and Walker have treated the categories "female" and "woman" as uncontested terrain that can be employed interchangeably everywhere.[32] But as Donna Haraway reminds us, "[t]here is nothing about being 'female' [or a woman] that naturally binds women. There is not even such a state as 'being' female, itself a highly complex category constructed in contested sexual scientific discourses and other social practices."[33] The benevolent intervention associated with Hosken, Daly, and Walker, like that of formal colonial powers, privileges the image of the "One" and "Same" everywhere. Their intervention speaks the "truth" of universal bodies/sexualities, human rights, and ethics, which they see as self-evidently present in those very words, hence unquestionable. Similarly, female genital practices are assumed to have kept their original and undisputed meanings. How those meanings came about as well as what was discarded during the time of their encoding is all but erased, creating in this sense a stable and unambiguous practice.

FRAN HOSKEN

Most prominent in anti-FGM discourse is the work of Fran Hosken, who coined the label FGM and whose commitment to abolishing the practices of female circumcision has made her a vocal and influential anti-FGM activist since the early 1970s. Hosken's benevolent intervention resembles that of the colonial civilizing discourse insofar as it appeals to master narratives of male total control over African women, tradition-boundedness, and ignorance. In Africa, according to Hosken, women are the property and sexual slaves of men:

> In Sub-Saharan as well as Arab-African and Middle Eastern societies, females are the property of males. Upon reaching puberty, a woman is traded from her father's family to her husband's family in return for a bride price. All marriages are arranged between the male family heads and represent an alliance between families rather than individuals. A woman's chief purpose is to produce and raise sons and render sexual services to her husband.[34]

Hosken argues that not only are the "victims" of the practices "illiterate and too young to speak for themselves," they are also "unaware of the rest of the world and of their own bodies' biological functions. They are quite unable to communicate their needs."[35] Hosken may be referring here to children but, throughout her work, she has attributed this same characteristic to women, whom she sees as rendered voiceless by their victimizers. In her view, tradition helps to "keep women 'in their place'—that means, without education, training, or modern tools; ignorant, illiterate, and isolated; and most of all, without the most important and basic facts on health, reproduction and sexuality, which every woman who is raising a family most urgently needs to know."[36] According to Hosken, "In Africa, women for the most part are the subsistence farmers. Therefore, the means to a good life is to control women and to own as many as possible. As a result, the methods to keep women under male control are drastic: excision and infibulation."[37]

The conceptualization of Other women's continued oppression is presented by Hosken through popularized images of foot binding in China, sati in India, genital mutilation and polygamy in Africa, purdah and veiling in Islamic nations, machismo in South America, and the chastity belt in Europe. The latter, however, is deemed as now irrelevant within a perspective that sees Euro-American women having progressively liberated themselves in most ways, unlike Third-World women. In Hosken's assessment, it is then the responsibility of Euro-American women as well as the Western medical scientists who "clearly" comprehend the problem of female genital practices to liberate those Others who lack such comprehension. And because "[b]y definition the goals of tradition and development are incompatible,"[38] Hosken persistently calls upon Western-based institutions to intervene to put an end to the barbarity of FGM. Hosken's argument and condemnation of genital practices is constituted largely through one privileged premise: that of the ignorant and male-dominated native woman Other(s) who now must be rescued, not only from the native men, but also from patriarchal traditions.[39]

Hosken asks, "Now that the truth about human sexuality has been established by Kinsey, by Masters and Johnson, and by the Hite Report, why are the facts not taught in every school and especially in the developing world."[40] She adds, "We are able to teach those who cling to distorted beliefs some better ways to cope with themselves, reproduction and sexuality: everyone has the capacity to learn."[41] Following this rationale, Hosken "started the information campaign with the child-birth picture [b]ooks which are designed to distribute this essential knowledge everywhere in the world."[42] For Hosken, the "biological facts" and "sexual truths" established by Kinsey, Masters and Johnson, and Hite are not embodiments of locally situated cultural perspectives based on particular values and interests, but rather a universal "reality." Armed with such Western "scientific truth" and the image of African women as sexually mutilated victims, Hosken does not need to consider the viewpoints of those who perform female genital practices. In fact, she suggests that learning the histories and the local meanings behind these practices is not an option that Western researchers should consider important:

> The cause of the practice of excision and infibulation is lost in the distant past; typically, no one in Africa today can give a plausible explanation for genital mutilation of girls that is not tied to myths, magic, misconceptions and ignorance of biological facts. One can only guess how long it has taken to bring about the unquestioned acceptance "as our custom and tradition" of these terrifyingly sadistic and permanently damaging mutilations, that are even now considered an essential requirement for marriage in many African countries.[43]

In addition, Hosken argues that "rural Africans are friendly and try to please: they will tell a researcher whatever they think he/she wants to hear."[44] The congruence between Hosken's notion of friendly Africans and colonizers' images of Africans as childlike is hard to miss. She is especially suspicious of contemporary ethnographical and anthropological literature that tends to address female genital practices in relation to their social and historical contexts and maintains that this literature, "written mostly by men, ignores the mutilations and conceals their true results and effects on African life."[45] One senses that Hosken is uncomfortable with ethnological approaches to female genital practices because they contradict her prefigured assumptions. By excluding such perspectives from her work, she is even able to forget—and to make us forget—the historical role that colonial anthropology itself played in the constitution of the colonial discourse on "female circumcision."

Africans' perspectives and contextualized ethnographies seem irrelevant to Hosken, who prefers to focus her attention on what she sees as the relationship between female genital practices and the "customs" of male violence in Africa: "Africa is the most violent continent demonstrating the direct relationship between family violence and civil or tribal warfare. What are called 'cultural traditions' in reality are practices that support the ritual abuse of women, systematically damaging women's health and strength to make sure of their subordination to men. . . . The result of these violent customs can be seen today all over Africa's ongoing tribal and civil wars."[46] Hosken uses the example of a case in Kenya in the early 1990s, in which at least nineteen high school girls were brutally raped and nine were crushed to death during a high school riot, as proof that rape in Africa is a tradition. While rape and wife beating are crimes that cut across racial, cultural, and geographical locations, Hosken normalizes them as "customs" that are no different from other expected cultural practices. Similarly, arranged marriages are stripped of their heterogeneity and become constituted through the language of "selling" in order to enforce the image of male control. It is this textual power to appropriate, distort, erase, and contain that connects contemporary eradication discourses with earlier colonial practices.[47]

Hosken's ability to maintain a total vision of African women and girls as "the victim[s] of male control—the sexually oppressed"[48]—allows her to call for Western intervention and to appear benevolent. Despite her obviously offensive and racist portrayals of Africa and Africans, her *Hosken Report* is the most widely cited document in anti-FGM discourse, while her periodical, *WIN News*, is the most persistent voice in the battle against female genital practices and has received very little serious scrutiny within Western feminism. Meanwhile, some eradication advocates (such as Evelyne Accad) dismiss any criticism of Hosken as a distraction and a refusal of the "academic feminists" to commit to the more serious work of liberating women.[49]

MARY DALY

Daly is one of the most prominent and influential cultural feminists from the second wave of feminism, who brought a much needed and important lesbian awareness and perspective to what was arguably a heterosexual-feminist-dominated women's studies field. However, like Hosken, Daly looks at female genital practices as evidence of universalized male domination and as representing one particularly vicious form of the internalization of female subservience in a world full of violence against women: "There are some manifestations of the sado-ritual syndrome that are unspeakable—incapable of being expressed in words because they are inexpressibly horrible. Such are the ritual genital mutilations—excision and infibulation—still inflicted upon women throughout Africa today, and practiced in many parts of the world in the past."[50] Having conceptualized male domination as an invasion of the entire global social fabric, Daly's mission is to help women to liberate themselves from the "phallocracy" by teaching them how to identify oppression:

> Women . . . are the real but unacknowledged objects of attack, victimized as The Enemy of Patriarchy—of all its wars, of all its professions. There are feminist works which provide abundant examples of misogynistic statements from authorities in all "fields," in all major societies, throughout the millennia of patriarchy. Feminists have also written at length about the actual rapist behavior of professionals, from soldiers to gynecologists.[51]

The feminist scholarship Daly discusses, which women should seek in order to learn the danger and the legacy of patriarchy, is written primarily by Euro-American women. Since she does not ask Euro-American women to read what African, Chinese, and Indian feminists have written about their own conceptions of patriarchy, one can only assume that the flow of education that Daly is advocating here and elsewhere throughout her text is one-way, going from Western to non-Western women.

For Daly, as for Hosken, culture is a static, bounded "thing" that people possess or that takes hold of them. In this sense, both regard culture as unchanging without the application of an external force. Thus, Daly's frustrations are directed most intently at those Western-educated natives and powerful institutions that are silent about the female genital practices that Euro-American radical feminists have worked so hard to uncover: "Why do educated persons babble about the importance of tribal coherence and tradition while closing their eyes to the physical reality of mutilation? Why do anthropologists ignore or minimize this horror? Why is it that the Catholic Church has not taken a clear position against this genital mutilation? Why do some African leaders educated in the West continue to insist upon the maiming of their daughters?"[52] Daly suggests that "[t]here has been a conspiracy of silence"[53] among the UN agencies, especially WHO and UNICEF, nongovernmental organizations, mission societies, church groups, and women's organizations, including the World Association of Girl Guides and Girl Scouts, Y.W.C.A., and the Associated Country Women of the World. With their stakes in maintaining global patriarchy, she argues, most refuse even to name female genital practices, lest they be forced to act against these unspeakable atrocities: "[They] all know what is going on. Or they have people in Africa who know. This quite aside from the Health Departments and hospitals in African countries and the M.D.s, especially gynecologists, who get the most desperate cases . . . The doctors know all. But they don't speak."[54] Daly is calling on these international agencies because she, like most eradication advocates, sees them as benevolent, if negligent, institutions. Like Hosken, Daly does not appear to be concerned about the atrocities committed against Africans, let alone African women, by some of these same agencies during the colonial era. Both seem to be suggesting that colonial rule did not go far enough in bringing civilization and rooting out barbarism. At the same time, such institutions are rarely sought out by Western feminists to intervene on their behalf and are often criticized by them for being patriarchal and for hindering various Euro-American women's rights. Daly seems to imply that given Africans' "lesser stages" of cultural development, any sort of intervention, including by "Girl Guides and Girl Scouts," will do, no matter how trivial from the viewpoints of those on the receiving end.

Daly's own project, detailed in *Gyn/Ecology: The Metaethics of Radical Feminism,* has emphasized histories and cultures that existed independently for Euro-American women before patriarchy took over. Daly urges us to know about and respect practices such as witchcraft and goddess worship, by which women can aspire and perhaps even return to "the remnants of naturally wild femaleness."[55] She hopes "that more feminists will give to the history of witches the serious study that it warrants, recognizing it as a part of our entombed history, a remnant of the old religion which pre-dated all patriarchal faiths and which was a Goddess-worshipping, matriarchal faith."[56] African, Chinese, and Indian women, on the other hand, defined only as objects of a "male sado-ritual syndrome," are assumed by Daly to have no such unique histories and cultures. It is the empowering remnants of Euro-American witchcraft that these Other(ed) women must emulate to be liberated from male domination. In an open letter, Audre Lorde provides a helpful criticism of Daly's shortsightedness:

[I]t was obvious that you were dealing with non-European women, but only as victims and preyers-upon each other. I began to feel my history and my mythic background distorted by the absence of any images of my foremothers in power. Your inclusion of African genital mutilation was an important and necessary piece in any consideration of female ecology, and too little has been written about it. To imply, however, that all women suffer the same oppression simply because we are women is to lose sight of the many varied tools of patriarchy. It is to ignore how those tools are used by women without awareness against each other.[57]

To emphasize Lorde's point, what Daly forgets is that the Euro-American feminist humanism on which she bases her benevolence is a master narrative that is deeply indebted to racism and colonialism.[58] Such a narrative has allowed Daly, like Hosken, to conceptualize women Others in advance as victims.

Daly even anticipates a backlash from Africans who might accuse Westerners of racism or neocolonialism, but urges her readers not to heed such objections:

Critics from Western countries are constantly being intimidated by accusations of "racism," to the point of misnaming, non-naming, and not seeing these sado-rituals. The accusations of racism may come from ignorance, but they serve only the interests of males, not of women. This kind of accusation and intimidation constitutes an astounding and damaging reversal, for it is clearly in the interest of black women that feminists of all races should speak out.[59]

Daly's frustration at Africans' seeming failure to appreciate such intervention echoes sentiments expressed by the colonial missionaries in the epigraph of this essay: Africans just don't seem to know what is best for them.

ALICE WALKER

Walker's benevolent rhetoric exhibits similar assumptions of the West's duty to intervene. Walker has been influential in generating a third wave of feminism through her criticism of the ways in which African American women have been represented and/or are ignored in various feminist texts. In *The Color Purple*[60] and *In Search of Our Mothers' Gardens: Womanist Prose,*[61] for instance, Walker has pointed to complexities in African American women's everyday life practices and struggles as well as their multiple and heterogeneous means of empowerment. However, when it comes to African women, Walker, like Daly and Hosken, has constructed very simplistic images of ignorant and dominated native subjects who have no sense of imagination and creativity and whose survival is dependent on Western intervention. Walker's novel *Possessing the Secret of Joy* is described as follows in the first paragraph of the publisher's summary:

> [This] is the story of Tashi, a tribal African woman who lives much of her adult life in North America. As a young woman, a misguided loyalty to the customs of her people led her to voluntarily submit to the *tsunga's* knife and be genitally mutilated (pharonically circumcised). Severely traumatized by this experience, she spends the rest of her life battling madness, trying desperately through psychotherapy—she is treated by disciples of both Freud and C. G. Jung—and even by Jung himself—to regain the ability to recognize her own reality and to *feel*.[62]

While Tashi voluntarily submitted to circumcision, she learned only later, through her contact with the West's "objective" eye, that her loyalty to custom was "misguided"; the customary justifications for circumcision, rooted in "myth," kept her ignorant of the "truth" of the tortuous physical and psychological implications of the practice. None other than the icons of Western psychological science correct the traumas of "tradition." In this sense, Tashi appears as rescued, psychologically, by the West and its capacity to reveal universal truths as antidotes to local myths.

Walker tells a story of an incident that occurred when she was a little girl in order to share with her "mutilated victims" how she came to feel, corporeally, the physical trauma of female genital practices. She tells us that her brother shot her in the eye with an air rifle, damaging the pupil, which then rendered her eye blind within minutes. Walker directly equates this incident, which she refers to as "visual mutilation," with female genital practices:

> I was eight when I was injured. This is the age at which many "circumcisions" are done. When I see how the little girls—how small they are!—drag their feet after being wounded, I am reminded of myself. How had I learned to walk again, without constantly walking into something? To see again, using half my vision? Instead of being helped to make this transition, I was banished, set aside from the family, as is true of genitally mutilated little girls. For they must sit for a period alone, their legs bound, as their wounds heal. It is taboo to speak of what has been done to them.[63]

After simplifying the practices and making them knowable only through the violence she endured as a little girl in the United States, Walker continues her analogy:

> No one would think it normal to deliberately destroy the pupil of the eye. Without its pupil, the eye can never see itself, or the person possessing it, reflected in the eye of another. It is the same with the vulva. Without the cli-

toris and other sexual organs, a woman can never see herself reflected in the healthy, intact body of another. Her sexual vision is impaired, and only the most devoted lover will be sexually "seen." And even then, never completely.[64]

In Walker's account, female genital practices are denied complexities, histories, and situated meanings, while African women are rendered ignorant and subservient. "[T]hough one is struck by the complicity of the mothers, themselves victims," Walker comments, "one must finally acknowledge that those who practice it [genital mutilation] are, generally speaking, kept ignorant of its real dangers—the breakdown of the spirit and the body and the spread of disease—and are themselves prisoners of ritual."[65]

Walker sees no choice but to heed her benevolent duty to rescue these "prisoners," with whom she connects through her eye incident. She explains that she was compelled to write *Possessing the Secret of Joy:*

> I wrote my novel as a duty to my conscience as an educated African-AmerIndian woman. . . . I know only one thing about the "success" of my effort. I believe with all my heart that there is at least one little baby girl born somewhere on the planet today who will not know the pain of genital mutilation because of my work. And that in this one instance, at least, the pen will prove mightier than the circumciser's knife. Her little beloved face will be light that shines on me.[66]

Walker's self-congratulation can be interpreted as a missionary effort to liberate the ignorant with "objective" education, to replace the "primitive" with the "civilized," the "traditional" with the "modern," while disregarding all the (heavy) colonialist baggage those dichotomies carry. As Emmanuel Babatunde notes, Africa, as usual, becomes a land of torture and mutilation. America, on the other hand, "is the center of healing. The intermediaries, as usual, are the missionaries."[67] This time, however, there is a small difference: "[T]he missionaries are African-Americans. America is also the land of well-motivated female freedom fighters who must take the battle of liberation to other lands on behalf of all abused women."[68] Disturbed by Walker's distorted image of African women, Seble Dawit and Salme Mekuria write:

> We take great exception to the recent Western focus on female genital mutilation in Africa, most notably by the author Alice Walker. Ms. Walker's new film "Warrior Marks" portrays an African village where women and children are without personality, dancing and gazing blankly through some stranger's script of their lives. The respected elder women of the village's Secret Society turn into slit-eyed murderers wielding rusted weapons with which to butcher children. As is common in Western depictions of Africa, Ms.

Walker and her collaborator, Pratibha Palmar, portray the continent as a monolith, African women and children are the props, and the village the background against which Alice Walker, heroine-savior, comes to articulate their pain and condemn those who inflict it. Like Ms. Walker's novel "Possessing the Secret of Joy," this film is emblematic of the Western feminist tendency to see female genital mutilation as the gender oppression to end all oppressions. Instead of being an issue worthy of attention in itself, it has become a powerfully emotive lens through which to view personal pain—a gauge by which to measure distance between the West and the rest of humanity.[69]

Walker's assumption is that African women do not have a unique and complex history outside the imagination of African American women in the United States. The fact that both Africans and African Americans share a history of racial oppression through colonialism and slavery allows Walker to ignore their differences and to forget that the particular feminism that informs her intervention is based on a particular cultural practice situated in specific historical formations.

CONCLUSION

The pressure generated by eradication advocates such as Hosken, Daly, and Walker has helped shape the anti-FGM policies of institutions ranging from WHO and the American Medical Association to grassroots organizations operating in various African countries.[70] Rather than seeking to understand the unique and different ways in which women are actively positioned in different social struggles, interventionists appear to tell universal and totalizing stories that effectively fit women into prefashioned and hierarchized categories while suppressing their particular histories. In fact, it seems to have been precisely the rhetoric of benevolence ("doing good") that lent credibility to colonizers' efforts to abolish both the irua ria atumia in Kenya and sati in India. By appropriating colonial feminism, colonizers were able to appear motivated not by the desire to dominate but the duty to help Africans and Indians.

More recently, some Western scholars and eradication advocates have begun to distance themselves from sensationalist labels such as FGM and have opted for less imperialistic and accusatory terms such as "cuttings," "alterations," "operations," "surgeries," "modifications," and "performances," as well as more local or regional terms.[71] Such scholarship has shown that the use of FGM as the standard label makes it difficult for alternative, more complex stories of female genital practices to be acknowledged and included in the discussion and decision-making processes. This terminological shift has been taking place partly as a result of criticisms by various African studies scholars and Third-World feminists (not to mention the performers of practices themselves) of Western feminists and African elites: for taking such practices out of their social, political, and historical contexts; for treating African women as ignorant, passive Others who must be rescued by their "enlightened" sistren and brethren; and for ignoring various ways in which African women themselves have appropriated and negotiated with ever-changing cultural practices throughout history.[72] Pushed to rethink racist and imperialist tendencies in their understandings of female genital practices, many writers have attempted to tone down the most egregious colonial tendencies. However, the categories "women," "female bodies," and "sexualities" continued to be viewed as naturally given and universal entities that are harmed or compromised by specific cultural performances.[73] According to such assumptions, female genital practices continue to be equated with a lack of sexuality. Contemporary feminist studies have generated much insight regarding ways in which bodies and sexualities are actively made and negotiated through human and nonhuman actors, and should not be understood necessarily as objects of oppression, as many eradication advocates have assumed. Such advocates have monopolized the debates about female genital practices, reproducing the same sad totalitarian image of victimized native women and girls.

Following Michel Foucault's criticism of the "repression hypothesis,"[74] I am calling for a responsible and accountable intervention that goes beyond the simple notion of the "loss" or "repression" of sexuality due to female genital practices. Rather than begin by asking what is the effect of such practices on sexuality, this essay suggests we should be asking a different question: what kinds of sexuality do female genital practices produce or shape for the performers? Such a change of direction can help eradication advocates realize that to intervene is not to come from nowhere in particular, and that the enviable and desirable sexuality and genitalia need not be only those naturalized in advance.

This essay does not embrace an anti-intervention approach or call for an end to representation of Third-World women by Euro-American women or those who reside in the West in general. Nor does it seek to deny the medical risks and/or consequences of some genital practices. Rather, it calls for a radical scrutiny of the assumptions embedded within eradication discourses in the hope of steering current debates about female genital practices in directions that are more mindful not only of the varied perspectives and realities of those who perform such practice themselves, but also of the power relations that are already in place between those who are doing the "rescuing" and those being rescued.

NOTES

1. Robert Edgerton, *Mau Mau: An African Crucible* (New York: Free Press, 1989).

2. As David Gollaher notes in *Circumcision: A History of the World's Most Controversial Surgery* (New York: Basic Books, 2000), the shift from the earlier anthropological nomenclature of "female circumcision" to the more sensational "FGM" was an important victory for the FGM abolitionists in that it precludes dissent, as mutilation is self-evidently dangerous. In *Affecting Performance: Meaning, Movement, and Experience in Okiek Women's Initiation* (Washington: Smithsonian Institution, 1994), p. 342, Corinne Kratz notes that the politically charged label also works to mobilize political action through horrific overtones. Generalized images of such practices are in this way made mobile, removed from their varying contexts and homogenized to fit a standardized meaning. For example, the infamously generalized "three forms" of female circumcision—"infibulation, clitoridectomy, and sunna," in order of presumed severity—appear in virtually every text and have become now an unquestioned reality. Such deterministic and reductive measurements erase the idea that there are multiple and heterogeneous female genital practices that are each differently situated in specific social, cultural, political, and historical locations (ibid.). In fact, female genital practices do have particular local names that tie them to their larger social networks of meanings, and by erasing such names from their discussions, various scholars and eradication advocates have been successful in making female genital practices appear isolated, unnecessary, dangerous, and easy to understand—for any one who does not speak the performers' language.

3. Mary Daly, *Gyn/Ecology: The Metaethics of Radical Feminism* (Boston: Beacon, 1978); Fran Hosken, *Female Sexual Mutilations: The Facts and Proposals for Action* (Lexington, Mass.: Women's International Network News, 1980); Hosken, *The Hosken Report: Genital and Sexual Mutilation of Females,* 3rd ed. (Lexington, Mass.: Women's International Network News, 1982); Hosken, *The Hosken Report: Genital and Sexual Mutilation of Females,* 4th ed. (Lexington, Mass.: Women's International Network News, 1993).

4. Alice Walker and Pratibha Palmer, *Warrior Marks: Female Genital Mutilation and the Sexual Blinding of Women* (New York: Harcourt Brace and Company, 1993).

5. Royal College of Obstetricians and Gynecologists, *Female Circumcision* (London: Royal College of Obstetricians and Gynecologists, 1997); Council of Scientific Affairs, American Medical Association, "Female Genital Mutilation," *Journal of the American Medical Association* 274, no. 21 (1995): 1714–16.

6. Stephanie Welsh, "Breaking the Silence about Genital Mutilation," *Chronicle of Higher Education,* May 31, 1996, p.B3.

7. Patricia Schroeder, "Female Genital Mutilation—A Form of Child Abuse," *New England Journal of Medicine* 331, no. 11 (1994): 739–40; Linda Burstyn, "Female Circumcision Comes to America," *Atlantic Monthly,* October 1995, pp. 28–35.

8. Richard Rueben, "New Ground for Asylum: Threatened Female Mutilation Is Persecution," *ABA Journal* 82 (1996): 36; Sheryl McCarthy, "Fleeing Mutilation, Fighting for Asylum," *Ms.* 7, no. 1 (1996): 12–16.

9. Burstyn, "Female Circumcision Comes to America."

10. Sue Armstrong, "Female Circumcision: Fighting a Cruel Tradition," *New Scientist,* February 2, 1991, pp. 42–47.

11. Bronwyn Winter, "Women, the Law, and Cultural Relativism in France: The Case of Excision," *Signs* 19, no. 4 (1994): 939–74.

12. Keith Cole, *Kenya: Hanging in the Middle Way* (Oxford: Church Army Press, 1959).

13. Olayinka Koso-Thomas, *The Circumcision of Women: A Strategy for Eradication* (London: Zed Press, 1987), p. 12.

14. Nawal El Saadawi, *The Hidden Face of Eve,* trans. Sherif Hetata (London: Zed Books, 1980), p. xiv.

15. Judith Butler, *Bodies That Matter: On the Discursive Limits of "Sex"* (New York: Routledge, 1993).

16. Acknowledging first that there are many feminisms among "First-World" feminists, Cheryl Johnson-Odim writes: "There is still, among Third-World women, a widely accepted perception that the feminism emerging from the white, middle-class Western women narrowly confines itself to a struggle against gender discrimination. . . . [M]any have defined it as a liberal, bourgeois, or reformist feminism, and criticize it because of its narrow conception of feminist terrain." "Common Themes, Different Contexts: Third World Women and Feminism," in *Third World Women and the Politics of Feminism,* ed. Chandra Talpade Mohanty, Ann Russo, and Lourdes Torres (Bloomington: Indiana University Press, 1991), p. 315.

17. See Assitan Diallo, "Paradoxes of Female Sexuality in Mali: On the Practices of *Magnonmaka* and *Bolokoli-kêla* Female Agency," in *Rethinking Sexualities in Africa,* ed. Signe Arnfred (Uppsala: Nordic Africa Institute, 2003), pp. 173–94; Micere Mugo, "Elitist Anti-Circumcision Discourse as Mutilating and Anti-Feminist," *Case Western Reserve Law Review* 47, no. 2 (1997): 461–80; Chandra Talpade Mohanty, "Under Western Eyes: Feminist Scholarship and Colonial Discourses," in Mohanty, Russo, and Torres, *Third World Women,* pp. 51–80; Wairimū Ngarūiya Njambi, "Dualisms and Female Bodies in Representations of African Female Circumcision: A Feminist Critique," *Feminist Theory* 5, no. 3 (2004): 281–303; and Richard Shweder, "'What about 'Female Genital Mutilation?' and Why Understanding Culture Matters in the First Place," in *Engaging Cultural Differences: The Multicultural Challenge in Liberal Democracies,* ed. Richard Shweder, Martha Minow, and Hazel Rose Markus (New York: Russell Sage Foundation, 2002), pp. 216–51.

18. See Jomo Kenyatta, *Facing Mount Kenya: The Tribal Life of the Gikuyu* (1938; London: Secker and Warburg, 1959); Kratz, *Affecting Performance;* Lata Mani, "Contentious Traditions: The Debate on Sati in Colonial India," in *Development: A Cultural Studies Reader,* ed. Susanne Schech and Jane Haggis (Oxford: Blackwell, 1987), pp. 292–97; Christine Walley, "Searching for 'Voices:' Feminism, Anthropology, and the Global Debate over Female Genital Operations," *Cultural Anthropology* 12, no. 3 (1997): 405–38.

19. Leila Ahmed, *Women and Gender in Islam: Roots of a Historical Debate* (New Haven: Yale University Press, 1992), p. 151.

20. Wairimū Ngarūiya Njambi, "Irua Ria Atumia and Anti-Colonial Struggles Among the Gĩkũyũ of Kenya: A Counter Narrative on 'Female Genital Mutulation,'" *Critical Sociology* 33, no. 4 (2007): 689–708.

21. Greet Kershaw, *Mau Mau from Below* (Athens, Ohio: Ohio University Press, 1997), p. 190. Practices of woman-woman marriages were treated in the same manner,

see Wairimū Ngarūiya Njambi and William O'Brien, "Revisiting 'Woman-Woman Marriage:' Notes on Gikuyu Women," *NWSA Journal* 12, no. 1 (2000): 1–23.

22. See Edgerton, *Mau Mau;* Wanyabari O. Maloba, *Mau Mau and Kenya: An Analysis of a Peasant Revolt* (Bloomington: Indiana University Press, 1993). But the abolition of irua ria atumia backfired, and what came to be known as the "female circumcision controversy" went on to become an unstoppable mobilizing force that eventually led to the downfall of the colonial regime in Kenya.

23. Cole, *Kenya,* p. 16.

24. See Cole, *Kenya;* Kershaw, *Mau Mau from Below;* Njambi, "Irua Ria Atumia."

25. Kershaw, *Mau Mau from Below;* E. S. Atieno Odthiambo and John Longsdale, eds., *Mau Mau and Nationhood: Arms, Authority and Narration* (Athens: Ohio University Press, 2003); Maloba, *Mau Mau and Kenya.*

26. Mani, "Contentious Traditions," p. 293.

27. Ibid.

28. Ibid.

29. Amina Mama, *Women's Studies and Studies of Women in Africa during the 1990s,* Working Paper Series 5, no. 96 (Dakar: Codesria, 1996).

30. Johnson-Odim, "Common Themes, Different Contexts"; Mohanty, "Under Western Eyes." I am aware that African feminists themselves are not a homogenous category, and many do not subscribe to nationalist feminism. Moreover, just as African women who perform female genital practices cannot be viewed as pawns of men and traditions, nationalist feminists themselves should be seen as active subjects who appropriate nationalist policies to their own ends.

31. Kratz, *Affecting Performance,* p. 242. I am not suggesting that the structures of colonialism always look the same from one historical moment to another. In fact, as Stephen Slemon suggests, "the specifics of its textual or semiotic or representational manoeuvres shift registers at different historical times and in different kinds of colonial encounters." "The Scramble for Post-Colonialism," in *De-Scribing Empire: Post-Colonialism and Textuality,* ed. Chris Tiffin and Alan Lawson (London: Routledge, 1994), p. 20.

32. Similarly, the category "female" or "woman" that informed the work of many feminists throughout much of the 1970s and 1980s turned out to be particularly based on the white, Christian, heterosexual, middle-class woman.

33. Donna Haraway, *Simians, Cyborgs, and Women: The Reinvention of Nature* (New York: Routledge, 1991), p. 155.

34. Hosken, *The Hosken Report* (1982), p. 66.

35. Ibid., p. 9.

36. Ibid.

37. Ibid., p. 10.

38. Hosken, *The Hosken Report* (1993), p. 18.

39. See Mohanty, "Under Western Eyes."

40. Hosken, *The Hosken Report* (1993), p. 11.

41. Ibid., p. 6. "Because this information is essential to lead a healthy and productive life," Hosken argues, "no one has the right to withhold, distort or otherwise manipulate the biological facts which make us free to lead responsible lives," ibid., p. 8.

42. Ibid.

43. Ibid., p. 72.

44. Ibid., p. 11.

45. Ibid., p. 72.

46. Ibid., p. 16.

47. Chris Tiffin and Alan Lawson, Introduction, in *De-Scribing Empire: Post-Colonialism and Textuality*, ed. Chris Tiffin and Alan Lawson (London: Routledge, 1994), p. 6.

48. Mohanty, "Under Western Eyes," p. 58.

49. Accad argues that, "like many zealous and committed individuals, she [Hosken] has been unjustly criticized by some feminists, especially in the academic community, for what they see as a reductionist, impassioned representation of the problem, and an 'Orientalist' approach." "Excision: Practices, Discourses and Feminist Commitment," *Feminist Issues* 13, no. 2 (1993): 49.

50. Daly, *Gyn/Ecology*, p. 155.

51. Ibid., p. 28.

52. Ibid., p. 158.

53. Ibid., p. 157.

54. Ibid., pp. 157–58.

55. Ibid., p. 231.

56. Ibid., p. 221.

57. Audre Lorde, "An Open Letter to Mary Daly," *Sister Outsider: Essays and Speeches* (Freedom, Calif.: Crossing Press, 1984), p. 67.

58. See Haraway, *Simians, Cyborgs, and Women.*

59. Daly, *Gyn/Ecology*, p. 154.

60. Alice Walker, *The Color Purple* (London: Women's Press, 1983).

61. Alice Walker, *In Search of Our Mother's Gardens: Womanist Prose* (San Diego: Harcourt Brace Jovanovich, 1983).

62. Alice Walker, *Possessing the Secret of Joy* (New York: Harcourt Brace Jovanovich, 1992), n.p.

63. Alice Walker, "Alice's Journey," in Alice Walker and Pratibha Palmar, *Warrior Marks: Female Genital Mutilation and the Sexual Blinding of Women* (New York: Harcourt Brace, 1993), p. 19.

64. Ibid.

65. Ibid., pp. 24–25.

66. Ibid., p. 25.

67. Emmanuel Babatunde, *Women's Rights Versus Women's Rites: A Study of Circumcision among the Ketu Yoruba of South Western Nigeria* (Trenton, N.J.: Africa World Press, 1998), p. 18.

68. Ibid.

69. Seble Dawit and Salme Mekuria, "The West Just Doesn't Get It," *New York Times*, December 7, 1993, p. A27.

70. See Koso-Thomas, *The Circumcision of Women;* Claire Robertson, "Grassroots in Kenya: Women, Genital Mutilation, and Collective Action, 1920–1990," *Signs* 21, no. 3 (1996): 615–42; Nahid Toubia, *Female Genital Mutilation: A Call for Global Action* (New York: Women Ink, 1993); and WHO/UNICEF/UNFPA, *Female Genital Mutilation: A Joint WHO/UNICEF/UNFPA Statement* (Geneva: World Health Organization, 1997).

71. See especially Elizabeth Herger Boyle, *Female Genital Cutting: Cultural Conflict in the Global Community* (Baltimore: Johns Hopkins University Press, 1993); Stanlie

James and Claire Robertson, *Genital Cutting and Transnational Sisterhood: Disputing U.S. Polemics* (Urbana: University of Illinois Press, 2002); Ellen Gruenbaum, *The Female Circumcision Controversy: An Anthropological Perspective* (Philadelphia: University of Pennsylvania Press, 2001); Isabelle Gunning, "Arrogant Perception, World Traveling, and Multicultural Feminism: The Case of Female Genital Surgeries," in *Critical Race Feminism: A Reader,* ed. Adrien Katherine Wing (New York: New York University Press, 1997), pp. 352–60; and Hope Lewis, "Between *Irua* and 'Female Genital Mutilation:' Feminist Human Rights Discourse and the Cultural Divide," in Wing, *Critical Race Feminism,* pp. 361–70.

72. See Babatunde, *Women's Rights Versus Women's Rites;* Dawit and Mekuria, "The West Just Doesn't Get It"; Diallo, "Paradoxes of Female Sexuality in Mali"; Shweder, "'What about 'Female Genital Mutilation?'"; and Walley, "Searching for 'Voices.'"

73. See Njambi, "Dualisms and Female Bodies."

74. Michel Foucault, *The History of Sexuality: An Introduction,* trans. Robert Hurley (New York: Vintage Books, 1978).

12 Benevolence and Humiliation: Thinking Migrants, Integration, and Security in Europe

Prem Kumar Rajaram

> Confessions, apologies: why this thirst for abasement? A hush
> falls. They circle round him like hunters who have cornered a
> strange beast and do not know how to finish him off.[1]
>
> —J. M. COETZEE

The reception of migrants in Europe, particularly in light of common European Union (EU) immigration policy, has two significant aspects. One is the series of exclusionary and restrictive policies that create an impression of "fortress Europe." The other is a collection of practices, discourses, and legislation that seeks to inculcate into the recent migrant or refugee a sense of *being European.* This collection of ostensibly benevolent policies and practices of integration also serves (a) to remind the immigrant of his or her fundamental Otherness or "difference" needing modification, (b) to discipline those cultural or social practices that exhibit overly non-European aspects, and (c) to create a *partial* sense of belonging. The policies of integration that exist to Europeanize the migrant are not simply benevolent: they are also humiliating. As Ghassan Hage argues in reference to assimilation policy, "the point of emphasising that 'everyone should be like us', is never to make everybody like us. It is more to stress the difference between 'us' and 'those who are trying to be like us.'"[2]

A constructed problematic of integration is the principal lens through which migrant communities are viewed in Europe. Such integration is considered in terms of a larger history of nation building: to what extent will the advent of different migrants effect or disrupt the commonality of and in the nation? There are similarities to be found in policies of integration and strategies of exclusion underpinning "fortress Europe." They are both grounded in particular notions of community and foreignness where identity and belonging are hegemonically linked to the nation-state.[3] They are also grounded, ultimately, in the tension between association and differentiation endemic to European colonies of the nineteenth and twentieth centuries. This is a tension that comes from a concern about restricting, containing, or enclosing non-European identities, thereby differentiating and separating native from ruler but also outlining the terms of his/her association across different fields. Once those boundaries came into question, through social upheaval and mobility or through the weakening of the racial lineage, the conditions of differentiation and association came to be defined in terms of standards of behavior. Discernible cultures became the basis for inclusion, and the basis for exclusion was a demonstrable lack of understanding of norms and patterns of behavior.[4] This, as we shall see, is apparent in the recent debate on migrant integration in Europe.

If the boundaries of the nation-state are made clear through patterns of inclusion and exclusion that create a dominant political or cultural identity, then inclusion is premised on practices of devaluation or negation of those elements or traits of a marginal group that disrupt the coherence of a dominant group. The pattern of inclusion and exclusion is maintained within the state, for example, through ostensibly inclusive policies of integration directed at the recent migrant.

The essay begins by locating its argument within recent transnational migration literature. The second section briefly explores aspects of developing common European migration policy that deal with integration. The section following develops the security context within which migration is increasingly located by studying the murder of the Dutch filmmaker Theo van Gogh by a Dutchman of immigrant roots and the portrayal of this murder at the first European ministerial-level conference on integration held in Amsterdam a week later. The final section traces a rhetoric of benevolence in policy and discourse about integration. Here I note in particular the trope of a gift of community that is fundamental to integration policy. The benevolence of the gift, as I will show, conceals an antecedent humiliation. The gift is disciplinary; it simultaneously outlines the limits of community and demands of the migrant that she perform an identity acceptable to the norm.

INTEGRATION AND A PROBLEM OF FOREIGNNESS

Integration policy is about a problem of foreignness.[5] It concerns the relation of social unity to social stability, the issue of trust and reciprocal obligations, and the extent to which these are limited to national communities. Foreignness is a problem; it exists because of politics and a political thought that centers on the establishment and maintenance of national (territorially delineated) communities.

The problem of foreignness (and, consequently, the problem of integration) is most stark in those assessments and studies that see the nation-state as the fundamental organizer of social, judicial, political, and cultural life.[6] Christian Joppke depicts a "liberal state" that is the principal actor in the integration of migrants. The liberal state recognizes different communities at the institutional and juridical level. It implements a range of different policies to integrate migrants into a society whose boundaries are pre-given. Joppke's argument in favor of the state as arbiter of difference and value is performative. The assertion that the state is a central and necessary actor in integration repeats an image of essentialized communities that strengthens the claim that the state is primarily responsible for integration. It collapses state, nation, and society into a tripartite and symbiotic whole, each element inseparable from the others. The liberal state, with its purported careful institutional control of difference, is to be preferred, Joppke suggests, to variants of multiculturalist thinking. In his view, these variants render all cultural difference of equal value and thus destroy the very notion of value.[7] Bonnie Honig suggests that those who are inclined rather to *celebrate* foreignness repeat unintentionally the sense that foreignness is a problem. Theirs is a celebration of postnationalism and the erosion of the state: they hit upon the specific concern of those scholars who see foreignness as a harbinger of the erosion of community values and norms.[8]

The variant of transnationalism that Andreas Wimmer and Nina Glick Schiller identify is, however, not principally an empirical demonstration or celebration of the demise of the state as the central organizing unit of social and political life. These critics adopt techniques of analysis derived from a territorial imagination that sees bounded national communities overseen by an integral and coherent state as lenses or filters for understanding migration and politics. In their view, a "reified and essentialized notion of community" confines narratives of belonging, politics, and social action within territorial boundaries.[9] This is "methodological nationalism": "the assumption that the nation/state/society is the natural social and political form of the modern world."[10]

An important aspect of methodological nationalism is its spatialization of cultures, whereby "multiculturalism" comes to denote a collection of distinct, bounded cultural groupings with specific values. This process is illuminated in Ayşe Çağlar's study of the public and political representation of Turkish migrants in Berlin, seen as an ethnicized and ghettoized community analytically inseparable from a particular marginal urban space.[11] In such discourse, the community of Turkish migrants is essentialized and thereby rendered knowable and amenable to state integration policy. This form of seeing and representing makes invisible those (sometimes transnational) spaces of interaction, negotiation, and belonging of the Berlin Turkish community. It impairs the possibility of understanding techniques and "negotiations of belonging and sociality" of Berlin Turks beyond the given codes and categories of ethnicity and community.[12]

Çağlar's argument is important for two reasons. First, like Wimmer and Glick-Schiller's work, it critiques a methodological procedure and epistemological bent. Çağlar makes the case that public and governmental representations of migrants and their integration use codes and categories (akin to "methodological nationalism") that repeat a sense of ethnicized communities. Such codes and categories function as a way of making migrant communities knowable and governable, and trickle down (not without some corruption along the way) from national-scale governmental representations to municipal ones. The unruly migrant, replete with a range of religious, political, and social characteristics, is transformed into a tractable and generalizable subject understood primarily through codes of ethnicity and community. This allows for generalizing statistical practices such as the comparison between different types of migrants and across host societies.[13]

Talal Asad argues that statistics not only reflect a given social situation, but also actively construct it in particular ways. In his view, when social power becomes exercised through (or behind) the veil of statistics, experience is no longer subjective; it cannot be dialogic. Moreover, he asserts, "[s]tatistics converts the question of incommensurable cultures into one of commensurable social arrangements without rendering them homogeneous. . . . I do not say that statistical practices solve the philosophical problem of incommensurability; I say that statistical practices can afford to ignore it. And they can afford to ignore it because they are part of the great process of conversion we know as 'modernization.'"[14] Statistical practices, enabled by the use of codes and categories to define and understand migrants and migrancy, may be understood as a form of governmentality that creates two identities. Such practices vindicate the image of the state as necessary organizer of a society, and they articulate a self-fulfilling representation of migrant communities: migrants may conform to (stereo)type in order to have their political claims heard. The essentializing of community, the creation of codes and categories allowing thereby for a managerial state to act, obstructs more fluid perceptions of community and society.

The second matter that Çağlar emphasizes is that of space and scale. The essentialized notion of community manifests itself spatially. The national space is the given scale of analysis for Joppke. The state acts nationally; subscales, comprising various local spaces, become difficult to discern in an argument centered on the policy activities of the state. The state appears as an indivisible and unified whole, enveloping a distinct and clearly boundaried society. Çağlar shows how the policy imaginary manifests a "ghetto imagery" that marginalizes Turks in Berlin. The national-scale logic of essentialized communities is repeated and given flesh spatially at the city scale. Statist notions of problematic and essentialized foreign communities lead to an urban imaginary that locates them in a secluded and marginal ethnicized ghetto. In Çağlar's example, this framing restricts the study of migrant interaction in spaces across Berlin.

National-scale conceptions and representations of migrants are reflected in other scales. The methodological nationalism that Wimmer and Glick Schiller identify sees scales as natural, hierarchical, and distinct. The national scale, where integration purportedly takes place, is made distinguishable from other scales (such as "transnational" or "local") by an epistemology that naturalizes it as the normal space of politics.

The pathology is not the problem of foreignness but rather *how* this "problem" is constructed. Constructing a problem of foreignness is a performative ruse. It institutes the state as the arbiter of claims made by essentialized communities and as principal organizer of social and political life. The model of the nation-state prefigures how identity and difference are constructed.[15] Codes and categories of analysis obscure relational networks that transcend pre-given boundaries based on ethnicity. The result is a construction of society that exaggerates the role of the state and sets in motion an integration policy based on a form of multiculturalism where the onus is on preserving ethnic difference, which is itself understood in static spatial terms.

Integration becomes then a largely one-way process. The onus is placed on the state to recognize migrants, while migrants themselves are effectively reduced to suppliants seeking admission to a pre-given nation/state/society. Relational networks and negotiation techniques exercised by migrants across alternative spaces and scales often counter such humiliation. Recognition typically occurs not only at the national institutional and juridical scale but also at the municipal level and at other nongovernmental scales and spaces. However, as Çağlar shows, attention to spatial and scalar transgressions by migrants in their strategies of negotiating membership must be considered alongside public and statist discourses that seek to confine and reduce migrant identity. This essay pays greater attention to these discourses, which vary in relative strength across time and space, than to migrant practices. The aim is not to exaggerate the capacity of the state to dominate society but rather to point to its contemporary force in Europe, partly due to the securitization of migration and integration.

INTEGRATION AND EUROPEAN UNION

Discussions on common EU Immigration Policy culminated in November 2004 with the adoption of the Hague Programme by the European Council. The Programme has its genesis in the Amsterdam Treaty and the Tampere Programme. The Amsterdam Treaty, coming into effect in 1999, called for a common and coordinated EU migration and asylum policy to come into effect by 2004. The Tampere Programme (1999–2004) set a series of goals, focusing principally on maintaining a balance between the abolition of internal borders and the strengthening of external ones. The objective of the Hague Programme is to carry further the development of a common approach to immigration, including the formulation of common immigration and asylum policy. The central framework for thinking about common migration policy continues to be its relation to the goal of developing an area of "freedom, security and justice."[16]

The Tampere and Hague Programmes are responses to the risks identified following the removal of internal border controls when the need for reinforcing the external borders of the EU "became apparent."[17] In the period from 1999 to roughly around 2002, migration debates centered on punitive measures and were highlighted by the perceived economic and social risk posed by irregular migration and by concerns after the New York and Madrid terrorist bombings about the security risk posed by immigrants. From 2003, greater attention has been paid to issues of integration;[18] this appears due to two distinct issues: the perception that demographics require an inflow of new sources of labor and a series of violent or otherwise highly visible incidents attributed to migrant communities.[19]

The European Commission has in the Hague Programme understood "integration" as an after-the-fact mode of managing migration. Integration of migrants is crucial to the ongoing "stability and cohesion" of society. Here the commission essays an understanding of migration as a potential threat to the status quo. The concern, more precisely, is about *Europe's* capacity to accommodate recent and culturally different migrants into historically specific local institutions and cultural and political norms.[20] What is being presumed and inaugurated here is a stable, atomistic, and coherent European identity based on commonality. In this naming, a particular (a)historical movement of the nation-state, working to define and dominate its society, may be discerned. One can discern, that is, the state performing itself, interiorizing those it can interiorize and exteriorizing those it cannot in order to outline itself and maintain its organizing and regulating role over society.

The European Commission, in its first annual report on migration and integration, writes,

> *Admission and integration policies are inseparable* and should mutually reinforce each other. With respect to integration in the labour market, it will be important, at Member States' levels, to reflect further on the structures and instruments in place, in particular on the capacities to identify skills and labour shortages and to ensure higher participation of immigrants in the labour market.
>
> In parallel, Member States are also increasingly concerned about the integration of the newly arrived in particular ensuring *that immigrants understand and respect the fundamental norms and values of the host society* and with respect to language abilities, which are major barriers to integration. Inevitably Member States *will be reluctant to open up for further economic migration, unless they are able to integrate newcomers well into all aspects of society.*[21]

The commission notes that admission and integration are inseparable, for economic and security reasons. The construction of an integration problematic along those lines pays heed to national concerns about polity and community. The construction of the problem of integration through an identity/difference prism is, Didier Bigo suggests, a mode of governmentality.[22] This restricts and contains how we may conceive of community and of the characteristics of community.

Discussing convergence on approaches to integration at the European level can appear anomalous given differentiation in migration and integration processes, policies, and goals in nation-states across Europe. Adrian Favell notes that while there is a body of comparative work on integration across individual European states, it is impeded by the fact that "issues of immigration and integration are formulated in very distinct and context-specific ways."[23] A common link is that the answer to the question of integration *into what* is pre-given: "one, single, indivisible (national) 'state', and one, simple, unitary (national) 'society.'"[24] Policy is thus performative: integration policy attempts to create a national and indivisible state and society even as these entities are the purported, pre-given basis for thinking integration. It is beyond the scope of this essay to list the varying imaginations of state and society being performed by integration policies across Europe. While events since 2001 have led to the discussion of integration as a central element of common European migration policy, at the practical level, integration continues to be the prime responsibility of individual states. (It is too deeply connected, as Favell says, with how national polities imagine themselves to be in danger of ceding power to Brussels as EU capital). It is important to note, however, that the European Union cannot be defined solely as a collective of functionalist institutions whose involvement in policy issues can be measured only quantitatively.

The European Union is also marked by a spatial politics aimed at creating a consensus that European public space is networked and connected.[25] This spatial politics works "through symbolic representations of European space and its future development."[26] The commission's representation of European space as one potentially subject to disruptive and threatening flows of migrants creates an "ideational foundation" for the integration of migrants.[27] This is centered on the maxim that "immigrants understand and respect the fundamental norms and values of the host society."[28] The spatial politics involved in giving a sense of networked and connected European space is also a performative practice. By speaking of common interests to a collective of "member states," the commission is outlining that which it names as its justification: a common European public space where states work in ways that have consequences for each other.

Evidently, the limits of the European Union cannot be discerned by noting policy areas where there appears to be no quantitatively measurable evidence of its involvement. Spatial practices and discourses performatively create a geography of connection as the context for integration policy at the national (and subnational) level. Symbols and metaphors—here the metaphor of the foreign migrant who does not understand European norms and values—signal a shared, interconnected, and networked public space within which national integration policies must operate. In what follows I trace aspects of the metaphoric bases of this networked space (largely in reference to the securitization of the issue of migration) and the nature of the ideational foundations of networked, if not common, integration policy in Europe.

THE VAN GOGH MURDER

The Dutch filmmaker Theo van Gogh was shot and stabbed on November 2, 2004 in Amsterdam. His killer was Mohammed Bouyeri, a Dutch-born citizen of Moroccan Muslim descent. The number of death threats received by van Gogh, a prickly figure at the best of times, multiplied following television screening of his short film *Submission*, which is meant as a critique of Islamic conceptions of gender roles. The film uses somewhat crude and provocative imagery, interspersing nudity with Qu'ranic verses and scenes of domestic violence.[29]

Following the murder and a series of retaliatory attacks on Muslim schools and on mosques, the Dutch presidency of the European Commission opened a conference of European integration ministers on November 9 with a speech by the Dutch minister for integration, Rita Verdonk. The minister began with these words: "The Netherlands is a country in mourning. One week ago, on 2 November 2004, film maker and columnist Theo van Gogh was murdered in Amsterdam. He was brutally murdered in the street, in broad daylight. This murder shocked Dutch society to its core. And we haven't got over the shock yet."[30] Placing an account of the murder at the forefront of a conference on integration imputes a particular meaning to the event. Verdonk positions the question of integration in an interpretative framework run through with both security and cultural concerns. Her speech continues:

> *We know the arrested suspect's motivation* because he was carrying documents that made it clear that he was driven by the same malicious force that is behind the attacks in New York and Madrid: the destructive hate that is associated with fundamental Muslim terrorism. There is a large Islamic community in the Netherlands. *A community that is part of our society. A community that we value and that is dear to us. But this murder raises serious doubts. Doubts that we have been too lax.*[31]

Van Gogh's murder is rendered meaningful in its association with terrorist attacks in New York and Madrid. This connection, in turn, reinforces systems of naming and interpretation by which such events are utilized repeatedly as "codes that we cast like nets over time and space—in order to reduce or master differences, to arrest them, to determine them."[32] Such coding gives definitive meaning to incidents as far removed historically and geopolitically as the murder of a Dutch filmmaker, the killing of 191 individuals on Spanish trains, and the ongoing Iraqi insurgency. This process allows a conceptual and scalar leap. The evidence of documents suggests that van Gogh's murder is an act of transnational terrorism. Thus, the problematic becomes "fundamental Muslim terrorism" and its incidence in "a community that is part of our society." Integration is securitized: it is not simply a matter of cultural difference and what to do with it, but of dealing with deathly threats, destructive hate, and the malicious force of Islamic fundamentalism.

In Edward Said's sense, Verdonk's beginning is transitive; it begins "with (or for) an anticipated end."[33] Beginnings designate, Said says, a moment in time, a place, a principle, or an action. These do not stand in isolation but point to an earlier beginning; the source or motivation of the work is located within a wider idea of "precedence and/or priority."[34] In beginning in a particular way, a text thus locates itself within a judgment on what among events that have preceded it is meaningful or relevant. The meaning of a work is socially and otherwise located. According to Said, beginnings also "indicate, clarify or define a *later* time, place or action."[35] In other words, how a work begins "is the first step in the intentional production of meaning."[36]

Verdonk produces a meaning of migrants and of integration that is trans-fixed by the possibility of danger emanating from within the Muslim community. Difference becomes a metaphor for a problem of identity and security. Integration becomes a battle for Muslim minds. Arthur Waldron writes of van Gogh's alleged killer, "[t]o add irony to gruesomeness, two years earlier this same Mohammed Bouyeri, his impeccably tolerant and liberal views expressed in perfect Dutch, had been featured in the media as a shining model of the success of Holland's official multiculturalism."[37] Bouyeri, after shooting van Gogh and cutting his throat to the spinal bone, pinned a letter with a knife to his stomach. Ian Buruma notes that the letter was "written in the clear prose of an educated Dutchman."[38] Maria Margaronis observes that it "mingled Islamic formulas with the hippest Dutch street slang" and suggests that "it is Bouyeri's Dutchness that has so deeply disconcerted the security services: He is no foreign fighter but an Amsterdam homeboy."[39] Bouyeri's letter did indeed speak to a wider disaffection; the important point though is not his relative difference or likeness, but the hybridness of radical Islam in Holland. Communities and cultures said to foster violence are not ghettoized.

The response to Bouyeri's acts also suggests the instability of (migrant) citizenship. Ashley Carruthers argues that citizenship is not only a juridical category but a form of social performance. The idea of citizenship as performance points to the problematic of community. A citizen is not necessarily a member of the community; the migrant citizen, in particular, must also prove that he or she can perform traits of national belonging with regard to dress, language, and gender and work roles.[40] Belonging is thus accrued and conferred differentially upon different groups of migrants, with regard to their class, ethnicity, or religion over time. Conceived in this way, Bouyeri's strange hybridity points to a complex transnational accumulation of belonging, culminating in the palimpsest of the letter he places on van Gogh's body. Carruthers's framework may also partly account for the relative ease with which Bouyeri is dismissed from the Western fold and cast as alien: while a citizen of Europe, he does not perform his identity/belonging well. Newspaper reports were keen to take note, for example, that at the time of the murder Bouyeri was "dressed in a long Middle Eastern-style shirt"[41] and wore a beard.

Bouyeri was sentenced to life imprisonment for van Gogh's murder on June 26, 2005, after having refused to accept the authority of the court to try him. In the aftermath of the murder, there were heightened attempts to differentiate host communities from migrant, emphasizing difference and the insecurity that comes with it. Verdonk demanded that Muslims decide "which side they were on."[42] The idea of a particular spatialized culture under siege took hold, not only in the Netherlands but also elsewhere in Europe. The British home minister,

David Blunkett, proclaimed on national television that al Qaeda "is on our doorstep, and threatening our lives.'"[43] The code snowballs the event, moving it away from a disaffected individual toward al Qaeda.

THE BENEVOLENCE OF INTEGRATION

The conference on integration that Rita Verdonk's speech opened acknowledges the performative aspect of citizenship. In the conference's conclusions, the "national contact points for integration" who represented their states in the conference note that "shared citizenship is rooted in the knowledge and practice of liberal democratic values and requires active involvement in and engagement with society."[44] Toward this end, the conclusions lay great emphasis on "introductory programs" for migrants. Such programs are based on the belief that "newcomers must understand *unambiguously* what is expected of them upon entry and the host society must commit to the elimination of obstacles to full participation."[45] While the conclusions also note that a concept of "shared citizenship" should underlie the introductory programs, the onus remains on the migrant to develop those performance skills necessary to engage with and participate in "society."

The conference conclusions have two intertwined themes, dialogue and discipline. Dialogue is understood as a means of bridging distances between communities: "broad based dialogue is essential in confronting the frustration that often leads to social tension and distancing." But dialogue involves discipline: "*Barriers to integration (e.g. discrimination), resistance within communities to change* (e.g. in upholding negative cultural practices), and engagement with the host society must be prominent on the policy agenda. This dialogue should focus on openness and a commitment to mutual respect, while promoting motivation for change from within the community itself."[46] Dialogue thus addresses a resistance to change and is designed to promote a motivation to change. The onus here is on the migrant to prove or perform belonging. The version of community being described is teleological; the basis of "community" (commonality) is equivalent to what it effects (commonality also).[47] This is a community of common values and is structured by social engagement—a sense that everyone has a common responsibility to the society at large.

Such conceptions impose the state as a particular "frame of mind" directing the identification of foreignness and of community.[48] When the ministers for integration talk about integration and resistance needing to be "on the policy agenda," they are repeating a series of conflations: that between state and society, state and state apparatus, and state and democracy. Didier Bigo argues that because states in liberal-democratic societies receive their authority from those governed, the tensions between notions of state and democracy are over-looked.[49] The result is that "citizens are then conceived as nationals, understood by opposition to foreigners, and migrants are framed through various cultural discourses as foreigners, or as citizens of different national origin, who do not fit the 'national standard' of norms and values."[50] The threat from which the state promises deliverance is intelligible only from within the frame of mind imposed by the state. Thus, in the ministers' text, there is not only a forceful enveloping of members of the community within the code "citizenship" (remembering Derrida's notion of a code as something that masters difference), but also an enveloping of society.

Sara Ahmed and Anne-Marie Fortier write that this sort of community "presumes a citizen whose affiliation with those who are like them comes with exerting social control over, and maintaining strong borders against, 'outsiders.'"[51] The bald statement that migrant resistance to integration must be worn down (and the suggestion that it stems from negative cultural practices) disciplines migrant identity. Humiliation is thereby embedded in frames of thinking emanating from the state. So too is the idea of benevolence. The state acts to encourage the participation of migrants in a society by training them to divest themselves of "negative cultural practices."

At the same time, these constructions of migrant resistance to integration, and of a migrant who must be motivated to change to make herself more amenable to a liberal-democratic society, establish a sense of the host community as both vulnerable and virtuous. The community is virtuous insofar as it is the repository and guarantor of, in Bigo's terms, a national standard of morals and values. It is vulnerable because political participation in that virtuous society must be imparted on the basis of trust. Trust cannot be assumed of migrants, because a statist frame of mind casts them as outsiders. The fear generated by a sense that trust is finite, that not everyone can be transformed into moral and trustworthy subjects of responsible communities, generates a political technology whereby the circulation of anxiety becomes a form of domination.[52]

As a repository and guarantor of virtue, this society is invested with a remarkable moral weight. It becomes amenable to "with us or against us" narratives, and it establishes a discourse of benevolence that couches a series of humiliating discourses and practices. Rita Verdonk's call for Muslims to decide "which side they were on,"[53] made at a public memorial service for van Gogh and before several hundred people, resonates with George Bush's clarion call, "[E]ither you are with us or with the terrorists."[54] Both seek to memorialize troubling and complex events: the murder of a filmmaker by a streetwise Amsterdam resident who is a Muslim and the September 11, 2001 attacks carried out by Muslims who were also long-standing residents of Western countries. These memorializations serve as an emotive fount, drawing people together, while simultaneously declaring the limits of this drawing together, against an Othered enemy. Both use a polarizing language of a war on terrorism to move the call that you be "with us" to a demand that you be "like us." Ahmed and Fortier write of the community identified in Bush's demand:

> To be "with us" is an imperative to "be like us": if others are *not* to be identified as terrorists . . . (an identification that involves the threat of violence as well as actual violence), they must *mimic* the forms of civility and supposedly democratic governance that constitute the foundations of this community. In other words, the appeal to community to justify the war on terrorism is more than simply an appeal: it actually requires others to enter the community by becoming more "like us," if they are to survive.[55]

In such communities, where the dominance of particular normative identities is reinforced, it is difficult to engage in a dialogic or otherwise nonhumiliating way with migrants. Indeed the question of whether humiliation may be entrenched in migrant integration programs is placed out of bounds. The state is cast as vulnerable, rather than the migrant who is subject to humiliating conjecture and policy.

This depiction of a virtuous and vulnerable community under threat enables the disguising of acts of power as benevolence. Integration policy that cajoles the migrant into performing or mimicking the rites of belonging is subtended by the expansive claim of the community centered on its virtue before a deviant and dangerous Other. The integration of migrants, through a demand that they become more "like us" under threat of annihilation, is cast as a benevolent act. Or rather, it is a humiliating act disguised as a benevolent one enabled by the heightened sense of righteousness caused by a virtuous community under threat.

This call to be like us, to integrate, is an invitation or a gift. It is, in Verdonk's statement, an invitation to move away from deviance and embrace virtue. Such an embrace requires time and energy; it requires disciplining and rests on an antecedent humiliation. The migrant must humiliate him/herself, modify his/her identity, as a precondition for beginning integration measures. A gift or invitation can also be humiliating if the right to refuse is denied.[56] The ostensible benevolence of a gift or invitation by a greater power can actually be compulsion, particularly where a community of adherents to liberal democratic values is conflated with society as a whole (which is itself dominated by the state). There is no room for maneuver; the demand to mimic "us" is grounded in strongly emotive and absolutist terms.

The gift ties the recipient into a relation of debt. It is this relation of common indebtedness that maintains trust. However, integration as gift-giving is conducted within the context and institutions set by the state as described. Derrida's (and Levinas's) conception of the gift is one that must aspire to altruism. It must not be premised on a notion of reciprocity.[57] By contrast, Pierre Bourdieu is interested in the asymmetry of the gift. He notes that gifts can "set up conditions of lasting asymmetry," particularly when they link groups or people separated by telling social or economic gulfs that cannot be bridged. The consequence is that the gift holds no possibility of return; reciprocity, Bourdieu says, is preempted by the social gulf.[58]

In my analysis, such reciprocity is precluded because of a prior sociopolitical context that sees the migrant as an inherently untrustworthy foreigner. The "gulf" between citizen and foreigner is a political strategy that ties the migrant into a relation of dependence. The demonstration of belonging (of having accepted the gift of integration) comes not from an equivalent gift but in a performance that demonstrates adherence to the gift of integration. The relation of dependence is characterized here not chiefly by an incapacity to reciprocate but by a prior definition of the allowable terms and nature of this reciprocation. The call to reciprocation is thus a call to humiliation; it is a call to enter into a relation of dependence characterized by the demonstration of the abnegation of one's identity before that of the norm. This, as Bourdieu says, leads to a condition of permanent dependence.

CONCLUSION: TOWARD A COMMUNITY OF DIFFERENCE

In the preceding pages, I have tried to demonstrate by means of a particular example that the integration of migrants in Europe is run through with a discourse of benevolence that conceals an antecedent humiliation. Integration is seen as benevolent insofar as the pre-given community is conceived metaphorically as an invitation or gift afforded to foreigners. The statist framing of society, in which integration is premised on a unitary and indivisible community, points to an identity/difference problematic where the onus is on sameness or identity to assert and protect itself over a threat of difference. Humiliation occurs through a dialectic of discipline and dialogue that invites the migrant to change while there is no possibility of inviting a reciprocal change or accommodation in the host community.

A response to complex operations of humiliation disguised as benevolence is difficult to conceive. At the root of current policy and practice, as I have argued, is a form of "methodological nationalism": the tendency to understand peoples in terms of nationally or ethnically rooted cultures. Multiculturalism thus becomes the integration of a differently rooted and spatially located culture into a given and clearly outlined society. Integration in a *community of difference* that is *not* based on ethnic or national markers would allow for cross-cultural and multi-scalar engagement. It would begin by questioning the assumptions of methodological nationalism and tracing identity negotiation processes across spaces and scales. It must also perhaps begin with abandoning the desire for a prior common space for thinking commonness and community. This does not mean the removal of inequality (unequal power positions are difficult to do away with), but it does involve as a normative goal the sense that the common space for thinking community is fundamentally open to negotiation.

Thinking a community of difference puts the logic of benevolent integration aside. Such logic, as I have shown, is premised on a sense of clearly defined communities from whence notions of foreignness and nonbelonging may be formulated. Crucial to this is a statist frame of mind that leads to communities and cultures being considered in situ: located within a particular space (performatively) enveloped by the state. A community of difference, by contrast, understands cultures and conceptions of belonging as always subject to processes of negotiation and contest. An important consequence of this delinking of culture and state-centered space is the possibility of reciprocity. In this formulation, integration is not a benevolent gift across a social gulf but a multilateral process involving mutual engagement and accommodation. Crucially, where values conflict (and there will always be conflicts that cannot be resolved by dialogue) the response does not center on disciplinary measures to eradicate "negative cultural practices."[59] Within a community of difference the response to a conflict in values is not to be premised on exclusion; values are rather to be presented in terms of an ongoing discussion, inviting the possibility of change and accommodation over time.

Cultural difference and the trope of multiculturalism need to be historicized in debates about immigration. Thinking about responsibility, politics, and identity involves thinking beyond the spatial, scalar, and temporal rigidities of the state. Acts and policies of integration undertaken by states (and the forms of exclusion and humiliation they generate) betray a wider globe: a globe of despairing economic and social gulfs and of daily fear and insecurity. As Jan Pieterse argues, we cannot see politics of identity negotiation and contests for recognition as compartmentalized or separate from wider global processes and structures.[60] The politics of integration is a global politics: it is a site or zone where global contests of power and the disparities that they reveal become manifest.

NOTES

1. J. M. Coetzee, *Disgrace* (London: Secker and Warburg, 1999), p. 56.
2. Ghassan Hage, "On Having Ethnography: Mimic Me If You Can," *Australian Journal of Anthropology* 9, no. 3 (1998): 288.
3. Steven Lukes, "Humiliation and the Politics of Identity," *Social Research* 64, no. 1 (1997): 36–51.
4. Ann Laura Stoler, "Sexual Affronts and Racial Frontiers: European Identities and the Cultural Politics of Exclusion in Southeast Asia," *Comparative Studies in Society and History* 34, no. 3 (1992): 514–51.
5. See Bonnie Honig, *Democracy and the Foreigner* (Princeton: Princeton University Press, 2001).
6. Ibid., p. 2.
7. Christian Joppke, "The Retreat of Multiculturalism in the Liberal State: Theory and Policy," *British Journal of Sociology* 55, no. 2 (2004): 243.
8. Honig, *Democracy*, p. 2.
9. Andreas Wimmer and Nina Glick Schiller, "Methodological Nationalism and Beyond: Nation-State Building, Migration, and the Social Sciences," *Global Networks* 2 (2002): 324.
10. Ibid., p. 308.
11. Ayşe Çağlar, "Constraining Metaphors and the Transnationalisation of Spaces in Berlin," *Journal of Ethnic and Migration Studies* 27, no. 4 (2001): 601.
12. Ibid., pp. 601, 606.
13. Jan Niessen and Yongmi Schibel, European Commission, *Handbook on Integration for Policy Makers and Practitioners,* Directorate-General for Justice, Freedom and Security (Brussels: European Communities, 2004), p. 54; reproduced at http://europa.eu .int/comm/justice_home/doc_centre/immigration/integration/doc/handbook_en.pdf (accessed October 28, 2005).
14. Talal Asad, "Ethnographic Representation, Statistics and Modern Power," *Social Research* 61, no. 1 (1994): 84.
15. Craig Calhoun, "Nationalism, Political Community and the Representation of Society: Or, Why Feeling at Home Is Not a Substitute for Public Space," *European Journal of Social Theory* 2, no. 2 (1999): 217–32.
16. Council of the European Union, "The Hague Programme: Strengthening Freedom, Security and Justice in the European Union," in *Texte en Conseil Européen—Bruxelles, 04 & 05 novembre 2004: Conclusions de la présidence—Brussels, November 2004,* 14292/04 (Brussels: Commission des communautés européennes), p. 11; reproduced at http://europa.eu.int/comm/justice_home/news/information_dossiers/2005–2009/docs/ presidency_conclusions_en.pdf (accessed October 28, 2005).
17. Jan Niessen, *Five Years of EU Migration and Asylum Policymaking under the Amsterdam and Tampere Mandates* (Brussels: Migration Policy Group, 2004), p. 6.
18. Commission of the European Communities, *First Annual Report on Migration and Integration,* 16 July 2004, COM (2004) 508 final (Brussels: European Commission); reproduced at http://66.102.7.104/search?q=cache:6PuGl_QrJcQJ:europa.eu.int/comm/ justice_home/funding/doc/com_2004_508_final.pdf+%22First+Annual+Report+on+ Migration+and+Integration%22&hl=en (accessed October 28, 2005).

19. Ibid.

20. Adrian Favell, "Integration Nations: The Nation-State and Research on Immigrants in Western Europe," *Comparative Social Research* 22, no. 1 (2003): 18.

21. Commission of the European Communities, *First Annual Report,* p. 9 (emphasis added).

22. Didier Bigo, "Security and Immigration: Toward a Critique of the Governmentality of Unease," *Alternatives: Global, Local, Political* 27 (2002): 65.

23. Adrian Favell, "Integration Policy and Integration Research in Europe: A Review and Critique," in *Citizenship Today: Global Perspectives and Practices,* ed. T. Alexander Aleinikoff and Douglas Klusmeyer (Washington, D.C.: Brookings Institute/Carnegie Endowment for International Peace, 2001), pp. 349–99; reproduced at http://www.sscnet.ucla.edu/soc/faculty/favell/CARN-PUB.htm (accessed September 13, 2005).

24. Ibid.

25. James W. Scott, "A Networked Space of Meaning? Spatial Politics as Geostrategies of European Integration," *Space & Polity* 6, no. 2 (2002): 147–67.

26. Ibid., p. 149.

27. Ibid.

28. Commission of the European Communities, *First Annual Report,* p. 9.

29. As of February 22, 2005, the film could be downloaded from http://www.mediamatic.net/article-200.8323.html&lang=nl. There have been moves by van Gogh's production agency to restrict its availability. A transcript of the film is available at http://www.submission.eu.tt (accessed February 22, 2005).

30. Rita Verdonk, "Opening Speech Delivered by Minister Verdonk at the Integration Conference, 'Turning Principles into Action' on 10 November in Groningen," *Justitie,* 2004; reproduced at http://www.justitie.nl/english/Press/Speeches/2004/101104 Openingspeech_delivered_Verdonk_integrationconference.asp (accessed February 22, 2005).

31. Ibid.

32. Jacques Derrida, *Acts of Literature,* trans. Nicholas Royale, ed. Derek Attridge (London: Routledge, 1992), p. 419.

33. Edward Said, *Beginnings: Intention and Method* (New York: Columbia University Press, 1975), p. 72.

34. Ibid., pp. 4–5.

35. Ibid., p. 5.

36. Ibid.

37. Arthur Waldron, "Europe's Crisis," *Commentary* 119, no. 2 (2005): 49; reproduced at http://www.commentarymagazine.com/Archive/DigitalArchive.aspx?panes= 1&aid=11902050_1 (accessed September 13, 2005).

38. Ian Buruma, "Letter from Amsterdam: Final Cut," *New Yorker,* January 3, 2005; reproduced at http://www.newyorker.com/fact/content/?050103fa_fact1 (accessed September 13, 2005).

39. Maria Margaronis, "Dutch Tolerance Tried," *Nation,* December 20, 2004; reproduced at http://www.thenation.com/doc/20041220/margaronis (accessed September 13, 2005).

40. Ashley Carruthers, "The Accumulation of National Belonging in Transnational Fields: Ways of Being at Home in Vietnam," *Identities: Global Studies in Culture and Power* 9 (2002): 426.

41. Buruma, "Letter from Amsterdam."

42. "Thousands Make a Racket at Van Gogh Rally," *Expatica,* November 3, 2004; reproduced at http://www.expatica.com/source/site_article.asp?subchannel_id=1&story _id=13525&name=Thousands+make+'deafening'+racket+at+Van+Gogh+rally (accessed February 23, 2005).

43. David Blunkett, quoted in Waldron, "Europe's Crisis," p. 49.

44. "Integration Policy Conference Conclusions of the Presidency, 11 November 2004," *Justitie,* 2004; reproduced at http://www.justitie.nl/themas/meer/integratiebeleid/ europees_integratiebeleid/conclusions.asp (accessed February 22, 2005).

45. Ibid.

46. Ibid. (emphasis added).

47. Sara Ahmed and Anne-Marie Fortier, "Re-imagining Communities," *International Journal of Cultural Studies* 6, no. 3 (2003): 253.

48. Bigo, "Security and Immigration," p. 67.

49. Ibid.

50. Ibid.

51. Ahmed and Fortier, "Re-imagining Communities," p. 253.

52. Bigo, "Security and Immigration."

53. "Thousands Make a Racket."

54. Maja Zehfuss, "Forget September 11," *Third World Quarterly* 24, no. 3 (2003): 518.

55. Ahmed and Fortier, "Re-imagining Communities," pp. 253–54.

56. William Ian Miller, *Humiliation* (New York: Cornell University Press, 1993).

57. Jacques Derrida, *Given Time: 1. Counterfeit Money,* trans. Peggy Kamuf (Chicago: University of Chicago Press, 1992).

58. Pierre Bourdieu, "Marginalia: Some Additional Notes on the Gift," in *The Logic of the Gift: Toward an Ethic of Generosity,* ed. Alan Schrift (New York: Routledge, 1997), p. 238.

59. "Integration Policy Conference."

60. Jan Nederveen Pieterse, "The Case of Multiculturalism: Kaleidoscopic and Long Term Views," *Social Identities* 7, no. 3 (2001): 405.

13 Hearts, Minds, and Wetlands: Stakeholders and Ecological Restoration from the Everglades to the Mesopotamian Marshlands

William E. O'Brien

> [T]his program will need to develop strategies for public participation, public awareness, and public decision-making in its development and activities. In the end, the marshdwellers must speak for themselves, displaying all the internal differences of opinion that enrich open dialog, debate, and consensus. The program will need to work with the widest range of stakeholders in creative and purposeful venues throughout its life, building the blocks of civil society.[1]
>
> —USAID

> But there are problems with the stakeholder model, most evident in its performative effect. Minority players in environmental conflict continue to feel marginalized; capital continues to determine what is both feasible and desirable; the "manageability" of environmental risk is rarely questioned.[2]
>
> —Kim Fortun

THE BENEVOLENCE EFFECT OF STAKEHOLDER PARTICIPATION

Official environmental management institutions, as with other elements of governance, present themselves as benevolent solvers of technical problems and as neutral mediators of varied social, economic, environmental, and political interests. Calls for stakeholder participation, such as in the United States Agency for International Development (USAID) quotation above, for instance, suggest a drive among managers to relinquish some of their control to ensure a democratic voice to people and groups impacted by plans. As environmental management has become globalized through the institutionalization of sustainable development, such calls for participation are expressed in an expansive number of governmental, multilateral, and even nongovernmental agencies that speak a more or less common policy language. This essay considers the benevolence claims evident in official calls for stakeholder involvement in two cases of ecological restoration—one in Florida's Everglades in the United States, the other in southern Iraq's Mesopotamian Marshlands.

With half a world between them, and in widely divergent social and political contexts, these two massive-scale restoration efforts are linked not only by their size, their mutual task of addressing ecosystem degradation caused by drainage and channelization, and the redemptive involvement of U.S. environmental agencies.[3] They are also situated in a globalized discourse of "managerial ecology" that emphasizes expert knowledge and technical proficiency, but also promotes "adaptive management" in the face of scientific uncertainty, and explicitly seeks stakeholder involvement in planning and implementation to ensure the social feasibility of plans. This approach promises more sensitive expressions of expert knowledge that replace the "top down" control that predominated in earlier versions of scientific environmental management.[4] Framed by managerial ecology, both the Everglades and Mesopotamian Marshlands cases emphasize scientific learning and attentive listening as benevolent alternatives to past managerial arrogance.

Yet my own conclusions echo the disappointment expressed by Fortun in my epigraph. The official invitation to stakeholder involvement acts as a "benevolence effect"; in other words, this invitation generates what appears as a performance of "environmental justice" that promises participation, yet also regulates the enrollment of actors into the process in ways that interfere least with the application of expert knowledge. Stakeholder participation becomes normalized under managerial ecology as yet another technical component of the planning process, undermining the transformative potential of empowerment as a tool in shaping ecologically and socially just outcomes. The difficulty in fulfilling the promises of stakeholder involvement is particularly evident for groups that are most often the subject of such rhetoric: those that are most vulnerable both to the negative impacts of environmental degradation and to exclusion from the planning process. The rhetoric typically focuses on such groups while ignoring the unequal abilities of different types of stakeholders to influence outcomes.

ADAPTING TO CONFLICT THROUGH MANAGERIAL ECOLOGY

Using benevolent rhetoric to justify and legitimize official acts is a persistent theme in liberal governance that applies historically to ecosystem degradation as well as restoration; what has changed is the paradigm of public perceptions of environments, which has altered frameworks of environmental management. The histories of both case studies point to modern visions of human progress that ultimately contributed to ecosystem decline: drainage of parts of the Everglades in the early twentieth century transformed "wasted" swamplands into productive soils, in part as a Progressive Era means of distributing land to farmers;[5] in southwest Asia, a "modernization" theme from the 1950s produced the networks of dams in the Tigris and Euphrates headwaters, constructed to control river water for hydroelectric power, that has drastically restricted water flow to the marshes in southern Iraq.[6]

In both cases, modern pretensions of the progressive control of nature led to dramatic declines in ecosystems, evident in dwindling wildlife, water pollution, soil subsidence and salinization, and other problems. Today's calls for restoration of both ecosystems reflect a change in modern ecological discourses that recognizes the increased scale and intensity of environmental degradation throughout the twentieth century. Resource managers today express ambivalence regarding the promised modern connection between rationality, control of nature, and progress. Where environmental management was once rooted in "the belief in certain knowledge and the ability to control nature as if it were a machine,"[7] a new managerial ecology paradigm has emerged as a humbler version of applied expert knowledge that emphasizes a willingness to listen and learn, to both the ecosystems they are now trying to rehabilitate and the human communities that have something to gain or lose in the process.

Within this modified managerialism, the phrase "adaptive management" has emerged as a core element of planning that recognizes the uncertainty of knowledge, ecosystem complexity, and political conflict as integral elements of management.[8] Adaptive management, now embraced globally, promotes an iterative, trial-and-error approach to environmental management that encourages smaller-scale testing and refinement of projects to avoid large-scale mistakes. According to the National Research Council in the U.S.A, planning remains comprehensive and contained largely within resource management agencies, though "stakeholders" are called upon to work with scientists and engineers to develop goals and targets that both restore ecosystems and satisfy human communities.[9] To these ends, the rhetoric of stakeholder involvement has become ubiquitous in environmental management worldwide.

Managerial ecology and adaptive management therefore express official benevolence most effectively by also embracing stakeholder involvement, acknowledging both ecological and social uncertainties, and even potentially opening a space for alternative models of participation;[10] however, the paradigm remains ambivalent about the modern impulse of control. The new managerial ecology, according to Dean Bavington, continues to promise *eventual* certainty and clarity, despite "what appears initially as irreducibly complex and uncertain."[11] In this sense, the politics of environmental conflict appears in managerial ecology as yet another technical aspect of planning to be controlled and managed using modified rational principles.[12] And as a result, stakeholder participation risks being subsumed as a subset of natural science and engineering aspects of planning.

Subsuming environmental politics into a technocentric, managerial frame, as in the cases presented here, results in a performance of benevolence for various audiences. In the Everglades, attempts by the U.S. Army Corps of Engineers to promote "environmental justice" are intended to demonstrate to minority communities and others that concerns for the potentially uneven impacts of restoration plans are being addressed; however, the environmental justice concept is defined by the Corps in a way that leaves little scope for the kinds of involvement demanded by activists in such communities. A similar approach, which appears to insert stakeholders into a largely pre-formed planning agenda, is evident in the Iraq case as well.

Managerial ecology has emerged as what Suzan Ilcan and Lynne Phillips call a "global technology of government" that "intervene[s] upon and shape[s] the conduct of persons, activities and spaces on a global scale through a range of diverse authorities, development programs and complex techniques enlisted to solve certain problems."[13] Stakeholder involvement can also be considered as an example of what Mitchell Dean calls a "technology of performance" that presents itself as a technique "of restoring trust (i.e., accountability, transparency and democratic control)."[14] The need to rebuild such trust points to an emerging skepticism regarding scientific expertise since the late twentieth century.[15]

"THE MARSH DWELLERS" IN MESOPOTAMIAN MARSHLANDS RESTORATION

By all accounts, Mesopotamian Marshlands restoration is an urgent task. Two of the three marshes that define this part of southern Iraq, the Central and Al Hammar marshes, have declined by well over ninety percent, while the third, the Hawr Al Hawizah marsh, along the border with Iran, has declined by two-thirds.[16] The dramatic degradation of these marshes, located at the confluence of the Tigris, Euphrates, and Shatt al Arab River and occupied by human and nonhuman communities for millennia, is presented as having two major causes: first is the systemic reduction of water flowing from the Tigris and Euphrates headwaters due to dam construction that began decades ago outside the borders of Iraq, particularly the Southeastern Anatolia Project in Turkey.[17] However, most of the discussion about Marshland destruction centers on accelerated deliberate drainage of the marshes, largely since the Gulf War in 1991, as part of a revenge campaign by Saddam Hussein against Shiites and the Marsh Arabs in the south.[18] Though the work on this channelization system began in the late 1980s, ostensibly to promote commercial wheat production in the region and to protect against Iranian military incursions,[19] postwar drainage had dramatic impacts through the 1990s, destroying the livelihoods of people living in and around the marshes, along with wildlife habitat on a massive scale.

The benevolence effect of stakeholder involvement, as promoted by U.S. institutions, operates in several ways in the Mesopotamian Marshlands case. For a domestic audience, it reinforces Edward Said's characterization of the prevailing self-perception that the United States is "not a classical imperial power, but a righter of wrongs around the world, in pursuit of tyranny, in defence of freedom no matter the place or cost."[20] Through the restoration effort, made possible by the U.S. invasion, the oppressed Marsh dwellers have now been given a voice that was denied them under dictatorship—"the people" get the last laugh, thanks to the benevolence of U.S. intervention. Additionally, marshlands restoration helps portray globally that despite the destruction of the "Shock and Awe" invasion campaign in Iraq and prisoner abuses at Abu Ghraib and Guantanamo Bay, and despite its withdrawal from the Kyoto Protocol and backtracking on the Montreal Protocol, the United States under the Bush II administration is a promoter of both human rights and sustainable development.

Within the discourse of managerial ecology, however, the call for stakeholder involvement is an unsurprising commonplace. While stakeholders are conveniently propagandized in the Iraq case, they are an independently ubiquitous presence in a discourse produced through a vast range of governmental and multilateral agencies that include, yet go beyond, those from the United States. As such, the stakeholder has, in addition to its foreign policy propaganda value, an equally interesting role in the Iraq context as part of a transportable planning package. Operating as what Elleke Boehmer calls a "traveling metaphor," the stakeholder acts as a universal name that is transportable from site to site, regardless of territorial context, and that homogenizes as a means of managing difference.[21] The term functions as a generic means of locating "the people" as an integral element in a participatory planning process and reassures that planners care about popular input.

While the globalization of scientific management is tied historically to the colonial discourses Boehmer describes, the decentralized scientific discourse of managerial ecology employs stakeholders to perform globally as part of a traveling show that combines with scientific and engineering expertise. For example, prior to the U.S. invasion of Iraq, the United Nations Environment Programme (UNEP) presented this view regarding future restoration efforts:

UNEP has long advocated that only a river basin approach involving all stake-holders and emphasizing the connections between ecosystem components (land-air-water-biodiversity) offers a holistic and viable framework for the sustainable management of freshwater resources.[22] Packaged as a traveling metaphor in managerial ecology, the stakeholder is made mobile and universal, and is carried to south Florida, southern Iraq, and beyond, just as the "universal" knowledges of science and engineering are transferable as "immutable mobiles."

While USAID had since taken the lead role in the restoration effort in the Mesopotamian Marshlands, the initial planning for a postinvasion restoration effort was organized by a small group of Iraqi exiles who enrolled a team of scientific and engineering experts, ITAP (International Technical Advisory Panel), to create plans for a project called "Eden Again." Framed in the terms of managerial ecology, and bearing a strong resemblance to the Everglades restoration plans, Eden Again appeared as both science and marketing device aimed at enrolling larger and better-funded institutions into the restoration effort. In their report, released in February 2003 in anticipation of the U.S. invasion, ITAP's "inter-disciplinary group of scientists with expertise in hydrology, biology, ecosystem restoration, and soil science"[23] identified technical needs and possibilities for restoration; through the iterative approach of adaptive management, grandiose plans would not be attempted at once, but instead, demonstration projects would be implemented and stakeholders consulted in order to determine their technical as well as social feasibility. As the report states: "Development of a locally driven participatory process for all stakeholders within Iraq to guide the decision-making process and strengthen ownership of results is vitally important. The restoration options presented within this report are just that—options—that the local stakeholders can select through a comprehensive decision-making process."[24] When USAID took over the restoration effort in occupied Iraq, the planning approach and even some of the personnel of Eden Again were translated more or less directly into the new institutional arrangement. Additionally, USAID has assembled an even larger coalition of governmental and multilateral resource management agencies, and has displayed the rhetoric of stakeholder participation even more prominently: while the Eden Again technical advisory team was carefully constructed as a credible scientific enterprise to elicit donor support, the U.S. State Department (the institutional home of USAID) recognizes the importance of trumpeting the liberatory benefits of stakeholder participation in Iraq.

USAID's mastery over the rhetoric of stakeholder empowerment stems from its history as a development assistance agency. While the theme of empowerment has more radical roots in relation to activism concerning marginalized groups, the idea has been mainstreamed and promoted more recently as a prominent theme in neoliberalism, which operates as a means of encouraging privatization and market solutions,[25] mainstays of policies advocated by USAID. In fact, USAID's rhetoric explicitly distances its planning from more techno-centric forms of managerialism, stating:

> [T]he marshlands rehabilitation is a complicated multi-party collaborative effort requiring stakeholders to articulate their individual interests and con-cerns as a first step in reaching consensus around common goals and strate-gies. No one should underestimate the difficulty in achieving this as the re-maining marshlands face increasingly rapid total collapse. Still, this approach, which merges technical expertise with a collaborative process, has a far greater likelihood of success than one which is primarily technically driven.[26]

Yet, despite USAID's effective use of the language of stakeholder collaboration, there are noteworthy clues pointing to a continued technocentric orientation in planning. As with Eden Again, for instance, the planning team that defines the restoration agenda is composed overwhelmingly of natural scientists and engi-neers, with none of the "stakeholders" included: the stakeholders are to be "given" a voice in this project as the plan is put into action.[27] Furthermore, col-laborating institutions are exclusively governmental and multilateral resource management agencies. USAID's partners in restoration include the U.S. State Department's Bureau for Oceans and International Environmental and Scien-tific Affairs, the U.S. Army Corps of Engineers, the U.S. Geological Survey, the Environmental Protection Agency, and the Fish and Wildlife Service. USAID also expresses interest in incorporating experts working with the mul-tilateral Ramsar Convention on Wetlands and participants from Iraqi ministries and science communities. All of these participants are fully immersed in the technocentric assumptions of managerial ecology. There is no call for the types of alternative, collaborative planning approaches, such as advocacy research, done at the behest of communities that might actively shape agendas.[28]

Along with the relatively well-developed natural scientific elements in the management plan, the stakeholders themselves appear as elements that require management. Beyond remote sensing, soil mapping, sampling and analysis, studies of flora and fauna, and hydrological monitoring and modeling, "Marsh dweller" demographics, economics, and public health are also to be mapped and analyzed as a means of defining the human aspects of ecological restoration. This generically standardized approach could be applied at restoration sites in any part of the world. As Ilcan and Phillips state, "The international dispersion of such standardized grids has played a significant role in transforming a quali-tative world into information and rendering it compliant to control."[29]

DISCIPLINING ENVIRONMENTAL JUSTICE IN EVERGLADES RESTORATION

Control is also a theme in Everglades restoration in south Florida, which is further along in its implementation. My focus here is on the U.S. Army Corps of Engineers (the Corps) and its attempts, along with those of its state level partner, the South Florida Water Management District (SFWMD), to implement environmental justice in its planning process for Everglades restoration in Florida. As a federal agency operating under the mandate of Executive Order (EO) 12898, the Corps must demonstrate to a number of audiences—congressional, activist, and others—that they are working toward the effective pursuit of environmental justice.[30] A successful performance regarding environmental justice works to enhance the image of the Corps as an agency open to reform in their never-ending quest for environmental legitimacy in the face of an ever-skeptical public.

The Everglades have been dramatically modified over the past century. While some lands directly to the south of Lake Okeechobee were drained by settlers by the 1920s, devastating floods from hurricanes in the 1920s and 1940s led to more dramatic transformation resulting from the creation of the Central and Southern Florida (C&SF) Project, approved by Congress in 1948. Through the C&SF project, the Corps constructed a series of canals, dikes, levees, and other structures, creating three large water catchment areas, and drained what became the vast Everglades Agricultural Area (EAA), now occupied by large sugar farms and a few towns. The purpose of the project was to ensure a steady supply of water to coastal urban areas and to control flooding as well as to promote agricultural development. Only the southern third of this once vast wetland ecosystem was set aside as Everglades National Park, created in 1947. Drainage and diversion have been successful in the goals of providing water and flood control, but have also resulted in significant degradation of the ecosystem. Impacts including soil subsidence, water pollution, and habitat degradation have led to dramatic declines in fish and wildlife populations, while ocean saltwater has intruded into freshwater aquifers. Even the Everglades National Park is currently under threat due to blocked water flow from the north and from both air- and water-borne pollution.

As a result of these problems, the Corps has been forced to rethink the C&SF Project and design a plan for restoring the Everglades. Officially, the task is codified in the Comprehensive Everglades Restoration Plan (CERP), approved by the U.S. Congress in 2000, which adopts the adaptive management frame of managerial ecology that has become so globally ubiquitous. The stakeholder model has been prominent in Everglades restoration, and CERP was approved as a result of the support of a coalition of federal and state governmental agencies and stakeholders, including environmentalist groups, sugar corporations, urban government officials, Native Americans, and land developers, among others. However, this coalition was fragile to begin with, and, only a few years into the plan, hostilities over the important details threaten to split it apart. Among the many contentious, better-publicized issues in Everglades restoration, environmental justice issues barely appear as a blip on the radar screen. Yet issues that can be termed as environmental justice are present due to the multiplicities of black, Hispanic, and Native American communities impacted by the plans in culturally and ethnically diverse south Florida, and several environmental justice organizations have attempted to influence the CERP process. Environmental justice activists have raised issues surrounding potential impacts on drinking water quality, land acquisition plans, and the racial makeup of CERP staff, as well as the potential for gentrification in urban areas as further development in the Everglades is halted.[31]

Environmental justice is incorporated into CERP as one of a number of social goals housed in what is called the "Environmental and Economic Equity Program."[32] In addition to its numerous engineering projects, CERP also includes several "programs," such as this one, that apply across projects, intended both to facilitate project completion and to enroll interested communities into the planning process. Closely related to the Environmental and Economic Equity Program is the Public Outreach Program, designed to inform the public about CERP. The Environmental and Economic Equity Program is designed to achieve objectives ranging from promoting government contracts for minority-owned businesses to collecting social baseline data on the various affected communities and institutionalizing procedures for addressing environmental justice concerns.

The very fact that the Corps is explicitly addressing such issues should be recognized as an important step. It represents a significant capitulation by a federal agency to pressures by social activists that is in many ways encouraging. At the same time, environmental justice is new conceptual territory for an agency that had not, prior to EO 12898, expressed explicit regard for the impacts of its plans on minority communities. In their own words, CERP planners talk about "reaching in and reaching out," as many staff members within the agency need training in the meaning and demands of environmental justice.[33] This incorporation is part of a wider attempt of the Corps to open its planning process to greater public involvement and to shed its image as a top-down agency, beholden to special interests.

However, old institutional habits die hard, and the Corps encodes environmental justice in a manner that is least disruptive to the normal workings of the agency. The CERP approach to incorporating environmental justice works to depoliticize and subsume the concept, placing it into a familiar framework of managerialism. This articulation treats environmental justice disputes as but one more element to be "managed" through rational planning techniques, yet one more task to be pursued by the numerous task forces in CERP. Environmental justice in this sense emerges as a technique of government in which a particular, domesticated conception is normalized into Corps discourse that makes it possible to structure, shape, and control the process, on agency terms, within a rhetorical performance of empowerment and partnership.

Stephen Sandweiss points out that the success of environmental justice as a movement has depended on its "collective action frame"—that is, its ability to tap into "an aggressive, grassroots focus on political empowerment, voiced in the language of social and economic justice"[34]—which could make one wary of adopting the technocentric, legalistic discourse of managerial ecology, as embodied by agencies such as the Corps. This managerial framework has, in fact, frustrated activists who have urged the Corps to take procedural justice issues more seriously. As one environmental justice activist in the region wrote in a plea to the Corps,

> I realize now that the Corps' understanding of EJ [environmental justice] . . . is 180 degrees different from what our communities know and expect. . . . [F]or best results, the Corps needs to hear from us what OUR issues are in the CERP, and not the other way around. It is the antithesis of environmental justice for you to formulate policies and then tell us what you're going to do! . . . You have some of the best, most knowledgeable, committed environmental justice folks in the nation residing in Florida, and many of us are intensely focused on the CERP, and we are not being included in crafting this plan.[35]

While the Environmental and Economic Equity Program, which houses the environmental justice activities in CERP, attempts to promote meaningful participation, the involvement of such communities, in practice, so far does not appear all that much different from the standard review-and-comment process of public involvement in federal planning.

Given the difficulty that the Corps has in accommodating the collective-action frame of environmental justice, it has had to pursue other avenues to demonstrate and publicly perform its commitment to environmental justice. In this regard, economic equity and public outreach programs have been lashed together with environmental justice as the most visible attempt to present an image of effective action. In the Corps's outreach newsletters, for instance, CERP concern for minority involvement is relayed, in part, through the foregrounding of photographs of people of color. In fact, almost all of the newsletter entries present relatively superficial nods to minority communities. The most prevalent items are those announcing the presence of a CERP information booth at community events, such as African American, Hispanic, and Haitian cultural festivals. Furthermore, presence at these events is oriented more toward "getting the word out" regarding CERP than attempting a meaningful inclusion of communities in the planning process. In that regard, environmental justice activists have expressed frustration that "outreach," as pursued in CERP, seems to be an attempt more to enlist minority support for already-formulated restoration plans than to provide for more substantial forms of dialogue and input.

The other visible nod to environmental justice prominent in CERP publications is the promotion of the Economic Equity Program that solicits contract bids from minority-owned businesses. While a welcome addition, the program conflates minority business opportunity with environmental justice, and seems premised on the hope that offering the possibility of jobs will quell any dissent.

Beyond planning, there are contentious issues in implementation as well. According to its environmental justice guidelines, the Corps is to "address as [being] feasible, significant and adverse environmental impacts" on minority communities. Yet it remains unclear under what circumstances the Corps and SFWMD's environmental justice policies lead to action. Perhaps the biggest test case to date regards a debate over the implementation of Aquifer Storage and Recovery (ASR) technologies as a key component of CERP. ASR systems are deep injection wells that are used to store excess water that falls on the land surface, water that is currently flushed out to sea. ASRs would pump that water down into the Floridan aquifer (situated below the aquifer where drinking water comes from), where it would be stored until needed during the dry season. The Corps and SFWMD see such technologies as key to the restoration project because they allow a range of interests (especially those of agriculture and urban areas) to be satisfied with a continuous water supply. ASRs emerged as an environmental justice issue, at least in the minds of activists, because 200 out of the 333 planned wells would be constructed around the perimeter of Lake Okeechobee, and there were several contested issues regarding the safety of the technology. Thus, the large minority communities in the area would disproportionately feel any negative environmental impacts. The region is demographically split between black, Hispanic, and white residents, many of whom had relied upon the lake for their public drinking water, which is already virtually undrinkable due to pollution from ranching operations upstream as well as sugar production. Local environmental justice activists claim that the poor water quality of poor communities results from their status as a sacrifice zone as water managers defer to powerful agricultural interests, and that the promotion of ASRs has been yet another instance of government agencies' disregard for their health.

The most contentious safety issue centered on proposed legislation in Florida that would have relaxed quality standards for water pumped into the wells. The Corps and SFWMD endorsed the move, which critics argued could potentially, under certain circumstances, have led to drinking water contamination by fecal coliform bacteria and other pollutants. In this case, the agencies did not pursue investigation of ASR implementation as an environmental justice issue, deeming the potential impact as not significant or adverse, which sparked intense criticism from environmental justice organizations. Ultimately, due to a wider public outcry regarding a variety of uncertainties surrounding the technology, unrelated to environmental justice per se, the Corps and SFWMD agreed not to pump untreated water into ASRs.

The Corps performs environmental justice in relation to both legal demands of EO 12898 and those of minority communities attempting to influence the CERP process. While projecting an image of benevolence and concern, the approach works to rewrite such demands in terms that the agency can more easily control, allowing the Corps to shape what counts as an adequate response. It takes a concept born in social movement activism and domesticates and normalizes it under managerial ecology, creating what Peter Brosius calls a "discursive displacement" in which official sources deploy a rhetoric of reform, yet shaped to their own agenda.[36] However, the approach should not be dismissed, in that it opened a space for such an important issue to be addressed, even though it ultimately addresses the issue in ineffectual ways. In this sense, environmental justice planning in CERP emerges as what Fortun calls a "double bind," referring to "situations in which individuals are confronted with dual or multiple obligations that are related and equally valued, but incongruent."[37] The Corps and SFWMD need to at least appear sensitive to environmental justice issues, even though their priorities may lie elsewhere.

For CERP planners, the double bind is managed through an effort to codify environmental justice in terms that allow the agency to attempt to meet its multiple obligations, particularly to more powerful stakeholders, while addressing minority concerns with all apparent sincerity and no necessarily malevolent intent. Yet in the power struggles of CERP some obligations demand more Corps attention than others, and thus environmental justice is conveniently configured in ways that ultimately have a considerably smaller practical impact, which regularly disappoints activists involved in the process.

CONCLUSION

It may seem ironic that stakeholder participation has emerged as a ubiquitous mantra in environmental management at a time when the resolution of environmental problems has become ever more professionalized in policy analysis and legal and natural scientific discourses. Because it goes against the grain, the populist promise of stakeholder rhetoric is difficult to fulfill, particularly for groups that are most vulnerable both to the negative impacts of environmental degradation and to exclusion from the planning process. As the cases presented here suggest, stakeholders are largely appropriated by a technocentric process that, as Fischer puts it, "is largely concerned with the rationalization of social institutions and practices to better conform to and facilitate the logic of the technological juggernaut."[38] The benevolence effect of participation is enhanced by a tendency to characterize stakeholders, implicitly or explicitly, as vulnerable groups, ignoring their unequal abilities to influence outcomes. For instance, the impact of the sugar industry and land developers in shaping Everglades restoration is dramatically significant,[39] while it will be interesting to see what role major oil corporations play as stakeholders as they vie for access to petroleum reserves under Iraq's marshes. As Fortun notes, stakeholder participation has important potential as a step forward in environmental planning and decision making; however, the tendency to subsume such groups in a managerial discourse makes likely the outcomes she laments in the epigraph to this essay—that marginalized groups tend to stay marginalized, that capital disproportionately shapes what outcomes are possible, and that the possibility of controlling risk is rarely questioned.

NOTES

1. USAID [U.S. Agency for International Development], *Strategies for Assisting the Marsh Dwellers and Restoring the Marshlands in Southern Iraq: Interim Status Report,* Bureau for Asia and the Near East, Integrated Water and Coastal Resources Management IQC, 2003; reproduced at http://www.iraqmarshes.org/Documents/Publications/Project Publications/Scoping%20Trip%20Report%20—%20final%20%209-30-03.pdf (accessed December 17, 2004), p. 33.

2. Kim Fortun, *Advocacy after Bhopal: Environmentalism, Disaster, New Global Orders* (Chicago: University of Chicago Press, 2001), p. 272.

3. USAID administrator Andrew Natsios even referred to the Mesopotamian Marshlands as "their Everglades," quoted in Brookings Institution, *The Iraqi Marshlands: Can They Be Saved? Assessing the Human and Ecological Damage,* forum sponsored by the British Embassy and the Brookings–SAIS Project on Internal Displacement

(The Brookings Institution, Washington, D.C., May 7, 2003); reproduced at http://www.brookings.edu/comm/events/20030507.pdf (accessed December 17, 2004), p. 4.

4. See Dean Bavington, "Managerial Ecology and Its Discontents: Exploring the Complexities of Control, Careful Use and Coping in Resource and Environmental Management," *Environments* 30, no. 3 (2002): 3–21; Bavington and Scott Slocombe, "Moving beyond Managerial Ecology: Counterproposals," *Environments* 31, no. 3 (2003): 1–4.

5. See Nelson N. Blake, *Land into Water/Water into Land: A History of Water Management in Florida* (Tallahassee: University Presses of Florida, 1980).

6. Hassan Partow, UNEP [United Nations Environment Programme], *The Mesopotamian Marshlands: Demise of an Ecosystem,* Early Warning and Assessment Technical Report, UNEP/DEWA/TR.01–3 Rev. 1, (Nairobi, Kenya, 2001); reproduced at http://www.grid.unep.ch/activities/sustainable/tigris/mesopotamia.pdf (accessed December 17, 2004).

7. Bavington, "Managerial Ecology," p. 7.

8. See Bavington, "Managerial Ecology."

9. National Research Council, *Adaptive Monitoring and Assessment for the Comprehensive Everglades Restoration Plan* (Washington, D.C.: National Academies Press, 2003), p. 22.

10. See Bavington and Slocombe, "Moving beyond Managerial Ecology"; Fikret Berkes, "Alternatives to Conventional Management: Lessons from Small-Scale Fisheries," *Environments* 31, no. 1 (2003): 5–19.

11. Bavington, "Managerial Ecology," p. 8.

12. See Bavington, "Managerial Ecology."

13. Suzan Ilcan and Lynne Phillips, "Making Food Count: Expert Knowledge and Global Technologies of Government," *Canadian Journal of Sociology* 40, no. 4 (2003): 444. The phrase "technologies of government" comes from Foucauldian studies of governmentality and is described by Mitchell Dean, *Governmentality: Power and Rule in Modern Society* (Thousand Oaks, Calif.: Sage, 1999), p. 31, as a technical means to "impose limits over what it is possible to do." Ilcan and Phillips define global technologies of government as "the dispersion of a wide range of techniques (e.g., numerical, classificatory, spatial, visual, and discursive) that work beyond the nation-state to govern conduct," "Making Food Count," p. 444.

14. Dean, *Governmentality,* p. 169.

15. Frank Fischer, *Citizens, Experts, and the Environment: The Politics of Local Knowledge* (Durham, N.C.: Duke University Press, 2000).

16. Partow, UNEP, *Mesopotamian Marshlands,* pp. 29–33.

17. See Partow, UNEP, *Mesopotamian Marshlands;* Brookings Institution, *Iraqi Marshlands.*

18. See USAID, *Strategies for Assisting the Marsh Dwellers;* also Committee on International Relations, *United States and the Iraqi Marshlands: An Environmental Response,* Hearing before the Subcommittee on the Middle East and Central Asia, February 24, 2004, serial no. 108–74; reproduced at http://commdocs.house.gov/committees/intlrel/hfa92186.000/hfa92186_0.HTM (accessed December 17, 2004).

19. Partow, UNEP, *Mesopotamian Marshlands.*

20. Edward Said, *Culture and Imperialism* (New York: Vintage, 1993), p. 3.

21. Elleke Boehmer, *Colonial and Postcolonial Literature* (Oxford: Oxford University Press, 1995), p. 52.

22. Partow, UNEP, *Mesopotamian Marshlands,* p. 1.

23. ITAP [International Technical Advisory Panel], *Building a Scientific Basis for Restoration of the Mesopotamian Marshlands: Findings of the International Technical Advisory Panel Restoration Planning Workshop,* convened by Eden Again Project and The Iraq Foundation, February 2003; reproduced at http://www.edenagain.org/publications/pdfs/bldgscientificbasis.pdf (accessed December 17, 2004), p. 2.

24. Ibid.

25. See Dean, *Governmentality.*

26. USAID, *Strategies for Assisting the Marsh Dwellers,* p. 4.

27. Ibid., p.2.

28. Following the U.S. invasion, local residents dismantled many of the water control structures (beyond the control of the restoration project), flooding significant portions of the marshes. While project scientists have expressed optimism that at least certain portions of the marshes are recovering, they are also concerned about the potential impacts of haphazard water releases and fear that previous ecological damage, such as soil salinization, will hamper restoration efforts in large areas. Furthermore, planned dam construction on the Iranian side of the border would further restrict water flow, and it remains uncertain whether the restoration project will proceed according to initial plans, given ongoing security and funding problems and lack of political will; many residents seem no longer to desire the marsh-dwelling way of life, having become used to more lucrative dry-land farming. See Andrew Lawler, "Reviving Iraq's Wetlands," *Science* 307, no. 5713 (2005): 1186–89, and Curtis J. Richardson, et al., "The Restoration Potential of the Mesopotamian Marshes of Iraq." *Science* 307, no. 5713 (2005): 1307–11.

29. Ilcan and Phillips, "Making Food Count," p. 445.

30. The "environmental justice" label in the U.S. context emerged in the early 1980s to depict issues surrounding the disproportionate exposure to environmental hazards faced mainly by peoples of color. For example, see Robert D. Bullard, *Dumping in Dixie: Race, Class, and Environmental Quality* (Boulder, Colo.: Westview Press, 1994), and David E. Camacho, ed., *Environmental Injustices, Political Struggles: Race, Class, and the Environment* (Durham, N.C.: Duke University Press, 1998). President Clinton signed EO 12898 in 1994, requiring federal projects in the U.S. to be accountable for their potential impacts on minority and other disadvantaged communities. The order resulted from pressure from environmental justice activists.

31. Frank Peterman and Audrey Peterman, "Position Paper on Restudy/GCCSF Draft Restudy Report" (Miami: Earthwise Productions, 2000).

32. USACE and SFWMD [U.S. Army Corps of Engineers and South Florida Water Management District], *Environmental and Economic Equity Program Management Plan: Comprehensive Everglades Restoration Plan,* final report, August 2001; reproduced at http://www.evergladesplan.org/pm/pm_docs/eee/eee_sept_17.pdf (accessed December 17, 2004).

33. Naniann Regalado (U.S. Army Corps of Engineers), "We're Glad You Asked . . . ," *CERP Perspectives Newsletter,* Spring 2002, p. 13; reproduced at http://www.everglades plan.org/docs/cerp_persp_spring_2002.pdf (accessed December 17, 2004).

34. Stephen Sandweiss, "The Social Construction of Environmental Justice," *Environmental Injustices, Political Struggles: Race, Class, and the Environment*, ed. David E. Camacho (Durham, N.C.: Duke University Press, 1998), p. 32.

35. Audrey Peterman, e-mail message to the U.S. Army Corps of Engineers, January 26, 2001.

36. J. Peter Brosius, "Analyses and Interventions: Anthropological Engagements with Environmentalism," *Current Anthropology* 40, no. 3 (1999): 277–309.

37. Fortun, *Advocacy after Bhopal,* p. 13.

38. Fischer, *Citizens, Experts, and the Environment,* p. 14.

39. The *Washington Post,* for example, published a series of investigative articles documenting the influence of these industries over the Everglades restoration process. See Michael Grunwald, "Between a Rock and a Hard Place: Wetlands Shrink before Growing Demands of Industry, Consumers," *Washington Post,* June 24, 2002, p. A1; Grunwald, "An Environmental Reversal of Fortune: The Kissimmee's Revival Could Provide Lessons for Restoring the Everglades," *Washington Post,* June 26, 2002, p. A1; Grunwald, "Growing Pains in Southwest Fla.: More Development Pushes Everglades to the Edge," *Washington Post,* June 25, 2002, p. A1; and Grunwald, "A Rescue Plan, Bold and Uncertain: Scientists, Federal Officials Question Project's Benefits for Ailing Ecosystem," *Washington Post,* June 23, 2002, p. A1.

Contributors

Patrick Brantlinger is James Rudy Professor of English, Emeritus, at Indiana University. He edited *Victorian Studies* for a decade and is author of *Dark Vanishings: Discourse on the Extinction of Primitive Races; Who Killed Shakespeare? What's Happened to English since the Radical Sixties; The Reading Lesson: Mass Literacy as Threat in British Fiction; Fictions of State: Culture and Credit in Britain; Crusoe's Footprints: Cultural Studies in Britain and America;* and *Rule of Darkness: British Literature and Imperialism.* With William Thesing, he is editor of *A Companion to the Victorian Novel.* He is currently working on a study of postcolonialism and Victorian literature.

Leigh Dale is author of *The English Men: Professing Literature in Australian Universities* and, with Helen Tiffin, Alan Lawson, and Shane Rowlands, co-author of the annotated bibliography *Post-Colonial Literatures in English.* Her co-edited books include *The Body in the Library* and *Colonialism and Commerce.* She edits the journal *Australian Literary Studies,* and teaches Australian and post-colonial literatures at the University of Queensland.

Helen Gilbert teaches theater studies at Royal Holloway College, University of London, and is co-convenor of the College's interdisciplinary Postcolonial Research Group. Her books include *Performance and Cosmopolitics: Cross-cultural Transactions in Australasia;* the award-winning *Sightlines: Race, Gender and Nation in Contemporary Australian Theatre;* and *Post-Colonial Drama: Theory, Practice, Politics.* She is editor of *Post-Colonial Plays: An Anthology* and (with Anna Johnston) of *In Transit: Travel, Text, Empire.*

Alan Lester is Professor of Historical Geography at the University of Sussex, U.K. He has written on historical geographies of South Africa and, more recently, on the projects and networks that characterized British colonialism in the early nineteenth century. His latest books are *Imperial Networks: Creating Identities in Nineteenth Century South Africa and Britain* and *Colonial Lives across the British Empire: Imperial Careering in the Long Nineteenth Century,* edited with David Lambert.

Wairimū Ngarūiya Njambi is Associate Professor of Women's Studies and Sociology at the Harriet L. Wilkes Honors College, Florida Atlantic University. Her research and teaching areas include science and technology studies, feminist science studies, postcolonial studies, cultural studies, and critical race and sexuality studies. Her work has appeared in journals including *Feminist Theory, NWSA Journal, Meridians, Gender and Society,* and *Critical Sociology.*

William E. O'Brien teaches environmental studies and geography at the Harriet L. Wilkes Honors College, Florida Atlantic University. His research and teaching interests have included the cultural meanings of "nature," the intersection of race, ethnicity, and environment, and geographies of environment and development in the Global South. His recent work has appeared in journals such as *Ethics, Place & Environment, Human Ecology,* and *Historical Geography;* he is currently writing a book about the racial segregation of state parks in the American South during the Jim Crow era.

Lisa O'Connell teaches eighteenth-century British literature at the University of Queensland. Her research interests include the rise of the novel, church-state relations, and the development of settler colonial cultures. She has published articles on eighteenth-century theater, popular anthropology, travel narratives, sentimental fiction, and courtesan memoirs. She is currently a postdoctoral fellow at Johns Hopkins University.

Kirsten Holst Petersen is Associate Professor at Roskilde University, Denmark, where she lectures in English and cultural studies. Her area of research is postcolonial literature, with particular emphasis on Africa and on women's writing. She is editor or co-editor of *Religion, Development and African Identity; Displaced Persons;* and *Chinua Achebe: A Celebration.*

Chris Prentice teaches postcolonial literatures and theory at the University of Otago, Dunedin. Her current research focuses on discourses of cultural difference evident at the intersection of postcolonial political and cultural concerns and the effects of globalization. She has published essays on aspects of this topic in edited collections and journals such as *SPAN, New Literatures Review, Ariel,* and *Continuum* and is currently working on a book that theorizes such concerns more broadly.

Rajeswari Sunder Rajan is Global Distinguished Visiting Professor in the Department of English, New York University. Her major books include *The Scandal of the State: Women, Law and Citizenship in Postcolonial India; Real and Imagined Women: Gender, Culture and Postcolonialism;* and the edited collections *Crisis of Secularism in India* (with Anuradha Needham); *Signposts: Gender Issues in Post-Independence India;* and *The Lie of the Land: English Literary Studies in India.*

Prem Kumar Rajaram is Assistant Professor in the Department of Sociology and Social Anthropology at the Central European University in Budapest. He has previously worked at the Department of Geography, National University of Singapore. He is co-editor with Carl Grundy-Warr of *Borderscapes: Hidden Geographies and Politics at Territory's Edge*. His principal research interests are borders and issues of belonging/nonbelonging and the detention of refugees in Europe, Australia, and Malaysia.

Sarah Richardson is a Senior Lecturer in the Department of History at the University of Warwick, UK. Her recent publications include (with Anna Clark) *The History of Suffrage, 1760–1867* and (with Kathryn Gleadle) *Women and British Politics, 1760–1860: The Power of the Petticoat.*

Chris Tiffin teaches nineteenth-century literature at the University of Queensland. He is editor of *South Pacific Images,* and co-editor of *De-Scribing Empire* (with Alan Lawson), and *South Pacific Stories* (with Helen Tiffin). He has compiled a bibliography of novelist Rosa Praed and (with Lynnette Baer) a listing of her papers, and is the author of articles on nineteenth-century colonial authors, bibliography, and electronic editing.

Philanthropic and Nonprofit Studies

Dwight F. Burlingame and David C. Hammack, editors

Thomas Adam, editor. *Philanthropy, Patronage, and Civil Society: Experiences from Germany, Great Britain, and North America*

Albert B. Anderson. *Ethics for Fundraisers*

Peter M. Ascoli. *Julius Rosenwald: The Man Who Built Sears, Roebuck and Advanced the Cause of Black Education in the American South*

Karen J. Blair. *The Torchbearers: Women and Their Amateur Arts Associations in America, 1890–1930*

Eleanor Brilliant. *Private Charity and Public Inquiry: A History of the Filer and Peterson Commissions*

Dwight F. Burlingame, editor. *The Responsibilities of Wealth*

Dwight F. Burlingame and Dennis Young, editors. *Corporate Philanthropy at the Crossroads*

Charles T. Clotfelter and Thomas Ehrlich, editors. *Philanthropy and the Nonprofit Sector in a Changing America*

Ruth Crocker. *Mrs. Russell Sage: Women's Activism and Philanthropy in Gilded Age and Progressive Era America*

Marcos Cueto, editor. *Missionaries of Science: The Rockefeller Foundation and Latin America*

William Damon and Susan Verducci, editors. *Taking Philanthropy Seriously: Beyond Noble Intentions to Responsible Giving*

Gregory Eiselein. *Literature and Humanitarian Reform in the Civil War Era*

David C. Hammack, editor. *Making the Nonprofit Sector in the United States: A Reader*

Jerome L. Himmelstein. *Looking Good and Doing Good: Corporate Philanthropy and Corporate Power*

Warren F. Ilchman, Stanley N. Katz, and Edward L. Queen II, editors. *Philanthropy in the World's Traditions*

Warren F. Ilchman, Alice Stone Ilchman, and Mary Hale Tolar, editors. *The Lucky Few and the Worthy Many: Scholarship Competitions and the World's Future Leaders*

Thomas H. Jeavons. *When the Bottom Line Is Faithfulness: Management of Christian Service Organizations*

Amy A. Kass, editor. *The Perfect Gift*

Index

abolition of slavery, 4, 13–14, 16–17, 21, 32, 43, 61–69, 71n9; antislavery reformers, 32, 91; subsequent disappointment at, 70. *See also* slavery

Aborigines, 4, 13–14, 17–20, 23, 26n34, 41, 74–75, 83; attrition of, 41; in economic systems, 19–20; Protectorate of, 44; superior to Irish, 22

Aborigines Committee, 18, 37–44; analysis of colonialism, 39

Aborigines Protection Society, 17–18, 40, 82

Africa, 8–9, 17, 23, 64, 110, 160–161, 169; as barbarous land, 172–173; as feudal estate, 105–107, 109, 112–113; West Africa, 43. *See also* Cape Colony, Kenya, Sierra Leone

African Institution, 62

Africans, 8–9, 104–109, 167; and education, 111–112. *See also* Hottentots, Kikuyu, Kohesan, Xhosa

Ahimsa. See nonviolence

altruism, 3; as test of benevolence, 2, 13

Ambedkar, B. R., 145

Anti-Corn Law League, 97

Anti-Slavery Society, 17

Annual Register, 61

Aoteaora. *See* New Zealand

apprenticeship (transition from slavery), 34, 36

Argus (Melbourne), 74

Arnold, Matthew, 43

Arthur, Governor George, 33

Australia, 8, 13, 18–20, 39–42, 44; Chinese labor proposed for, 58–59; model for removing indigenous peoples, 78. *See also* New South Wales, Tasmania, Victoria, Western Australia

Backhouse, James, 33

Bagehot, Walter, 25n15

Baker, Ernest, 6

Barlee, F. P., 76

Barrow, John, 62

benevolence: altruism a test for, 2, 11; ambivalence of, 120, 126; asymmetrical, 103; coexisting with racism, 108–113; conflicting with expertise, 199, 206–209; conflicting with law, 63–64; coinciding with economic theory, 16–17; colonial, 11, 17, 19, 84, 106, 123–124, 127; deferring reform, 16; early meaning of, 11n6; and economics, 2, 19–20, 97; and environmental justice, 10; feminist rhetoric of, 162, 170; Gandhi on, 142; and imperialism, 5–7, 14, 17, 19, 106–107, 125–126, 137; imposing humiliation, 181, 191, 193; informing official acts, 199–201; never disinterested, 2, 11, 13–15, 136; Nietzsche on, 13; power disguised as, 192; as practice, 2, 13; supplanted by political economy, 4, 14–15, 23, 52; and religion, 3–4, 13, 22; viewed negatively, 1, 81–82

Bentham, Jeremy, 52, 55, 60n21

Berlingske Aftenavis (Danish newspaper), 112

Helen Gilbert is Professor of Theatre at Royal Holloway, University of London. She is author of *Sightlines: Race, Gender, and Nation in Contemporary Australian Theatre* and *Post-Colonial Drama: Theory, Practice, Politics,* and is editor of *Post-Colonial Plays: An Anthology* and (with Anna Johnston) of *In Transit: Travel, Text, Empire.*

Chris Tiffin teaches in the School of English, Media Studies, and Art History at the University of Queensland. He is editor of *South Pacific Images* and co-editor of *De-Scribing Empire* and *South Pacific Stories.*